IN SIGHT
OF SURRENDER

IN SIGHT OF SURRENDER

*The U.S. Sanctions Campaign
against South Africa,
1946–1993*

Les de Villiers

PRAEGER

Westport, Connecticut
London

Library of Congress Cataloging-in-Publication Data

De Villiers, Les.
     In sight of surrender :   the U.S. sanctions campaign against South
Africa, 1946–1993 / Les de Villiers.
          p. cm.
     Includes bibliographical references and index.
     ISBN 0–275–94982–6 (alk. paper)
     1. United States—Foreign economic relations—South Africa.
2. South Africa—Foreign economic relations—United States.
3. Economic sanctions—South Africa. I. Title.
HF1456.5.S6D45   1995
337.73068—dc20   94–29920

British Library Cataloguing in Publication Data is available.

Library of Congress Catalog Card Number: 94–29920
ISBN: 0–275–94982–6

First published in 1995

Praeger Publishers, 88 Post Road West, Westport, CT   06881
An imprint of Greenwood Publishing Group, Inc.

Printed in the United States of America

The paper used in this book complies with the
Permanent Paper Standard issued by the National
Information Standards Organization (Z39.48–1984).

10 9 8 7 6 5 4 3 2 1

Copyright Acknowledgment

The author and publisher gratefully acknowledge permission from Investor
Responsibility Research Center to reprint Figure 1: Top U.S. Companies in
South Africa—May 1987 originally published in *Wall Street Journal*, June 4,
1987 and Table 2: The Anatomy of Withdrawal originally published in J.
Kibbe and D. Hauck, *Leaving South Africa: The Impact of U.S. Corporate
Disinvestment*, IRRC, July 1988.

A nation that is boycotted is a nation that is in sight of surrender.

President Woodrow Wilson

Contents

Abbreviations

AAO	Anti-Apartheid organization
ACOA	American Committee on Africa
AEB	Atomic Energy Board
AFL-CIO	American Federation of Labor and Congress of Industrial Organizations
AGM	Annual General Meeting
AMCHAM	American Chamber of Commerce
AMSAC	American Society of African Culture
ANC	African National Congress
ANCYL	African National Congress Youth League
ANLCA	American Negro Leadership Conference on Africa
ASSOCOM	Associated Chambers of Commerce
AZAPO	Azanian People's Organization
BOSS	Bureau of State Security
CAAA	Comprehensive Anti-Apartheid Act
CIA	Central Intelligence Agency
CORE	Congress of Racial Equality
COSATU	Congress of South Africa Trade Unions
CP	Conservative Party
CRS	Congressional Research Service
CSIR	Council for Scientific and Industrial Research
DP	Democratic Party
DTA	Democratic Turnhalle Alliance
EPG	Eminent Persons Group
FCI	Federated Chamber of Industries
FNLA	National Front for the Liberation of Angola
FLS	Frontline States
FSAM	Free South Africa Movement
GAO	General Accounting Office
HSRC	Human Sciences Research Council
IAEA	International Atomic Energy Agency
IBR	Institute for Black Research

ICAO	International Civil Aviation Organization
ICCR	Interfaith Center of Corporate Responsibility
IDASA	Institute for a Democratic Alternative for South Africa
IFP	Inkatha Freedom Party
ILO	International Labor Organization
IMF	International Monetary Fund
IRRC	Investor Responsibility Research Center
JEC	Joint Executive Authority
JMC	Joint Monitoring Commission
JSE	Johannesburg Stock Exchange
LDC	Less developed country
LIBOR	London Interbank Borrowing Rate
MDM	Mass Democratic Movement
MK	Umkhonto we Sizwe
MPC	Multi-party conference
MPLA	Popular Movement for the Liberation of Angola
NAACP	National Association for the Advancement of Colored People
NAFCOC	National African Federated Chamber of Commerce
NASA	National Aeronautics and Space Administration
NATO	North Atlantic Treaty Organization
NGO	Non-governmental organization
NP	National Party
NSC	National Security Council
NSSM	National Security Study Memorandum
NUM	National Union of Mineworkers
OAU	Organization of African Unity
OPEC	Organization of Petroleum Exporting Countries
PAC	Pan Africanist Congress
PFP	Progressive Federal Party
PLO	Palestinian Liberation Organization
PRWM	Polaroid Revolutionary Workers' Movement
PWV	Pretoria-Witwatersrand-Vereeniging [region]
SAAF	South African Air Force
SABC	South African Broadcasting Corporation
SABRITA	South Africa-British Trade Association
SACC	South African Council of Churches
SACP	South African Communist Party
SADF	South African Defense Force
SADCC	Southern African Development Coordinating Council
SAFTO	South African Foreign Trade Organization
SAIC	South African Indian Congress
SAPA	South African Press Association
SCC	Standstill Coordinating Committee
SCLC	Southern Christian Leadership Conference

SWAPO	South West African People's Organization
TEC	Transitional Executive Council
TUCSA	Trade Union Council of South Africa
UDF	United Democratic Front
UDI	Unilateral Declaration of Independence
UN	United Nations Organization
UNITA	Union for the Independence of Angola
UNTAG	United Nations Transitional Assistance Group
UPU	Universal Postal Union
ZANU	Zimbabwe-Africa National Union
ZAPU	Zimbabwe-Africa Political Union

Preface

This book traces the economic and trade sanctions campaign against South Africa from its modest beginnings in 1946 through its climax in the late 1980s, when South Africa appeared isolated in every respect. It concludes with the signing by President Bill Clinton in November 1993 of the South African Democratic Transition Support Act, adopted by the US Congress to restore normal economic relations with post-apartheid South Africa.

This is not a quantitative report on the economic and financial impact of sanctions against South Africa. That is better left to economists who will no doubt in future ply their craft, trying to quantify the harm done to South Africa's economy by these punitive measures. Although I picked up interesting, often contradicting, damage estimates during my research, these are mentioned only where they seemed to have directly influenced decision-making on either side of the sanctions issue. I also left in-depth theorizing and speculation about the political impact of sanctions as future fodder for the growing stable of political scientists hungering after new challenges. In this study such impact is revealed only by the actions and statements of men and women involved in the sanctions game over the years.

My decision to concentrate on US sanctions was determined by the following factors:

1. In the postwar world, the United States, as the undisputed leader of the West and the strongest economic power, held the key to successful sanctions against South Africa. The whole campaign was considered futile until this giant could be induced to join.
2. When comprehensive sanctions were eventually adopted by Congress, the United States was not only one of South Africa's major investors, but among its top trading partners.
3. The United States had the power to coerce Japan and cajole Britain and other industrial nations into following its direction on sanctions—much like a large vessel pulling the smaller ones along in its slipstream.

4. The United States, more than any other nation, had a history of sanctions with which the South African experience could be compared or against which it could be measured.

The more ambitious approach would of course have been a study of all sanctions against South Africa—including even those by states who had little or no business links with the target country and went along for the free ride by making symbolic gestures. This global option was passed up in favor of a more intensive exclusive study of US sanctions and the measures applied by other nations are mentioned only where appropriate and relevant.

I approached the subject of sanctions not merely as a disinterested observer. Serving in the 1960s and 1970s as a senior South African diplomat in the United States and Canada and eventually as the Deputy Secretary of Information in Pretoria, I have for many years been involved and in charge of the anti-sanctions campaign as it related not only to the United States but other countries as well. This, I believe, helped me to bring a special perspective to the subject that would otherwise not have been possible.

Does this former involvement on one side of the issue impede my sense of fairness or the objectivity that historians always strive for but never quite seem to fully achieve? Not necessarily.

Historian Arthur Schlesinger, at one time a member of the Kennedy White House staff, contributed landmark studies on both President Kennedy and his brother Robert F. Kennedy.[1] The perspective and valuable insights that came from Schlesinger, having been an "insider," far outweighed the element of partisanship or subjectivity in his work. Anthony Lake, who moved in and out of three administrations in positions of importance, is another prolific writer who contributed to our knowledge of foreign policymaking in the United States on issues relating, among others, to South and Southern Africa.[2]

In my own case, the following encounter may help reassure those who fear that I am too blinkered by my partisan past to tell both sides—or, in this case, the many sides of the US-South African sanctions story.

In spring 1993, I met with George Houser at his home in a rustic wooded area some thirty miles from New York City. We proceeded to a country restaurant where we spent several hours talking, returned to his house and talked some more—five hours in all. There was much to talk about. The discussion was friendly, jovial. and scholarly. Houser, now in semi-retirement, is the founder of the American Committee on Africa (ACOA), the anti-apartheid pressure group that pioneered sanctions against South Africa in the United States. In America his sponsors, friends, and associates over the years included Martin Luther King, Eleanor Roosevelt, Jackie Robinson, Sidney Poitier, Harry Belafonte, and other notables.

In his crowded study pictures of George Houser with these luminaries abound, some of them on the wall and other propped up in random fashion against books and other mementos. There was, however, nothing random about the way Houser commanded his troops into battle, so to speak, or the way he exploited the media and fired up many Americans with the idea of doing something about South African apartheid. With his hazel eyes, slightly sun-reddened face and gray goatee, George Houser could easily pass for a farmer in South Africa. He even concedes that the South African government did some positive things. Apartheid, however, was an "evil" system that had to be eradicated. He preferred sanctions to outright violence and race war, but he did not condemn alternative means.

Ending apartheid "at any cost" became a life's vocation for Houser after he had met Walter Sisulu, Albert Luthuli, and members of the underground in South Africa during a visit to Malan's South Africa in the early 1950s. Afterward he was blacklisted by Pretoria and kept out of the country for close to forty years. Only in the early 1990s was he allowed to return for a reunion with Sisulu and others.

Now George and I were sitting across the table with no war to wage. I had long since left the government post that pitched me against George Houser and his troops in a propaganda war. While our encounters in past debates were quite intense and at times acrimonious, they were always conducted with civility. Although the protesters and street forces that he unleashed on corporate America sometimes turned nasty and the "liberation movements" that he supported had embraced violence as a tool, this mild-mannered man rarely raised his voice in debate. His role model was Gandhi.

As I mused rather immodestly at my newfound ability to calmly and objectively compare notes with him after many years of intense personal and official involvement on opposite sides of the sanctions issue, Houser remarked: "I could do that too. After all, it's all past tense now."

It is said that history, like good wine, improves with age and that the "immediate past tense"—as this subject still is—makes for a certain lack of perspective that can only be attained many years after the event. On the other hand research so soon after it happened afforded me the opportunity to interview participants while their memories were still vivid.

My personal encounters with key personalities in the South African sanctions saga covered the full spectrum—ranging from political policymakers such as Chester Crocker to Cyrus Vance and P. W. Botha, and financial overlords like Chase Manhattan Bank Chairman Willard Butcher and South African Reserve Bank Governor Chris Stals. It was only through conversations with these people that crucial events and developments could be reliably reconstructed and policy decisions properly assessed and analyzed. While other students will in future undoubtedly produce a more complete story as documents still hidden from public scrutiny become available and new aspects surface, first-hand human sources may sadly be fewer, and the memory of those remaining, somewhat less lucid.

In writings about the subject, the terms "embargo," "boycott" and "sanctions" are often used interchangeably. I also alternate between these terms in describing the punitive measures imposed against South Africa over a forty-seven year period.

The word "embargo" derives from the Spanish *embargar* (to impede) which in turn comes from the Vulgar Latin *imbarricåre* (to barricade). It has come to mean "a prohibition by a government on certain or all trade with a foreign nation."[3] The term "boycott," after British landlord Charles Boycott who was targeted by the Irish for his refusal to lower rents, came to signify the act by one or more parties of abstaining "from using, buying, or dealing with as an expression of protest or disfavor or as a means of coercion."[4]

While the word "sanction" means approval or giving official authorization, our use of the word in its plural is obviously intended to denote the opposite. "Sanctions" in this study signifies "coercive measures" adopted by one or more nations acting against a nation "to ensure compliance or conformity."[5]

I will settle for Daoudi and Dajani's definition of these three terms as "actions initiated by one or more international actors (the "senders") against one or more others (the 'targets') with either or both of two purposes: to punish the targets by depriving them of some value and/or to make the "targets" comply with 'certain norms the senders deem important."[6]

Although the restrictions imposed on South Africa over the past half century ran the gamut from moral to cultural, diplomatic to sports boycotts, our focus is on US economic sanctions. This means everything that affected South Africa's economy, either directly or indirectly—trade sanctions, arms and oil embargoes, nuclear and other technology boycotts and, most important, withdrawal or withholding of investment.

In the view of many, this latter type of sanctions, referred to as "divestment" or "disinvestment," had the most debilitating effect. These two terms, however, have never been accurately formulated despite gallant attempts by the experts. In US sanctions jargon, "divestment," a derivative of "divest" and related to "divestiture," meaning the "sale, liquidation, or spin-off of a corporate division or subsidiary," came to signify the selling of shares in a corporation with South African links. "Disinvestment," on the other hand, indicates withdrawal by a US or other overseas corporation—selling or liquidating its assets in South Africa under pressure.

When the world's major banks, with devastating effect, refused to roll over their loans to South Africa in the mid-1980s, a new and clear distinction was made between "financial" sanctions on the one hand and "trade" sanctions on the other.

Much of the research behind this book came from a doctoral dissertation completed by me under the able promotership of Prof. Diko van Zyl, dean of the Department of History at the University of Stellenbosch. I also owe gratitude to Prof. Pieter Kapp of Stellenbosch for his input and Prof. Richard Hull of New York University, one of America's foremost Africanists who, as external examiner, shared his valuable perspective and insight.

NOTES

1. Schlesinger, Arthur M., *A Thousand Days: John F. Kennedy in the White House* and *Robert Kennedy and His Times.*

2. During the Nixon era in the late 1960s Lake was personal assistant to Henry Kissinger and in Carter's time Director of Policy Studies at the State Department. After a stint as professor at Mount Holyoke College he reentered government as National Security Adviser to President Clinton. At least two of his works—*Caution and Concern: The Making of American Policy Toward South Africa* and *The Tar Baby Option: An American Policy Toward Southern Africa*—relate specifically to South and Southern Africa.

3. *American Heritage Dictionary,* Deluxe Electronic Edition, 1993.

4. Ibid.

5. Ibid.

6. Daoudi, M. and Dajani, M., *Economic Sanctions—Ideals and Experience,* p. 7.

IN SIGHT
OF SURRENDER

1

Mobilizing the World's Conscience

> Mine is an appeal to a conscience—to the conscience of the world's, which this Assembly is.
>
> —*Vijaya Pandit*
> *UN General Assembly, 1946*[1]

In 1946 India became the first nation to impose trade sanctions against South Africa. But 1946 will be remembered for another more momentous and ultimately effective action against South Africa by the same nation. In October 1946, after realizing that its sanctions had failed, India decided to make an appeal to the conscience of the world to act in unison against racism in South Africa. It was the beginning of a campaign that would eventually lead to near total sanctions against Pretoria and apartheid.

India had first threatened to apply a trade boycott against South Africa in November 1944 when Natal province adopted the so-called Natal Ordinances designed to restrict Indian land ownership in that province. When South Africa's Governor-General withheld his approval for this discriminatory legislation, India shelved the idea. Toward the end of 1945, however, the South African central government announced similar legislation and India repeated its threat. This time the warning went unheeded. The discriminatory legislation passed, and in July 1946 India banned all trade with South Africa.

From the comments in leading Indian publications at the time, it is clear that this trade boycott was not intended purely as a symbolic gesture. When the idea of sanctions was first raised in November 1944, two leading Indian journals, the *Eastern Economist* and *Commerce,* were confident that South Africans would suffer more than Indians. South Africa, they argued, would find it hard to forgo Indian jute and hessian imports, while India could easily substitute wattle bark imports from South Africa. By completely depriving

South African industry and agriculture of basic packing materials, *Commerce* predicted, India could cause "considerable paralysis" of that country's economy.[2]

India's trade boycott failed as countries such as Australia, Kenya, Southern Rhodesia, and Hong Kong acted as "transit ramps" for re-exporting to South Africa these commodities from India and eventually Pakistan replaced India as a supplier. "It is probable that South Africa had to pay higher prices initially for the imports from India secured through third parties, and suffered in the process some deterioration in its terms of trade, but the loss on this account could not have been very considerable," concluded Professor K. N. Raj of the Delhi School of Economics in his assessment of this episode some years later. "The loss ultimately has been that of India, namely of the South African market in which it had earlier established itself and in which the demand for its products had been continuously growing."[3]

The Indian experience, according to Raj, showed that "if a small group of countries decide to go it alone, it is very unlikely that sanctions can achieve their objective, however large the share of South African trade enjoyed by the sanctioning countries might be and however vital the requirement of the South African economy for their products." The loss was likely to fall more heavily on them than on South Africa, he noted. Even countries with a considerable political stake in appearing to be on the "right side of such a boycott" found it difficult to resist the temptation, as Pakistan's entry into direct trade with South Africa has shown.[4]

India discovered as others did before that there were a few simple ground rules for success with sanctions. The country applying the sanctions has to be economically much stronger and larger than its target; it should account for a substantial portion of the intended target country's trade and financial well-being; and it should be able to close the loopholes.[5]

Sanctions as a weapon were used before the birth of Christ. In Ancient Greece, as far back as 432 BC, Pericles enacted a boycott decree against the Megarians. While Thucydides downplayed its significance, another historian, Aristophanes, regarded the Megarian sanctions decree one of the major causes of the Peloponnesian War. "The Megarians, since they were starving little by little, begged to have the decree withdrawn," he noted in his book, *Archarnians*. "But we were unwilling, though they asked us many times. Then came the clash of the shields..."[6] In this instance, as in many others in the distant past, the goal of sanctions was obviously not to avert bloodshed but to weaken the target nation before the outbreak of war. The notion that economic sanctions might be used as a substitute for armed intervention is a relatively modern one.

After World War I, with its ghastly toll in human lives, the "economic weapon" seemed to the newly formed League of Nations to be a sensible alternative to outright war in the enforcement of international law. While its other articles outline the type of transgressions that would warrant action by the League, Article 16, the principal sanctions article, prescribed specific actions to be taken. It required the cessation of "all financial, commercial or personal intercourse between the nationals of the Covenant-breaking State and the nationals of any other State, whether a Member of the League or not." League members also pledged under this article to "mutually support one another" in applying these punitive "financial and economic measures" to "minimize the loss and inconvenience" to themselves.[7]

In a 1919 speech in Indianapolis, one of the leading advocates of sanctions as a diplomatic tool, US President Woodrow Wilson, concluded confidently: "A nation that is boycotted is a nation that is in sight of surrender." Apply this economic, peaceful, silent, deadly remedy, he maintained, and there will be no need for force.[8] As it turned out, President Wilson failed to get Congress to ratify US membership of the League of Nations that was supposed to administer this "deadly remedy." Eventually, Germany and Japan defected, leaving the League without the necessary clout to make sanctions work.

In their review of the role of sanctions since World War I, G. C. Hufbauer and I. Schott concluded that "like other fashions, economic sanctions wax and wane in popularity." At the same time they found that over the years sanctions remained "part and parcel of international diplomacy, a tool to coerce target governments into particular avenues of response."[9] Despite a few minor successes by the League in its imposition of sanctions against a few smaller powers in the 1920s and 1930s, this "economic weapon" failed miserably when applied against Italy to dissuade it from invading Ethiopia. Although supporters of this type of action afterward maintained that sanctions against Mussolini would have succeeded if they had not been applied half-heartedly, the public perception persisted that it was a flawed tool.[10]

Sanctions as a weapon of first resort was "somewhat rehabilitated" by the role that the naval blockade of Europe and the preemptive buying of strategic materials by the Allies played in the ultimate defeat of Germany and Japan during World War II.[11] It was with this and other lesser sanctions successes of the immediate past in mind that India set out to boycott South Africa in 1946—hoping to hurt it economically. Even though its sanctions failed, India set in motion another campaign that would eventually succeed. In October 1946 it took its battle with South Africa to the newly formed United Nations and managed to place the treatment of its people and other colored races at the top of the world organization's agenda. It also thwarted South Africa's attempt to annex South West Africa (Namibia), opening the Pretoria government to endless and sustained attacks on an additional front.

India's offensive against South Africa at this fateful first UN session in New York was spearheaded by widowed Vijaya Lakshmi Pandit—sister of Jawaharlal Nehru, who two years later became independent India's first prime minister. Utilizing her skills as a distinguished lawyer and her experience on the hustings since 1920, Mrs. Pandit made an impassioned and effective plea not only on behalf of the "oppressed" Indians but all "non-Europeans." In New York to assist Pandit were a South African Indian leader, H. A. Naidoo, as well as Dr. A. B. Xuma, the president of the Black African National Congress (ANC).

Some years later Albert Luthuli, then president of the ANC and Nobel laureate, would compliment India on the way it had "taken up the cudgels on behalf of the oppressed South African majority" and "dragged the whole scandal of apartheid into the open."[12] Apartheid at that time was, however, still an obscure word bandied about by opposition leader, Dr. Daniel Malan, and his Reunited National Party, which seemed unlikely to make it into government soon. Pandit was attacking segregation as practiced by Smuts.

As the debate progressed, the line of division became one of color, with the White nations suggesting that the South African Indian question be referred to the International Court of Justice for arbitration. The Whites were for the letter and the non-Whites for the spirit of the UN Charter.[13] A resolution was adopted that called for the treatment of the Indians in South Africa in accordance with the treaty obligations under the League of Nations as well as the Charter of the United Nations. Ostensibly mild, the significance of this resolution lay beyond its actual wording. It signaled the beginning of a protracted campaign against South Africa and its racial policies in the world organization. In her final speech before the votes were counted, Mrs. Pandit summed up as follows: "Mine is an appeal to a conscience—the conscience of the world, which the Assembly is."[14]

India asked for a political verdict in its favor and obtained it. It intended to make the treatment of South Africa's Indians and other South African racist actions a matter of world concern and censure. That too, it accomplished. But this is not all that India wanted. There was still the matter of South West Africa. Smuts had requested that this territory, administered by South Africa under a mandate from the defunct League of Nations, be allowed to become an integral part of his country. This request would be denied at the insistence of India.

Surveying the audience with an air of confidence as he spoke on the matter of South West Africa, the Indian delegate, Sir Maharaj Singh, closed with a stinging remark. "In December 1943," he recalled, "General Smuts in a speech on the Atlantic Charter used the following words: 'The old order is passing. The order to which I belong is dead.' He was right and his remarks apply to South Africa as well as to every other country in the world."[15] The old order had indeed passed and the new one held little promise for Smuts and South Africa. They were facing a world demanding the unthinkable—full and equal rights for everyone regardless of race or color. Smuts, the world leader who lifted his own country to heights above its level of competence, had become, in the words of Alan Paton, "only the leader of a small white aristocracy seeking to cling to its privilege in a changing world."[16]

The outcome of the South West Africa debate was a foregone conclusion and Smuts left before the final vote. On 14 December 1946, his Secretary for Foreign Affairs, D. D. Forsyth, performed the painful duty to be present when the members of the Trusteeship Council voted thirty-seven to zero, with nine abstentions, against incorporation and in favor of placing the territory under international trusteeship. Back in South Africa, Smuts found his supporters "dazed and amazed" by the events at the United Nations. "The refusal of South West Africa's incorporation into the Union [of South Africa] and the Indian rebuff have come as a great shock to them, even more than to me, who could understand these events in their larger international setting," Smuts wrote. "South Africa will in future have to keep in view how strong world feeling against her policy is," he predicted. "It may yet bring forth many woes for our country and people."[17]

While India's sanctions against South Africa turned out to be a failure, its attempt to awaken the "world's conscience" to the plight of Indians and Blacks was a resounding success. Soon there would be demands in the United Nations from a growing lobby of Third World nations, supported by the Communist bloc, for action instead of words of condemnation. Initial success came in 1956 when South Africa was forced to withdraw from the United Nations Educational, Scientific and Cultural Organization (UNESCO). Next, on 29 June 1961, the International Labor Organization (ILO) adopted a resolution calling for the withdrawal of South Africa from the organization on the grounds of its apartheid policies.

Emboldened by these early successes in barring South Africa from agencies of the world organization, Afro-Asian members implored the UN to take punitive action against South Africa. On 6 November 1962 member states were urged by majority vote in the General Assembly to sever diplomatic relations with South Africa, to close their ports to all vessels under the South African flag, to prohibit ships of member states from entering South African ports, to boycott South African goods, to refrain from exporting to South Africa, and to refuse landing and passage facilities to all South African aircraft. While this resolution had no binding power, it showed that "conscience of the world," as Mrs. Pandit dubbed the General Assembly in 1946, had indeed been awakened to the cause. It demonstrated impatience on the part of a world no longer content simply to condemn South Africa but clamoring instead for sanctions. To add weight to such resolutions, the General Assembly needed, however, to win over the Security Council, where permanent members such as the United States, Britain, and France were still resisting drastic punitive measures.

In 1946 India alone had neither the strength nor the size to make sanctions work against South Africa. Instead of hurting the target country, it deprived itself of useful exports and income. It discovered that unless trade sanctions are universal and near total, they do not work. Ultimately, however, it was not even the United Nations that held the key to successful sanctions but its strongest member, the United States. Until this superpower could be convinced to throw its weight behind the sanctions effort, all these resolutions at the United Nations would amount to nothing more than pure posturing—leaving South Africa unscathed and free to pursue apartheid.

To get the United States to support punitive measures against South Africa in the immediate postwar years seemed almost impossible. South Africa's "domestic policies" held a low priority in Washington. In US government circles, obsessed with the new danger of Communism, South Africa was regarded as a staunch and valuable ally—and in the American business community, a lucrative outpost of capitalism in Africa.

NOTES

1. Calpin, G. H., *Indians in South Africa,* p. 204.

2. *Commerce,* New Delhi, 10 November 1944.

3. Raj, K. N., "Sanctions and the Indian Experience," *Sanctions Against South Africa,* ed. Ronald Segal, pp. 99-102.

4. Ibid.

5. According to experts the "sender" of sanctions should preferably have a GNP ten times that of the "target country." Hufbauer, G.C.and Schott, J.J., *Economic Sanctions in Support of Foreign Policy Goals,* p. 56.

6. Fornara, Charles, *Plutarch and the Megarian Decree,* Yale Classical Studies, p. 24.

7. Dexter, Byron, *The Years of Opportunity—The League of Nations 1920-1926,* pp. 215-226.

8. Padover, Saul K., ed., *Wilson's Ideals,* p. 108.

9. Hufbauer and Schott, op. cit., pp. 8-9.

10. Scott, George, *The Rise and Fall of the League of Nations,* pp. 353-368.

11. Hufbauer and Schott, op. cit., p. 10.

12. Houser, George, The *International Impact of the South African Struggle for Liberation,* UN Center Against Apartheid, Department of Political and Security Affairs, No. 2/82, January 1982, p. 12.

13. Calpin, op. cit., p.246.

14. Ibid., p. 204.

15. Ibid.

16. Paton, A., *Hofmeyr,* p. 437.

17. Van der Poel, J., *Selections from the Smuts Papers,* Vol. VII, p. 105.

2

Caution, Compromise and Muddle

US policies toward South Africa since World War II have been
marked by caution, compromise and muddle, by inconsistency
between rhetoric and action.

—*Anthony Lake*
Adviser to US Presidents[1]

In trying not only to awaken the world's conscience but to spur its most
powerful nation into action against apartheid, India and its supporters in the
United Nations faced an uphill battle. In contrast to firm and decisive action
on other world fronts, US policymaking toward South Africa in the immediate
postwar years was, according to Anthony Lake, marked by caution, compromise, and muddle.[2]

Try as it might, the United Nations could not move the United States during the Truman and Eisenhower years to support its verbal condemnation of
South Africa, let alone consider punitive measures. Until 1958 the United
States chose to abstain from casting a vote whenever the General Assembly
or its agencies condemned South Africa's racial policies. This was done in
accordance with the South African contention that such resolutions constituted interference in its domestic affairs and therefore a contravention of
Article 2 (7) of the UN Charter.

While the United States, under Truman from 1945 until 1952 and under
Eisenhower from 1953 until 1960, may have appeared uncertain and muddled
in its approach, South Africa itself emerged with a new sense of domestic
purpose and direction after Malan replaced Smuts in the general election of
1948. On 26 May 1948, South Africa's White electorate chose the clear
direction offered by Malan's apartheid over the uncertainty of another five

years under Smuts. Soon to become the most hated word around the globe
since Nazism, with which it was frequently equated, apartheid was in reality
a refined version of the segregation applied in South Africa from the very day
that Black and White first encountered each other. It was old-style petty segregation coupled with a larger vision of self-governing Black nations. In contrast to the confused past practices, apartheid left little to imagination or dis-
cretion. Soon after he was sworn in as prime minister, Malan embarked on a
legislative spree, adding bricks and mortar until the fortress of apartheid
stood seemingly invincible against the Black threat.

So-called petty apartheid laws separated White and Black from cradle to
grave, stipulating where they could be born, educated, and work, where they
could live, travel, play sport, and be buried. Grand apartheid was embodied
in laws too, giving Blacks the opportunity and encouragement to become
citizens of their traditional homelands instead of seeking rights in "White"
South Africa. New laws in the first decade included the Prohibition of Mixed
Marriages and the Immorality Acts, the Group Areas Act and the Population
Registration Act of 1950. The latter, considered to be one of the cornerstones
of apartheid, classified South Africa's population according to racial origin
and required all adults to be entered on a central register as either White,
Indian, Colored or Blacks—divided according to tribal affiliation and origin.
After Malan retired in 1954 the construction of "fortress apartheid" was
continued by his successors. First, Premier Johannes Strijdom, and after his
death in 1958, his successor, Dr. Hendrik Verwoerd, oversaw the tedious
work.

The National Government tackled the outside world with the same self-as-
sured vigor that characterized its approach to domestic problems. Within
months after he took over in May 1948, Malan repealed the indirect representation in parliament granted to South Africa's Indians by Smuts shortly before
he left office. Any type of vote for Indians in the central government, Malan
argued, would lead to similar demands by other "non-Whites." Indians, he
contended, were not permanent residents and therefore not entitled to a role
in South Africa's affairs. On 14 May 1949, South Africa rejected a call by the
United Nations for a round-table discussion of South Africa's treatment of its
Indian population, which it considered a purely domestic matter. When the
UN General Assembly passed a resolution on 2 December 1950, insisting that
South Africa negotiate with India under the auspices of the three-man UN
commission, the leader of the South African delegation, Interior Minister T.
E. Dönges, summarily rejected it as the "most naked form of intervention."[3]

On the question of South West Africa, Malan informed the UN Trusteeship
Council that he felt no obligation to submit reports on developments in the
territory, and during October 1948 he announced that the territory would
henceforth be administered as an integral part of South Africa. The UN
Trusteeship Committee asked the International Court of Justice on 6
December 1949, to decide whether the Malan government was entitled to ab-

sorb South West Africa in defiance of the world organization. Seven months later, on 11 July 1950, the Court advised that South Africa was still bound by its obligations under the League of Nations mandate and therefore not entitled to change the territory's status without UN approval. Malan's government ignored the ruling, and on 30 August 1950, the territory held its first elections as part of South Africa, resulting in a sweeping victory for the National Party. Prime Minister Malan welcomed this triumph as a mandate for apartheid and "anti-Communist" policies in the territory. The stage was set for a protracted battle with the United Nations over control of South West Africa.

On 29 November 1953, the General Assembly passed two resolutions on South West Africa, one establishing a seven-man commission to study and report to the Assembly on the situation in South West Africa and the other demanding that the territory be placed under UN trusteeship. These and numerous other resolutions adopted by the General Assembly had little effect without the support of the United States or other major Western powers. The United States consistently abstained in accordance with a precedent set by Truman's Secretary of State, Dean Acheson, in 1952. In that year Acheson felt obliged to overrule Eleanor Roosevelt and others in the US delegation who argued that the United States should support an anti-apartheid resolution, co-sponsored by India and several Asian and Arab nations, on moral grounds. The United States, Acheson instructed, "should not intervene for what are called moral reasons in the internal affairs of another country." This would be "merely a cover for self-indulgent hypocrisy."[4]

Although there was no first-hand contact between Malan or his successors, Strijdom and Verwoerd, with either Presidents Truman or Eisenhower, relations with the United States in the military, diplomatic, scientific, and economic fields were mostly cordial and productive. In its new role as leader of the so-called Western world against the Soviet Union and its Communist allies, the United States welcomed all the assistance it could get. South Africa fitted into the global picture as a bastion against Communism in Africa. It was not only strategically located along the important Cape sea route but a supplier of vital materials. In 1948 the Malan government was one of the first to send an air crew to assist in the US-inspired Berlin airlift—a step that prompted the Truman administration to upgrade its diplomatic representation in South Africa to ambassadorial level in March 1949. To further underline its willingness to fight Communism, South Africa volunteered a South African Air Force (SAAF) squadron to assist in the battle against North Korea and Red China. At the end of August 1950, the UN and the United States accepted its offer, and two months later South African pilots joined the action in the Korean War effort.

Building on a friendship that developed between United States and South Africa during World War II, not only on the battlefield but on the highest level between Field Marshall Smuts and US President Franklin Roosevelt, a lend-lease agreement was signed and a number of US air bases established in

South Africa. During August 1949 both South Africa's Defense Minister Frans Erasmus, and his Chief of Staff, Lt. Gen. Ben Beyers, toured military facilities in the United States to determine the type of US equipment that would be suitable and available for the training of South African defense forces.[5]

On 10 November 1951, South Africa announced that it had reached agreement with the United States regarding the supply of military equipment. Furthermore, as a founder member of the International Atomic Energy Agency (IAEA), South Africa enjoyed full cooperation from the United States and other major nuclear powers. South Africa's Atomic Energy Board (AEB), established in 1949, started a development program in the early 1950s, and in 1957 President Dwight Eisenhower announced that it would be part of a group of six nations pooling their atomic resources and expertise. Apart from South Africa and the United States, Britain, Canada, France, and Australia were included in this arrangement.

Cooperation in space projects started in 1957 when South Africa's Council for Scientific and Industrial Research (CSIR) helped to keep track of the Soviet satellite, Sputnik I. Toward the end of the Eisenhower years, in September 1960, agreement was reached on the establishment of three facilities in South Africa by the US National Aeronautics and Space Administration (NASA).

Trade between South Africa and the United States expanded from a total of $230 million in 1946 to almost $400 million in 1960. In that year South African imports from the United States reached $288 million compared with $108 million in exports, giving the United States a favorable trade balance of $180 million. Despite a slight dip in the early 1950s, US investment in South Africa grew from $212 million in 1953 to $350 million in 1960.

Returning from his assignment as Eisenhower's emissary to South Africa in 1961, Ambassador Philip Crowe enunciated the priorities that guided US policy toward South Africa in the 1950s. South Africa stood firm, he pointed out in a letter to *US News and World Report* on 18 December 1961, while most of the 40-odd nations between Cairo and Cape Town were either neutral or under Communist influence. "The net of it," Crowe concluded, "is that South Africa has faced the issue of Communism squarely and is willing to go a long way toward combating it. Russia's threats and saber-rattlings do not scare her as they seem to frighten most of the emerging nations of the continent."

For many years South Africa played this anti-Communist theme to the hilt in an effort to keep the United States and other major Western nations from succumbing to increasing pressures at the United Nations against apartheid and its conduct in South West Africa. In May 1954 Malan took India to task, classifying it together with China as a Communist state, intent on fomenting trouble in South Africa by supporting the Black-led Defiance Campaign and other protests. In August 1954 Malan once again accused Nehru of using the Indian communities in posing a Communist threat against the European powers in Africa.[6] The South African leader was in tune with his times, as an article in *Newsweek* on 22 November 1955, shows. The magazine revealed an "actual blueprint" showing that the Kremlin "decided to give the highest priority" to the "infiltration of Africa from Tunis to Cape Town, from Dakar to Madagascar" and the "enlistment of all existing Communist and Communist-front organizations behind nationalist movements in each country and territory." In South Africa, *Newsweek* claimed, "opponents of Prime Minister Johannes G. Strijdom's apartheid or racial segregation policy will be given full support" in an effort "to whip up the same kind of militant agitation that now threatens France's hold on North Africa."

In subsequent years the South African authorities would frequently raise the specter of Communism whenever it came under attack in the United Nations or other world forums. After a policy speech by South African Foreign Minister Eric Louw at the 1961 UN session was expunged, Information Minister Frank Waring ascribed this "unprecedented happening" as "the logical result of the admission to United Nations membership of 26 newly-independent States" who "reinforced the Afro-Asian-cum-Communist-cum-Western-socialist-humanist bloc in the United Nations Assembly that has been sitting in judgment of South Africa since 1946."[7]

But Communism was not only a useful theme abroad. It served the South African government well in the justification of harsh measures aimed at containing and crushing growing domestic resistance and unrest at home.

Although there was a potpourri of protest movements that mushroomed as apartheid cast its growing shadow over the South African landscape, the African National Congress (ANC) took center stage. Aimed at defending the rights and privileges of Blacks, the ANC was established on 8 January 1912—barely two years after the Union of South Africa gained its independence from Britain and even two years before the National Party was formed. Until the outbreak of World War II, the ANC limited its actions mostly to appeals and manifestos, bringing Black complaints to the attention of the White authorities. Occasionally it invoked passive resistance. In the 1920s the ANC allied itself with the South African Communist Party (SACP), a White-dominated movement formed in 1921 to promote workers' causes. This partnership came to an abrupt end in 1930, when the more moderate Dr. Pixley ka Isaka Seme succeeded Josiah Gumede as leader of the ANC.

Issues of special concern in the 1930s were the termination of the indirect franchise enjoyed by Blacks in the Cape and Natal and the passage of the Native Trust and Land Act of 1936, which stipulated where Blacks could own land. The ANC formed the All-African Convention to present a united front against these affronts. In 1939 this umbrella organization was renamed the Non-European Front and expanded to include once again the SACP. During the war years the ANC and the SACP formed the African Mineworkers' Union, while a group of young black intellectuals established the ANC Youth League (ANCYL). In their ranks were Nelson Mandela, Walter Sisulu, and Oliver Tambo, who were all destined to play a major role in the ANC. In the immediate postwar years the ANC and SACP pact was strengthened when the two groups signed an agreement with the South African Indian Congress (SAIC). This new alliance threw its weight behind a boycott of Smuts' Native Representative Council—a body created for Blacks as an alternative to direct representation in parliament.

Malan and his National Party thus inherited in 1948 from Smuts and his United Party an increasingly militant alliance that stood ready to challenge apartheid. Under pressure from the Youth League, the ANC opted for mass action together with a number of other organizations under the newly formed Congress Alliance. On 1 May 1950, this alliance between the ANC, the SACP, and the SAIC launched nationwide strikes and demonstrations that soon led to clashes with the police, resulting in a number of shooting deaths. The government responded by passing the Suppression of Communism Act in June 1950, which outlawed the SACP and other organizations deemed subversive. By its definition, the Act regarded Communism as "any doctrine or scheme which aims at bringing about any political, economic, social or industrial changes in South Africa by the promotion of disorder or disturbances or which aims at encouraging feelings of hostility between the White community and non-White community." By the time the Act was passed, the SACP, anticipating its banning, had already disbanded and gone underground. Its membership found a new home in the ANC, which was still operating legally. Public protests against the new law were held throughout the country. One such demonstration in Cape Town on 14 June 1950, turned into a riot.

In December 1951 the ANC wrote to Prime Minister Malan, demanding that apartheid legislation be abolished and Blacks be given direct representation in parliament. He refused, and on 6 April 1952, the ANC and the SAIC held nationwide meetings to launch their Defiance of Unjust Laws Campaign. This movement gained further momentum as the Malan government proposed legislation to remove the Coloreds from the common voters' roll. What started as passive resistance and civil disobedience soon led to clashes with the police, arrests, and eventually, deaths. From the end of June 1952, the ANC and its non-White allies started deliberately breaking apartheid laws. Indians entered townships reserved for Blacks only, while Blacks refused to carry passes. Non-Whites used White entrances at railway stations and post offices and broke curfew regulations by roaming the streets in White areas late at night. In October 1952 alone 2,354 non-Whites were arrested on charges of violating the apartheid laws.

The Suppression of Communism Act had become inadequate. The new Public Safety Act 3 of 1953 gave government the power to declare a state of emergency by suspending laws and governing by decree, while the Criminal Law Amendment Act, also passed early in 1953, was intended specifically to cope with the Defiance Campaign. It made passive resistance against any law punishable. The Riotous Assemblies and Suppression of Communism

Amendment Act was passed on 3 February 1954, empowering the Justice Minister to prohibit, without giving reasons, public gatherings, and to ban anyone from attending.

In America this Defiance Campaign started to attract media attention. "Who among us can keep reading day after day the little news items from South Africa without a feeling of dismay of Negroes being arrested—thirty, fifty, a hundred at a time—fined, jailed and now flogged," wrote the *New York Times* on 12 August 1952. "Outsiders are watching the whole proceedings with a growing sense of dread, as well as disgust."

In October and November 1952 rioting broke out in Port Elizabeth and rapidly spread to various parts of South Africa, leaving several Whites and Blacks dead. The ANC condemned these incidents and denied involvement but the Justice Minister insisted that they were a direct result of the Defiance Campaign. While anti-apartheid activists abroad heralded this campaign as the long-awaited uprising of South Africa's Blacks and tried to use it as a springboard for sanctions and other punitive measures, the Nationalist government downplayed its significance. Speaking at the Natal National Party Congress in November 1952, then Native Affairs Minister Verwoerd, cautioned delegates against an "exaggerated view of the situation." This sort of behavior, he explained, "went in curves as in a graph—there were periods of peace and quiet and then came disturbances." In 1920, he reminded his audience, there were similar riots, arson, and bloodshed—and complaints by the liberals.[8]

On 26 June 1955 some 3,000 multiracial delegates representing the African National Congress, the South African Indian Congress, the South African Colored People's Congress, the South African Congress of Democrats, and the South African Congress of Trade Unions attended a meeting at Kliptown near Johannesburg. This Congress of the People gave birth to a Freedom Charter—based on the UN Universal Declaration of Human Rights and destined to become the touchstone of the resistance movement for many years to follow. "South Africa belongs to all who live in it, Black and White, and no Government can justly claim authority unless it is based on the will of all the people," the Freedom Charter declared. Those present demanded "equal treatment for all under the law" and claimed that "the mineral wealth beneath the soil, the banks and monopoly industry shall be transferred to the ownership of the people as a whole."[9]

Eighteen months later, on 5 December 1956, the government arrested 156 of the leading organizers of the Kliptown event on charges of high treason. The defendants—ranging from parliamentarians to priests, students, clerical workers, and laborers—were accused of attempting to overthrow the state and set up a Communist regime. On 17 December 1958, however, the prosecution, citing lack of evidence, withdrew its case against 61 of the accused, including African National Congress (ANC) President Albert Luthuli. Eventually all were acquitted after a trial that lasted four years.

In the meantime, Black activists scored a victory in their first boycott action inside South Africa. Starting as a protest against a fare increase of one penny, the boycott of the bus service between the Black township of Alexandria and Johannesburg soon turned into a political confrontation. In spite of the attempts by the authorities to end it, the boycott persisted for several weeks. Eventually it was agreed that the fares would remain unchanged, with employers paying a subsidy to make the service viable.

The Promotion of Bantu Self-Government Act adopted by the Verwoerd government at the beginning of 1959 to create separate independent homelands or Bantustans, where Blacks could exercise their political rights, resulted in further resistance and unrest. In June 1959 violent clashes between Blacks and the police erupted in and around Durban. It soon spread to other parts of Natal. Black organizers met in Durban on 26 November 1959, to plan another wave of passive resistance against the government's apartheid policies. The meeting was convened by banned ANC leader Albert Luthuli and attended by his followers as well as members of the Natal Indian Congress, the multiracial South African Congress of Democrats, and the South African Congress of Trade Unions.

Under discussion was Luthuli's appeal that "black buying and manpower" be used to "induce South Africa to mend its ways." Although he did not feel that "the economic ostracism" of South Africa was desirable from every point of view, Luthuli saw it as the only chance of a "relatively peaceful transition" to black majority rule. While expressing gratitude for "the way in which India at the UN has taken up the cudgels on behalf of the oppressed South African majority," he felt that it was "the growing world boycott, and the withdrawal—the very wise withdrawal—of foreign capital from the Union [of South Africa], which jolts them [the Whites] worst." Conceding that this economic boycott of South Africa would bring "hardship for Africans," Luthuli felt it was a price worth paying as it would shorten "the day of bloodshed."[10] In April 1959 a number of Black members who were opposed to the multiracial nature of the ANC defected. Under the leadership of Robert Sobukwe they formed the more militant, exclusively Black Pan Africanist Congress (PAC).

It was against this volatile background that visiting British Prime Minister Harold MacMillan delivered his historic and prophetic "winds of change" speech before the joint houses of parliament in Cape Town on 3 February 1960—at the conclusion of an extensive African journey. "The most striking of all the impressions I have formed since I left London a month ago is the strength of this African national consciousness," MacMillan cautioned his all-White audience, assembled in the ornate parliamentary dining room. "The wind of change is blowing through the continent. Whether we like it or not, this growth of political consciousness is a political fact."[11] Britain, said MacMillan, could not support South African apartheid but he also made clear his opposition to pressures for sanctions against South Africa. "I certainly do not believe in refusing to trade with people because you may happen to dislike the way they manage their internal affairs," the British leader said.[12]

At this time the Eisenhower administration had abandoned the Acheson rule of abstaining on UN resolutions critical of apartheid on the ground that it constituted "interference" in a member state's "domestic affairs." It could no longer ignore the growing voting strength of Black Africa as other former colonies followed Ghana to independence. Furthermore, on the US domestic front, the 1954 landmark Brown vs. the Board of Education decision by the Supreme Court had put civil rights on the front burner. During the 1958, UN session the United States voted against apartheid for the very first time. After registering the first US vote against South African apartheid at the UN on 30 October 1958, Assistant Secretary Joseph Satterthwaite, head of the newly formed Bureau of African Affairs at the US State Department, explained why it was necessary. The African people were looking to the United States for assistance, moral leadership, and understanding of their aspirations, he said.[13]

At least two years before Harold MacMillan lectured his distinguished White audience at the South African parliament about the winds of change in February 1960, the United States had already picked up the gusts and tilted its sails accordingly. But in the view of Eisenhower and his Secretary of State John Foster Dulles, South Africa still remained an ally in the struggle against international Communism. Not long after the UN vote of 1958, Satterthwaite, during an appearance before the Senate Committee on Foreign Relations, asked rhetorically whether it made sense indeed for the United States to express its opposition to apartheid when South Africa offered its unqualified support in the containment of the Soviet Union. This kind of ambivalence made it possible for South African Foreign Minister, Eric Louw, to dismiss another adverse American vote in the United Nations in 1959 as something that did not represent any fundamental change in American policy but simply the personal prejudice of a labor leader "well-known for his dislike of racial segregation" who just happened to be the head of the US delegation.[14]

Barely two months after the historic MacMillan speech a whirlwind ripped through an obscure black township near Johannesburg. On 21 March 1960, the newly formed Pan Africanist Congress (PAC) had started a nationwide protest by mustering its followers at police stations without passbooks, inviting arrest. At most stations the police managed to disperse the crowds without incident, but at the Transvaal township of Sharpeville they opened fire into an estimated crowd of 20,000 rock-throwing protesters, killing 67 and wounding 178. The reaction in Washington was unusually swift and strong. Without consulting its embassy in Pretoria or the White House, the State Department issued a statement on 22 March, expressing hope that "the African people of South Africa will be able to obtain redress for their legitimate grievances" and regretted "the tragic loss of life resulting from the measures taken against the demonstrators."[15] Despite strenuous objections

by the South Africans at the UN, the United States called a meeting of the
Security Council and joined in a resolution on 1 April 1960, "deploring the
policies and actions of the South African government." The South African
situation, it was resolved, "might endanger international peace and security."
Both Britain and France abstained.

In declaring the situation in South Africa a possible danger to world peace
and security, the United States for the first time opened the door to punitive
measures authorized under the UN Charter for such situations. The United
States placed apartheid permanently on the Security Council's agenda and in
November 1960 it fired off an aide-memoire to Pretoria urging it to abandon
"a policy that was so clearly in violation of the UN Charter."[16] American investors joined the capital flight from South Africa in the wake of the
Sharpeville shootings, causing the South African foreign exchange reserves
to plunge by $64 million. Gold slumped. Anti-apartheid activists abroad, who
once believed that South Africa's economy was invincible, started speculat-
ing optimistically about a possible collapse and the end of White rule.

At the Witwatersrand show grounds, after speaking before a business audience on Saturday, 9 April 1960, Dr. Verwoerd was shot twice in the head and
seriously wounded. The assailant, a wealthy British-born cattle breeder,
David Pratt, reportedly "hated Nationalists." The minister of Public Works,
Paul Sauer, who acted as prime minister until 31 May while Verwoerd recovered, caused a stir in National Party circles by calls for a "new approach" to
the Black problem. In a speech on 19 April 1960, at Humansdorp he argued
in favor of higher wages and the easing of passbook and other restrictions.
Sharpeville, Sauer concluded, had closed the "old book" of White-Black relations. Apartheid legislation should be changed, he said, to give Blacks "a
hope for a happy existence."[17] Foreign Minister Eric Louw wasted no time
rebuking Sauer and as well as those in the National Party who supported him.
The government's policy remained unchanged, he told parliament on 20 April
1960. Within a week Verwoerd would be in full control again, he added, to
give reassurances in this regard.

About a month later Prime Minister Verwoerd, while still recovering from
his wounds, did inform parliament that certain "changes" were indeed contemplated. They were, however, hardly a change in direction or policy—
merely cosmetic adjustments. In a message read in the House of Assembly
on 20 May 1960, Verwoerd merely intimated a more charitable approach on
the part of the authorities as far as police raids in the townships and the use
of liquor by Blacks were concerned. Employers were encouraged to increase
productivity to justify higher wages, and steps were promised to accelerate
the political and industrial development of the Black homelands.[18]

Within a few months the South African government managed to put down
the revolt and restore law and order. The state of emergency was lifted on 31
August 1960, and the uproar overseas subsided. Investors returned and foreign
funds started flowing in once again to a lucrative market that had regained a

good measure of stability. In November 1960 General Motors announced expansion plans. Substantial loans from US banks and multilateral lending institutions further helped South Africa toward economic recovery and growth.

Under this crust of recovered stability, however, a simmering undercurrent still remained, ready to erupt again like a volcano. The ANC and the PAC went underground, establishing bases in friendly African states from which they planned to launch the next phase—an armed struggle. Sharpeville and the insurrection that followed in its wake did not bring apartheid to an end, but it signified to some the beginning of the end. "It is my personal belief that history will recognize that Sharpeville marked a watershed in South African affairs," wrote anti-apartheid activist Bishop Ambrose Reeves a few years later. "Until Sharpeville, violence for the most part had been used in South Africa by those who were committed to the maintenance of the White minority." After Sharpeville, said Reeves, "for the first time both sides in the racial struggle in South Africa were committed to violence; the White minority to preserve the *status quo;* the non-White majority to change."[19]

More important, the Western world, including America, could no longer afford to stay aloof or discount South Africa's racial problems as a purely domestic affair. It had become a race war of sorts. So a new course was set that would increasingly and inevitably lead to greater pressures at the United Nations for punitive measures by its most powerful member, the United States. Until 1960 the United States was able to stand on the sidelines as a dispassionate, if not disinterested observer, noted Christopher Coker. It could refuse to choose between its economic interests and moral responsibilities and for most part it was not required to do so.[20] This was no longer possible.

The hardened American rhetoric toward the end of the Eisenhower administration, however, still fell far short of the expectations of those who demanded sanctions to bring apartheid to an end. Still, they did see a few cracks in the armor. Although it was still a matter of words instead of deeds, the US diplomats had at least been forced to become more virulent and strident in their condemnation of South Africa and apartheid. On the other hand, US business and official relations with South Africa were quickly restored and even expanded. It was also with great disappointment that apartheid's opponents heard on 13 September 1960, of the US National Aeronautics and Space Administration's decision to establish three tracking stations on South African soil. Equally disheartening was the prospect of seeing Eisenhower's hands-off policy continued by Vice President Richard Nixon, who was expected to win the presidential race.

Then the unexpected happened. Nixon lost to a young, relatively obscure senator from Massachusetts named John Fitzgerald Kennedy. "Now the trumpet summons us again against the common enemies of man: tyranny, poverty, disease," Kennedy declared in his inaugural speech in January 1961. To Blacks in Africa and America this signaled willingness to go beyond mere rhetoric in the fight against "tyranny" in South Africa. The South African government had, of course, its own totally different interpretation. "President John F. Kennedy pledged to those old allies whose cultural and spiritual origins we share, the loyalty of faithful friends," observed South African Information Minister Frank Waring. "South Africans assumed that they were included in this pledge [as] they do share with Americans their cultural and spiritual origins and the values that go with them."[21]

The South African Minister turned out to be wrong in his assumption. Both John Kennedy, and his successor, Lyndon Johnson, sided with Black Africans and Americans against the "tyranny" of apartheid. The growing strength of the African contingent in the United Nations and the increasing importance of Black Americans in domestic politics left them no other choice.

NOTES

1. Lake, Anthony, *Caution and Concern: The Making of American Policy Toward South Africa, 1946-1971*, p. 44.

2. Ibid.

3. *New York Times*, 3 December 1950.

4. Thomas, Franklin, ed., *South Africa: Time Running Out*, pp. 344-345.

5. Lake, op. cit., pp. 48-50.

6. *New York Times,* 2 August 1954.

7. Waring, Frank, Foreword, *The Case for South Africa: As Put Forth in the Statements of Eric H Louw,* ed. H. Biermann, p.10.

8. *The Star,* Johannesburg, 28 November 1952.

9. Luthuli, A., *Let My People Go,* pp. 158-160.

10. Ibid., p. 208.

11. *Souvenir of Visit of The Right. Hon. Harold MacMillan, Prime Minister of the United Kingdom to the House of Parliament on Wednesday, 3rd February, 1960,* Printed on Authority of Mr. Speaker, Cape Times Ltd., Parow, p. 8.

12. Ibid., pp. 12-13.

13. Thomas, op. cit., p. 346.

14. Coker, C., *Constructive Engagement and Its Critics*, p. 4.

15. Thomas, op. cit., p. 347.

16. Coker, op. cit., p. 6.

17. *Die Burger,* Cape Town, 20 April 1960.

18. *Die Burger*, Cape Town, 21 May 1960.

19. Houser, George, The *International Impact of the South African Struggle for Liberation,* UN Center Against Apartheid, Department of Political and Security Affairs, No. 2/82, January 1982, p. 14.

20. Coker, op. cit., p. 4.

21. Waring, op. cit., p.12.

3

Disengagement

It is generally accepted that disengagement is the middle ground
between sanctions and a do-nothing policy.

William Hance[1]

Disengagement, as applied by John F. Kennedy during his brief presidency
and continued by his successor, Lyndon Johnson, turned out to be a disappointment for those who expected them to push for racial equality in South
Africa with the same fervor as they did in America. It was, according to
American political scientist William Hance, the middle ground between
sanctions and a do-nothing policy—pleasing neither White South Africa nor
its detractors.

In November 1962 historian Arthur Schlesinger, then an aide in the
Kennedy White House, was summoned to the Oval Office. President John F.
Kennedy instructed him to assist UN Ambassador Francis Plimpton with the
text of a speech explaining to the world organization why America was opposed to sanctions against South Africa. Schlesinger paraphrased Kennedy's
instruction as follows: "Would the passage of a resolution recommending
sanctions bring about the practical result we seek? We do not believe this
would bring us closer to our objective—the abandonment of apartheid in
South Africa. We see little value in a resolution which would be primarily a
means for a discharge of our emotions, which would be unlikely to be fully
implemented and which calls for measures which could be easily evaded by
the country to which they are addressed—with the result of calling into question the whole efficacy of the sanctions process."[2]

After Sharpeville the Security Council had instructed Secretary General
Dag Hammarskjold to investigate on a first-hand basis South Africa's racial

policies. Although Hammarskjold made preliminary arrangements for this trip with Foreign Minister Eric Louw at a meeting in London during May 1960, the Congo crisis interfered and it was only on 6 January 1961, that Hammarskjold finally began a week-long visit to the land of apartheid. Returning on 12 January, after private discussions with Prime Minister Verwoerd, representatives of the ANC, and church leaders, Hammarskjold issued a communiqué describing his talks as "frank, constructive and helpful." On 23 January, however, he conceded before the Security Council that he had been unable to reach an agreement with Verwoerd "on arrangements that would provide for appropriate safeguards of human rights" in South Africa. The UN General Assembly therefore on 13 April 1961, urged member states "to consider taking such separate and collective action as is open to them under the UN Charter to bring about the abandonment of the policies." A proposal that diplomatic and economic sanctions be applied against South Africa was defeated by forty-two to thirty-four votes—twenty-one nations abstaining.

Verwoerd launched South Africa's largest peace-time police raid to date on 3 May 1961. It was aimed at non-White leaders who called for a general strike at the end of that month when the Union of South Africa was to become a republic. The strike action was first announced in March at a mass meeting in Pietermaritzburg attended by ANC and PAC delegates, with Nelson Mandela as the main speaker. Between 8,000 and 10,000 were arrested, but Mandela narrowly escaped and went into hiding. On 31 May 1961 South Africa heralded its new republican status in relative tranquillity as the strike fizzled. Only about 50 percent of the Black work force in Johannesburg stayed away from work. The authorities were putting the newly promulgated General Law Amendment Act of May 1961 to good use in maintaining law and order and crushing the Black opposition.

On 28 November 1961, the UN General Assembly responded with yet another resolution condemning South Africa. It was a milder substitute for two draft resolutions that had called not only for economic sanctions but for South Africa's expulsion from the UN—strongly opposed by United States and other Western states. During the debate in the UN General Assembly, South African Foreign Minister Eric Louw had threatened to turn any sanctions against those who applied them. Citing the use of South African harbors and services when the Suez Canal was closed in 1956, Louw believed shipping was one area where South Africa could retaliate. "Punitive action works both ways," he said.[3]

A year later, over objections from the United States and other Western nations, the UN General Assembly passed a strong resolution calling on member states to sever diplomatic relations with South Africa, to close their ports to all vessels under the South African flag, to stop using South African ports, to boycott South African goods, to refuse to export to South Africa, and to deny landing and passage facilities to all aircraft of the South African government and companies registered under South African law. With this tough measure on 6 November 1962, it had become clear to the Kennedy administration that the United States could no longer escape African pressures. Still, the sanctions contained in a November 1962 General Assembly resolution were considered an "unrealistic declaration" and "grandiose and ineffectual" by an "impatient" Kennedy.[4]

The matter surfaced again with fresh intensity in May 1963 when the newly formed Organization of African Unity called from Addis Ababa on the United States to choose between Africa and the White rulers of South Africa and the Portuguese territories. In both of these countries, the United States had strategic interests. It had established a military tracking station in South Africa and in June 1962 agreed to sell the Verwoerd government arms for use against Communist aggression. Its base on the Portuguese was important in the Cold War rivalry with the Soviet Union. These were some of the considerations that came up during a meeting held in the Kennedy cabinet room on 18 July 1963, to consider an appropriate response to renewed pressures from the OAU for sanctions against both South Africa and Portugal.

Assistant Secretary of State for Africa and former Michigan Governor Mennen (Soapy) Williams felt that a full military embargo was justified. Even though this would fall short of the sanctions proposed by the UN General Assembly in 1962, it would be a step in the right direction, he argued.[5] Adlai Stevenson, who replaced Plimpton as UN Ambassador, cautioned Kennedy that the United States was approaching a decisive situation from which the Africans will draw conclusions about the "long-run nature" of its policies. But there were senior officials who argued strongly against sanctions. It would, they pointed out, gain for the United States only a "transitory political truce with the African leaders, who would be satisfied with nothing less than a full economic embargo" and jeopardize the tangible advantages of cooperation with South Africa on a wide range of defense matters.[6]

Sanctions against South Africa had become necessary not only as a gesture to increasingly impatient African member states, but also to help deflect pressures for similar action against Portugal. In the case of Portugal, Kennedy feared that sanctions would lead to the loss of its strategic Portuguese Azores base. Sanctions against South Africa, it was felt, "could do something in African eyes to make up for restraint in the case of Portugal." Still, the prospect of a total UN arms embargo troubled both Kennedy and Secretary of State Rusk, as it might set "a precedent for collective sanctions which might lead the UN down a road imperiling its very existence."[7] Although Rusk favored a call on UN member states to refrain from supplying arms that could be used to suppress the Black African population, Kennedy eventually settled on an arms embargo that went one step further. The United States would sell no further arms to South Africa from the beginning of 1964 as long as South Africa continued to practice apartheid.

On 2 August 1963, UN Ambassador Adlai Stevenson relayed this decision to the Security Council and five days later he voted for a resolution by the Council calling on all states "to cease forthwith the sale and shipment of arms, ammunition of all types and military vehicles to South Africa." He expressed the hope that South Africa would reassess apartheid in the light of the constantly growing international concern over its failure to heed the numerous appeals made to it by various organs of the United Nations—as well as appeals by member states, including the United States. But he ruled out mandatory or coercive sanctions as "both bad law and bad policy." It was bad law because the founders of the United Nations intended to limit such severe measures to instances where there was "a clear and present threat to the peace." This threat did not exist in South Africa's case. It was bad policy "because the application of mandatory sanctions in this situation was unlikely to lead to the abandonment of apartheid," Stevenson felt.[8]

When the UN Security Council voted on 2 August 1963, for an arms embargo against South Africa, Britain and France abstained. In American circles there was dissension over the wisdom of the US initiative and its impact. It was felt that it could not satisfy for long the insatiable African demand for stronger measures against apartheid. Expressing this insatiable African demand at the time were Patrick Duncan and Philip Mason, two critics who presumed to speak for Africa and the disenfranchised in South Africa. They both wrote articles in the prestigious American magazine, *Foreign Affairs,* urging the United States to support the fight for "political and social justice" for Blacks in South Africa by applying far-reaching sanctions. In his article Duncan, the son of a former South African governor-general who lived in exile in London, rejected as insignificant Ambassador Adlai Stevenson's announcement that the United States had utilized its diplomatic and consular establishments in South Africa "to demonstrate by words and by deeds" its official disapproval of apartheid. These words, Duncan argued, had "limited value" and the only deed that Stevenson could cite was the American Embassy's invitation of non-Whites to its Fourth of July celebrations over the objection of the Verwoerd government. The United States should discourage investment in South Africa because American capital helped to prop up and strengthen apartheid, Duncan insisted.[9] British activist Philip Mason also criticized Kennedy for not going far enough in his support of sanctions against South Africa and called for disinvestment.[10]

Duncan warned that if apartheid were to continue much longer, or if the world were to stand aside from South Africa while the races "mutilated each other," race relationships everywhere could he poisoned.[11] This connection between the racial issue in South Africa and race relations elsewhere became a part of the litany in the early 1960s, according to Richard Bissell. "Both ideologically and tactically, Blacks were seen as standing together in various separate political struggles," he wrote. South Africa's problems were not only "a barometer of US racial attitudes, but also a determinant of racial peace in the United States and elsewhere." In this fashion, he said, "relations with South Africa became the most important foreign policy issue for US Blacks to include in their political platforms."[12]

For many years, however, action against South Africa was driven not by Black Americans but White activists. The original call for US sanctions came from the American Committee on Africa (ACOA) under leadership of its founder, George Houser, an ordained Methodist Minister. Since its inception in 1953, the ACOA had pressed for total US disengagement from South Africa. It supported the ANC ever since Houser conferred with Albert Luthuli, Z. K. Matthews, and Walter Sisulu during a trip to South Africa in the early 1950s. Eventually the ACOA would also extend a helping hand to the PAC and every other "genuine liberation movement" in South Africa.

On 10 December 1957, the ACOA had called for a "World-Wide Day of Protest" against apartheid as part of its Declaration of Conscience campaign. Featuring Mrs. Eleanor Roosevelt as chairwoman of the international sponsoring committee and Martin Luther King Jr. as vice chairman, this action elicited a response from Foreign Minister Eric Louw. On 12 December. he launched an attack on the ACOA in a radio broadcast from Pretoria, calling the organization "decidedly pinkish" and describing Executive Secretary George Houser as "a known leftist."[13] The ACOA got the attention of the South African government. Now all that remained was to get the American public and the lawmakers in Washington interested. Sharpeville helped it to do so. "Without Sharpeville we would never have had much success. Violence in South Africa was the only way we could have Americans sit up and take notice," George Houser admitted many years later. For the same reason the Soweto unrest helped to reinvigorate the campaign in 1976. Finally the wave of violence that started at the end of 1984 and persisted for several years, brought success. [14]

On 24 March 1960, barely days after the Sharpeville shootings, the ACOA attracted considerable media attention with a demonstration in front of the South African Consulate in New York. This was followed on 13 April with a protest meeting on the steps of New York's Town Hall to launch the South Africa Emergency Campaign, urging a boycott of South Africa and all its goods and establishing a fund for the "victims of apartheid." Speakers included Thurgood Marshall, general counsel of the NAACP and later a Supreme Court judge, Dr. Hastings Banda of Nyasaland (later president of independent Malawi) and Kenneth Kaunda of Northern Rhodesia (later president of Zambia).

In 1963 the ACOA managed to take its sanctions campaign beyond mere protest to real boycott action, when it, together with the Congress of Racial Equality (CORE), picketed the Brooklyn docks. The International Longshoremen's Association respected the ban and refused to unload a South African ship. Together with some 75 church, labor, student, and civil rights organizations, the ACOA established the Consultative Council on Southern Africa at a meeting in Washington attended by more than 600 delegates representing an array of other activist groups, including the National Association for the Advancement of Colored People (NAACP). This coalition started off by launching an attack on the US allotment of a sugar quota to South African producers.

In 1966 the ACOA, through its newly established Committee of Conscience Against Apartheid, started campaigning against loans and other involvement by US banks in South Africa. Kicking off with a demonstration of 300 in front of a First National City Bank branch in New York on 20 April 1966, and the closing of seventy accounts, the campaign soon snowballed. Between 1966 and 1969 the ACOA managed to mobilize several major churches and university campuses into threatening withdrawal of their funds from these banks unless the credit line to South Africa were dropped. During testimony before Congress in Washington the ACOA's George Houser specified the type of sanctions that he would like to see applied against South Africa:

1. US disengagement from the South African economy, including official persuasion of US companies to withdraw.
2. The placing of all US exports to South Africa under the provi sions of the Export Control Act.
3. Legislation to make it illegal for US firms in South Africa to practice racial discrimination.
4. A system of taxing companies continuing to do business in South Africa, using the proceeds to aid "victims of apartheid."
5. Elimination of the US quota for South African sugar.
6. Removal of the US space tracking stations.
7. Cessation of nuclear cooperation between the American Atomic Energy Commission (AEC) and the South African Energy Board.[15]

Far-fetched as these goals may have seemed at the time, they would ultimately become grist for the mill in a number of other activist groups that followed the ACOA on the road of sanctions against apartheid. Eventually most of them would be incorporated into American law. But in those days, even though South African Prime Minister Verwoerd publicly conceded that the Kennedy administration might get tougher with South Africa, Pretoria's officialdom dismissed Houser's efforts as the delirious dreams of a radical. After all, they argued, it would hardly be in America's strategic and economic interest to take such drastic action against a valued ally.[16]

For a while after Sharpeville, however, American policy was based on the belief that the days of the White regime were numbered. "There are few who doubt that the Republic of South Africa will blow up in due course," Undersecretary of State Chester Bowles wrote to Secretary of State Dean Rusk in the early 1960s. "When this occurs will we be able to say that we took every step or practical measure to prevent or temper the holocaust?"[17] So certain was the Kennedy administration that white South Africa was about to be devoured by the winds of change that the State Department cautioned its new ambassador Joseph Satterthwaite to prepare for a Black government "within eighteen months to five years."[18] The armed struggle launched by Umkhonto we Sizwe, or MK, the underground wing of the ANC, after the organization was banned, was seen as the final stage of an insurrection that would topple the Verwoerd regime.

Scores of attacks on military and strategic installations as well as "soft" targets in South Africa reinforced the belief that the end was near for White rule. Armed, however, with the Sabotage Act of 1962, which gave it wide powers to quell opposition and terrorism—including the death sentence for sabotage—the South African government regained control and restored order.[19] In August 1962 the ever-evasive Mandela was caught. He was already serving a five-year sentence for incitement and leaving the country illegally when on 11 June 1963, the police raided MK's secret headquarters at Lilliesleaf farm in the Rivonia outskirts of Johannesburg and trapped most of the other members of its High Command. The so-called Rivonia trial that followed led to life imprisonment at Robben Island for Mandela and the other underground leaders of the ANC.

In June 1963 South Africa's White rulers appeared to be firmly in control once again and quite invincible. The same Kennedy advisers who gave Whites in South Africa only months or at most a few years at the helm before they capitulate to the winds of change, drastically revised their estimates. According to Coker, Robert Good, who was the director of Research and Analysis in the State Department's Africa Bureau, conceded afterward that "he had been personally responsible for foolishly optimistic forecasts of the rate of political change" in South Africa.[20] Some years after he returned from his stint as US Ambassador in Pretoria, Satterthwaite in his testimony before a Congressional Committee gave South Africa at least a decade or much longer to put its house in order. The South African government was so strong politically and militarily and the economy of the country so sound, he felt, that it would be wishful thinking to expect that the "long hoped for breakthrough in racial relations will occur in the near or even foreseeable future."[21]

On 22 November 1963, not long after Ambassador Stevenson carried out Kennedy's instruction and voted in support of the UN Security Council's call for an arms embargo against South Africa, the young president was assassinated in Dallas. When the United States voted on 4 December 1963, in favor of a second call by the Security Council for an arms embargo, former Vice President Lyndon B. Johnson was already in the Oval Office. It is unlikely that the new president had any personal input. During the first few weeks of his tenure Johnson had to give his undivided attention to other much more pressing immediate policy decisions concerning Vietnam and the Cold War. Furthermore, his interest in matters African was at best superficial.

Despite a brief goodwill visit to the continent as vice president, Johnson knew precious little about Africa. The new president, it was said, once confided at being confused about Algeria and Nigeria because their names both ended in "geria."[22] But the Texan was a man with impeccable political instincts and he soon realized, as his predecessor had discovered, that apartheid can only be ignored at the risk of losing Black American support. South Africa therefore began to feature more prominently on the White House agenda. Speaking on 26 May 1966, during a reception for African leaders at the White House, Johnson commented on an increasing awareness in Africa that governments should represent the will of its citizens. "This makes all the more repugnant the narrow and outmoded policy which in some parts of Africa permits the few to rule at the expense of the many," he said in clear reference to Apartheid. "Just as we are determined to remove the remnants of inequality from our own midst, we are also with you—heart and soul—as you try to do the same." [23]

Described by officials as a "model" denunciation of apartheid and racism, Johnson's remarks were received with less enthusiasm by the left.[24] This was, the *New Republic* commented on 13 August 1966, the president talking out of the left side of his mouth while out of the right American business was saying something else. "The sheer scale of existing business investment itself offers assurance that the US government will not act 'rashly' by putting too much pressure on South Africa to alter her 'narrow and outmoded' policy," the magazine wrote. Another publication, *Commonweal,* wrote on 10 June 1966, that if Johnson's words "had been accompanied by equivalent action, say by the economic disengagement of the US from South Africa, we might celebrate." But by then Johnson, like his predecessors, had discovered that there were limits to what the United States could do. An official review of American policy toward South Africa that was started by the State Department in 1961 but completed only three years later, after Johnson had become president, recommended that the United States concentrate on achievable economic and social change in the fields of labor and education.[25]

Still, Mennen Williams, who continued in his post as assistant secretary for African Affairs, found that Johnson was not merely set to follow the direction set by Kennedy in regard to South Africa but willing to go further than his predecessor in backing up words with action.[26] Military cooperation between the two countries drastically diminished during the Johnson administration as the United States expanded the scope of the arms embargo in 1964 by banning the sale to South Africa of materials for the making of arms. There was also stricter observance of the 1963 UN arms embargo itself. Even the sale of light civilian aircraft that could also be used for military purposes, was prohibited.

Instead of merely responding to pressures at the United Nations the new Johnson administration decided to take the initiative. In 1965 National Security Adviser McGeorge Bundy approved a recommendation by the State Department, over objections by the Department of Commerce, to withdraw official guarantees for investors in South Africa and discourage future private investment in that country.[27] To obtain maximum exposure for these policy changes, America's UN Ambassador Arthur Goldberg was told to wait for the most opportune moment during a UN General Assembly debate to announce them. Goldberg himself lobbied strongly within the Johnson administration for a mandatory UN arms embargo, despite the risk of direct US collision with France as South Africa's principal arms supplier. He also favored a ban on nuclear cooperation with the Verwoerd government, a step that would have brought the State Department in conflict with the Department of Commerce.[28]

There were, however, limits. In 1965, when a controversial study under the direction of Amelia Leiss concluded that a massive naval blockade of South Africa would be needed to make sanctions work, the idea was promptly shelved by the United States, even though it allegedly had the approval of UN Secretary General U Thant. This 170-page report, titled "Apartheid and the United Nations Collective Measures," estimated that 30,000 assault and 63,000 other troops, 145 war ships, transport and supply vessels, and 500 aircraft would be needed for a 30-day campaign to subdue South Africa—at a total cost of $95 million. The publication acknowledged the valued assistance of an officer of the Military Academy at West Point.[29] As William Hance pointed out, there was, however, "no disposition in the government of either the United States or the United Kingdom to engage in large-scale economic sanctions backed by a naval blockade of South Africa."[30]

The real difficulty with sanctions, wrote J.E. Spence in 1965, was that it assumed on the part of the Western powers and "above all the United States" a "cool and calculating" willingness to "provoke a crisis" with unforeseen consequences. Verwoerd and his ministers were aware that any widespread disturbances would sharpen the dilemma for the Western powers and spur them into action. They were therefore taking "every precaution" against such disturbances. "As long as South Africa's foreign policy-makers can project an image of stability and economic prosperity," Spence concluded, action against their government in the form of sanctions were remote.[31]

In the mid-1960s, anticipating a decision against South Africa on the issue of South West Africa (Namibia) at the International Court of Justice in The Hague, Assistant Secretary Mennen Williams cautioned the Verwoerd government that the United States expected all parties to comply with the verdict. The implication was clearly that the necessary steps would be taken to enforce this decision, including sanctions. As former members of the League of Nations, Ethiopia and Liberia had filed the suit after South Africa continued to ignore the International Court's 1950 advisory finding that South Africa was still bound by a League of Nations mandate passed on to the UN. On 18 July 1966, the Court decided that neither Ethiopia nor Liberia had "established any legal right or interest in the subject matter of this claim." It ruled that only the defunct League of Nations, which originally mandated the territory to South Africa in 1920, was legally entitled to challenge South Africa over its administration of South West Africa.

Prime Minister Verwoerd welcomed this ruling in a nationwide radio address as a "major victory for South Africa." At the same time the largest Black nationalist organization in the territory, the South West African People's Organization (SWAPO), announced its intention "to rise in arms and bring about our liberation." The Organization of African Unity condemned the World Court's decision as having "diminished its prestige and created doubts regarding its integrity." The United States rejected the Court's decision as well and insisted that the previous advisory opinion remained in force. South Africa, the United States contended, was still bound to accept UN supervision.

In October 1966 the United States supported a UN General Assembly resolution "terminating" South Africa's mandate over South West Africa and establishing an ad hoc committee to decide on practical measures for the administration of the territory. This UN resolution was promptly dismissed by Prime Minister John Vorster, who assumed the leadership of South Africa after Verwoerd's assassination in September 1966. So began a new chapter in the protracted dispute over South West Africa/Namibia that started in 1946 with Smuts' request for UN permission to incorporate the territory and led to to repeated calls for sanctions against South Africa.

By this time, however, Mennen Williams had undergone a change of heart. In an appearance before a congressional committee toward the end of 1966, Williams questioned the wisdom of sanctions against South Africa, expressing doubts over the commercial and political strictures proposed by Goldberg at the United Nations. According to Williams, the web of interests binding the United States and South Africa together, especially South Africa's reliance on the West for capital, made comprehensive economic sanctions unnecessary and inappropriate. He voiced his opposition to the introduction of an embargo against South Africa similar to the one imposed against Rhodesia even though the objective was the same in both countries—majority rule.[32]

The unilateral declaration of independence (UDI) by Ian Smith's white government on 11 November 1965, led to British sanctions against the rebel colony. The Verwoerd government chose to maintain normal economic relations with its northern neighbor, providing Rhodesia with a valuable export corridor and access to much-needed oil and other vital supplies—a practice continued by the Vorster government in 1966 with the full support of the official white opposition United Party. Impatient with Britain's inability to bring the white rebels in Rhodesia to heel, the UN General Assembly on 16 December 1966, voted unanimously in favor of total sanctions. A few days earlier Britain had managed to avert Black African calls for an extension of the embargo to South Africa, saying that it preferred not to involve a third party in the dispute. As UDI persisted in Rhodesia for the next fifteen years, however, there would be more calls for an economic blockade of South Africa as punishment for its assistance to the Rhodesian rebels.

William Hance defined the South African policy direction followed during the Kennedy and Johnson years as one of "disengagement—the middle ground between sanctions and a do-nothing policy." Unfortunately, Hance added, disengagement was not clearly defined and left scope for "a whole range of steps from verbal condemnation up to and including sanctions." Depending on the measures chosen, disengagement could be a policy of "neutralism, non-cooperation, dissociation, intervention or withdrawal." It could either be a carrot or a stick, or both. While this approach irritated the South Africans, it did not move them to abandon apartheid. It fell short of Black American and African expectations. "At present," Hance contended in 1968, "the United States is variously seen as 'identified with,' 'involved,' 'implicated,' and 'responsible for,' or 'as partners' or 'accomplices' in apartheid."[33]

Although the United States under Kennedy's direction for the first time supported UN sanctions when it voted in favor of a UN Security Council call for an arms embargo, these sanctions were not mandatory. Throughout the 1960s the United States continued to resist stronger economic punitive measures. Even Robert Kennedy, brother of the deceased president, expressed reservations about sanctions in 1967 during an appearance in Kenya on his way back to the United States after visiting South Africa at the invitation of Verwoerd's opponents. Earlier he had sent a letter to thirty American business leaders stating his objection to financial disengagement because "the cost to non-whites might far outweigh any change in that government's policies."[34] An Executive Order by President Johnson in January 1968 constraining investment abroad, which affected US investment in South Africa, was not specifically aimed against apartheid but rather intended to improve the American balance-of-payments position.[35]

Both the Kennedy and Johnson administrations tried to make up for their shortcomings on the sanctions front by public posturing in the diplomatic field. In the early 1960s President Kennedy precipitated an official South African boycott of the Fourth of July celebration at the US Embassy in Pretoria by inviting Black South Africans. In May 1965 the Johnson White House instructed the aircraft carrier *USS Independence* to avoid Cape Town as a port of call to save its Black crew members from being subjected to apartheid.

The *Independence* was, however, not the only American naval vessel to land in troubled political waters around South Africa. On 4 February 1967, as the US carrier *Franklin Delano Roosevelt* eased into Cape Town harbor, another diplomatic storm erupted. The more pliable Prime Minister Vorster, who succeeded Verwoerd, had agreed to let crewmen of all races go ashore and attend specially arranged non-segregated social functions. Those in the Johnson administration who argued in favor of the call pointed out that refueling at sea would cost an additional $250,000, require the diversion of a tanker needed elsewhere, and deny the crew much-needed shore leave after nine months off Vietnam. Having heard about the *Franklin Delano Roosevelt's* intended call at Cape Town, the ACOA, NAACP, and Black Congressmen Charles Diggs and Donald Fraser sprung into action, bitterly attacking the decision. With the assistance of insider Wayne Fredericks, deputy to Assistant Secretary Mennen Williams at the State Department, the matter was reopened in discussions between legislators, the departments of State and Defense, and the White House. The *Franklin Delano Roosevelt* cut short its visit and departed on 5 February, leaving behind a disappointed Cape Town community that was ready to roll out the red carpet—and a South African government fuming over the latest snub by Johnson.

But while governmental relations between South Africa and the United States reached an all-time low, business partnerships flourished. "Even in the closing days of the Johnson administration American officials began to question whether negative sanctions were a very useful approach," writes Christopher Coker. "The arms embargo of 1963 had proved to be a broken reed. American equipment continued to be exported to the Republic [of South Africa] throughout the 1960s, with or without the Department of Commerce's knowledge."[36]

South Africa, however, was taking no chances. Thoroughly alerted by the happenings at the United Nations and continued discussions of further sanctions by the United States, it was busy "building up immunity." As early as 1965 oil companies were instructed by the South African government to stockpile a six-month supply at three tank farms at Durban, Port Elizabeth, and Cape Town. In 1968 similar instructions were issued to importers of chemicals and rubber to stock up.[37]

In the November 1968 presidential election Richard Nixon defeated Hubert Humphrey after Lyndon Johnson decided against running for another term and challenger Robert Kennedy was assassinated. Although the Vorster government welcomed this changing of the guard in Washington, the Kennedy-Johnson era had ended without much harm done. In its final days the Johnson administration had seriously begun to rethink its position. Among the influential voices in Johnson's ranks who argued strongly against sanctions was Undersecretary of State George Ball, who not only opposed the arms embargo of 1962 but expressed skepticism over its effectiveness against a country with South Africa's military strength and industrial self-sufficiency. There was, according to Ball, a growing resistance among conservative advisers in the Johnson administration to having South African policy shaped by a "sense of guilt at home," the "desire not to affront civil rights sentiment," and the effort to secure "the approbation of the nations of black Africa."[38]

The respected political commentator and former director of policy planning at the State Department, George Kennan, echoed the same sentiments when he took successive US administrations to task for belittling the real changes underway in South Africa, which were produced by a "conflict" between "official ideology" and "the stormy pace of economic growth."[39] Kennan was merely using an argument that would be heard frequently in the business community over the next few years as it made a case against sanctions. Instead of disinvestment and sanctions, they argued, investment and economic growth were needed to help hasten the end of apartheid. This same view was prevalent among the African policy experts who took charge when Richard Milhaus Nixon moved into the White House toward the end of January 1969. South Africa was looking forward to improved relations with the world's leading nation and further sanctions seemed a very remote possibility.

NOTES

1. Hance, William A, "The Case For and Against United States Disengagement from South Africa," *Southern Africa and the United States,* eds. William A. Hance, Leo Kuper, Leo, Vernon McKay, and Edwin S. Munger, p. 110.

2. Schlesinger, Arthur M., *A Thousand Days: John F. Kennedy in the White House,* p. 580.

3. *New York Times,* 10 November 1961.

4. Schlesinger, op. cit., p. 580.

5. Ferguson, Clyde, and Cotter, William R., "South Africa: What is to be Done?" *Foreign Affairs,* January 1978, p. 259.

6. Schlesinger, op. cit., p. 581.

7. Ibid.

8. Statement by Ambassador Adlai E. Stevenson, United States Representative in the Security Council on the South African Question, *Press Release by the US Mission to the United Nations, No. 4233,* August 2, 1963.

9. Duncan, Patrick, "Toward a World Policy for South Africa," *Foreign Affairs,* 42, October 1963, pp. 38-48.

10. Mason, Philip, "Some Maxims and Axioms," *Foreign Affairs,* 43, October 1964, pp. 150-164.

11. Duncan, op. cit. p. 43.

12. Bissell, Richard E., *South Africa and the United States,* p.11.

13. Ibid.

14. George Houser interview, May 1993.

15. George Houser testimony, *Hearings of the Subcommittee on Africa, House of Representatives,* 1966, Part I, pp. 190-200 and Part IV, pp. 541-543.

16. Barber, James, *South Africa's Foreign Policy,* 1945-1970, p. 191.

17. Bowles, Chester, *Promise To Keep: My Years in Public Life,* p. 428.

18. Chettle, John, "The Evolution of US Policy Toward South Africa," *Modern Age,* Summer 1972, p. 260.

19. The General Law Amendment Act 76 of 1962 became known as the Anti-Sabotage Act and later simply the Sabotage Act after its Clause 21 that dealt specifically with sabotage.

20. Coker, Christopher, *The United States and South Africa 1968-1985: Constructive Engagement and its Critics,* p. 6.

21. Satterthwaite, Joseph, "Policy Toward Africa for the 1970s," Hearings before the Subcommittee on Africa of the Committee on Foreign Relations, House of Representatives, 91st Congress, 2nd Session, 1970, p. 37.

22. Prinsloo, D., *United States Foreign Policy and the Republic of South Africa,* p. 28.

23. Johnson, Lyndon B., "The United States and Africa: A Unity of Purpose," *Department of State Bulletin,* 13 June 1966, p. 915.

24. Martin, Patrick H., *American Views on South Africa. 1948-1972,* p. 162.

25. "Department of State National Strategy Series—South Africa." Draft prepared by William R. Duggan and Waldemar B. Campbell, 28 October 1963.

26. Lake, Anthony, *Caution and Concern: The Making of American Policy Toward South Africa,* p. 97.

27. Memorandum from Gordon Chase to McGeorge Bundy, 3 November 1965, LBJ Library.

28. Shepherd, George W., *The United States and Non-Aligned Africa.* Optional Paper.

29. Leiss, Amelia ed., *Apartheid and the United Nations Collective Measures.*

30 Hance, op. cit., p. 28.

31. Spence, J. E., *Republic Under Pressure—A Study of South African Foreign Policy,* p. 75.

32. Williams, Mennen, "US Policy Towards South Africa," statement before the Committee on Foreign Affairs, House of Representatives, 89th Congress, 2nd Session, 1966, p. 4.

33. Hance, op. cit., p. 110.

34. Ibid., p. 119.

35. According to Anthony Lake, many individual investors compensated by buying stock in South African companies instead of directly investing in what was then a lucrative area for foreigners, Lake, op. cit., pp. 107-108.

36. Coker, op. cit., p. 9.

37. Doxey, Margaret, *Economic Sanctions and International Enforcement,* p. 122.

38. Ball, George, *The Discipline of Power,* p, 254.

39. Kennan, George, "Hazardous Courses in Southern Africa," *Foreign Affairs,* January 1971, p. 222.

4

The Tar Baby Option

> *tar baby, n.* A situation or problem from which it is virtually
> impossible to disentangle oneself.
>
> [After *Bre'r Rabbit and the Tar Baby*,
> an Uncle Remus story by Joel Chandler Harris.]
> *American Heritage Dictionary*

No one knows for sure who dubbed the Nixon-Kissinger approach to
Southern Africa the "Tar Baby Option." The label seemed to have sprung
spontaneously from State Department officials who felt that this new course
of action would bind the United States dangerously close to the unpopular
White rulers of Southern Africa.

Following Nixon into the White House as National Security Adviser was
former Harvard Professor Henry A. Kissinger. In February 1969 Kissinger
instructed his staff to undertake a number of strategic evaluations for different
parts of the world. In the first six months 61 comprehensive secret studies
were undertaken in accordance with the president's wish to review all the
important foreign policy questions affecting national security. National
Security Study Memorandum 39 (NSSM 39) dealt with Southern Africa and
was, as its name indicated, the thirty-ninth one to be undertaken. As the
predominant issue of the time, the Vietnam position was set out in NSSM 1.

Instead of relying on "*ad hoc* decisions" as previous administrations did,
Kissinger and Nixon employed the best brains at their command to find a
way to bring US policy toward the White regimes of Africa in line with
global US policy aims. The National Security Council Interdepartmental
Group for Africa that drew up NSSM 39 comprised representatives of the
Central Intelligence Agency and of the departments of State and Defense,
assisted by other departments and agencies including Treasury, Commerce,

the Joint Chiefs of Staff, the Agency for International Development (AID) and the National Aeronautics and Space Administration (NASA).

In NSSM 39 five objectives were listed—"without intent to imply priority":

1. "to improve the US standing in black Africa and internationally, on the racial issue;
2. to minimize the likelihood of escalation of violence in the area and the risk of US involvement;
3. to minimize the opportunities for the USSR and Communist China to exploit the racial issue in the region for propaganda advantage and to gain political influence with black governments and liberation movements;
4. to encourage moderation of the current rigid racial and colonial policies of the white regimes;
5. and to protect economic, scientific and strategic interests and opportunities in the region, including the orderly marketing of South Africa's gold production."[1]

NSSM 39 proposed five different options for accomplishing these goals. Kissinger had recommended, and Nixon had approved, Option Two—the so-called Tar Baby Option. It proposed closer cooperation with South Africa and a cozier relationship with the Portuguese rulers in Angola. Its premise was that "the whites are here to stay and the only way that constructive change can come about is through them." Although the arms embargo was to remain against South Africa, a more liberal view was taken on the distictions between civilian and military equipment. US naval calls to South Africa were to be allowed again as well as routine use of its airfields and tracking stations. Constraints on Export-Import Bank facilities for South Africa were to be relaxed and US exports and investment encouraged in accordance with the Foreign Direct Investment Program. Exchange programs in all categories, including military, were envisaged. Without actually changing the official US position that South African occupancy of South West Africa was illegal, the intention was to downplay this issue. Public US opposition was to be expressed against the use of force by African insurgent movements.[2]

An example of the "liberal treatment of equipment which could serve either military or civilian purposes," as suggested in the Tar Baby Option, was US approval of the sale in February 1970 of ten Lockheed Hercules C-130 transport aircraft to a South African air charter firm, Safair. In terms of another suggestion, the US Export-Import Bank in January 1972 guaranteed a ten-year loan to South Africa for the purchase of diesel engines. This reversed a ruling in 1964 by the Johnson administration to limit such loans to a maximum of five years. But the United States not only expanded Ex-Im Bank facilities for South Africa; it actually encouraged investment in that country. The visit of South African Admiral H H Biermann to the United States in May 1974 to hold meetings with Joint Chiefs of Staff Chairman Admiral Thomas Moorer and other top military and civilian officials was seen as further "highly visible evidence that the administration was implementing yet another Option 2 recommendation."[3]

The Vorster government had reason to be encouraged by the new approach introduced by the Nixon administration under the guidance of National Security Adviser and later Secretary of State Kissinger. American support for new sanctions seemed to be out of the question and ways were found by the Nixon administration and its allies in Europe to lessen the impact of the arms embargo. For a while Britain's new Conservative government contemplated lifting the arms embargo imposed by the Labor government against South Africa in accordance with the UN Security Council resolution of 1962. France, on the other hand, without much opposition from the United States, remained a steady supplier of arms to South Africa and even helped it develop a ground-to-air-missile, which Defense Minister P. W. Botha proudly described on 2 May 1969, as "the most advanced and effective weapon of its kind."[4]

Although the ritualistic condemnation of South Africa continued at the United Nations, US support for real economic sanctions against South Africa seemed quite remote. The 11-nation UN Special Committee Against Apartheid conceded on 25 September 1969, that the United Nations' economic sanctions against South Africa had failed. In its report the committee blamed the United States, Britain, Japan, and West Germany—South Africa's main trading partners—for this failure. These nations, the Anti-Apartheid Committee complained, not only ignored the boycott but actually increased their trade with South Africa since the world organization called on nations to impose sanctions in 1962.

On 21 November 1969, the UN General Assembly passed yet another resolution stressing the "urgent necessity" of widening sanctions against the rebel White government in Rhodesia by extending them to South Africa and Portugal. The General Assembly requested that the Security Council consider using force against apartheid and urged member states to press for the release from detention of "political prisoners" in South Africa. The United States vetoed the idea. On 13 March 1969, the Vorster government proceeded—over UN objections—with the South West Africa Affairs Act, which extended South Africa's apartheid legislation to the territory. When the International Court of Justice on 21 June 1971, ruled South Africa's administration and "continued presence" in the territory illegal, Vorster dismissed this latest opinion as an "international political vendetta" and vowed to continue leading all the population groups in Namibia toward self-determination.

On 6 March 1972, UN Secretary General Kurt Waldheim arrived in South Africa for discussions and a visit to Namibia in an effort to break the deadlock. Although he returned to New York with nothing more than "a number of ideas" for the future, he maintained that the trip was not pointless. Over UN objections, South Africa proceeded to establish a semi-autonomous Bantustan in Namibia's East Caprivi area on 23 March 1972. On 11

December 1973, the UN Security Council finally suspended Waldheim's talks with South Africa but on 6 June 1975, the United States, together with Britain and France, once again vetoed a resolution in the Council that would have imposed a mandatory arms embargo against South Africa because of its failure to withdraw from Namibia.

In January 1976, the United States could no longer refuse to act in the face of South Africa's continued outright defiance of the UN over Namibia. Together with its Western allies the United States voted for UN Security Council Resolution 385, which called for an end to political repression and racial discrimination in the territory, the release of political prisoners, the repatriation of exiles, and free elections under UN supervision. By then the South Africans had already proceeded with their own conference of tribal and ethnic-based political groupings at the Turnhalle in Windhoek in an effort to counter SWAPO's claim of being the sole representative of the peoples of Namibia.

Kissinger decided to personally try his hand at brokering a UN-approved independence for Namibia. Encouraged by Vorster's initial acceptance of his seven-point proposal for talks, he pursued the matter with SWAPO. But the outlawed organization rejected the Kissinger plan despite the South African government's show of good faith by undertaking to release a number of political prisoners. With Kissinger's initiative rebuffed by SWAPO, the new coalition formed at the Turnhalle in Windhoek—the so-called Democratic Turnhalle Alliance (DTA)—gained special significance. Notwithstanding attempts by SWAPO to discount them as tribalists, puppets, and White racists, the DTA seemed destined to hold the key to independence for Namibia.

During most of the Nixon and Ford era, Kissinger appeared to be tilting strongly toward the White regimes in southern Africa in a belief that this was the best way to confront possible Communist gains and protect American interests. Prime Minister Vorster did his utmost to prove the Americans correct in this assumption. No stone was left unturned to expose, hunt down, and incarcerate members and sympathizers of the banned ANC as well as its Communist cohorts. He portrayed these actions against Black nationalist movements as part of the struggle by the United States to prevent the Soviet bloc or the People's Republic of China from gaining a foothold in Southern Africa.

In 1969 the autonomous Bureau of State Security (dubbed BOSS by its critics) was established by Vorster in terms of the innocuous-sounding Public Service Amendment Act. Placed in the care of an old friend and former police officer, General Hendrik van den Bergh, BOSS was put in charge of all matters affecting state security and assigned a secret budget of its own. Under the leadership of the charismatic van den Bergh, who first came to public notice in the mid-1960s when he master-minded the capture of Mandela's colleagues at Rivonia, BOSS soon played a key role not only in security matters but in decisions affecting defense and foreign affairs. The

General Law Amendment Acts of 1961, 1962, and 1963 gave wide powers to the police to quell unrest and sabotage, believed to be Communist-inspired.

In the 1970s van den Bergh and BOSS also became key players in a covert propaganda campaign launched under the leadership of Dr. Cornelius (Connie) Mulder. Secret funds were channeled to Mulder's Department of Information through BOSS and P. W. Botha's Department of Defense to be utilized in a variety of projects, ranging from the purchase and establishment of publishing houses, television news networks and other media, to influencing key politicians, trade union leaders and other influential opinion makers and decision takers around the world—and ultimately the United States. This effort was born out of sheer frustration with the ineffectiveness of past propaganda programs that relied on mundane methods executed with modest means.

Toward the mid-1970s an extensive covert campaign was underway. It was aimed in large part at countering sanctions. A major seminar at the Rye Hilton near New York City, orchestrated by the South African Information Department and presented under the ostensible auspices of the South African Foreign Trade Organization (SAFTO), drew more than 200 top executives from major American corporations—people who, in the words of Patrick Martin, saw American policy toward South Africa as "involving issues touching upon or threatening their own interests."[5] The keynote speaker was former US Treasury Secretary William Simon. The purpose of the seminar was purely and simply the establishment of a network and support system for American businesses to enable them to defend themselves effectively against pressures from sanctions groups.

It was not only these secret propaganda tactics by Mulder's men, but also their unconventional diplomacy that would earn special praise from Prime Minister Vorster. Just when Vorster's widely publicized "outward policy" in Africa lost momentum after an historic visit to Malawi as the guest of President Hastings Banda in May 1970, the Department of Information facilitated meetings with Presidents Houphet Boigny of the Ivory Coast and Leopold Senghor of Senegal, as well as high-level contact with Israel. In January 1974 Mulder met with Governor Ronald Reagan in Sacramento and Vice President Ford in Washington. Arrangements were made independently by the Department of Information. South Africa's Ambassador in Washington was briefed only afterward. Understandably, this intrusion on Foreign Affairs' turf led to severe infighting with the Department of Information.[6]

Mulder used these top-level meetings to impress upon the leadership of America the importance of South Africa as a partner and ally in Africa. He asked for increased US involvement in South Africa, both militarily and economically. The response from Reagan was more openly sympathetic, in part because as governor he did not suffer the same constraints as Ford, who was by then set to take charge as Nixon prepared to leave in the shadow of Watergate. The agenda for the historic meeting with Ford on 22 January

1974, was quite specific. Mulder stressed South Africa's worth as a stable Western partner to the United States, its strategic location on the vital oil route and its role as a major supplier of crucial minerals to America. South Africa's Sasol formula for the extraction of oil from coal, it was suggested, could well serve to help the United States meet its increasing energy demands in the future despite OPEC. In exchange South Africa wanted the United States to lift the restrictions imposed against it over the years, especially in the military field. First, it was suggested, an American vessel could pay an unobtrusive visit to a South African harbor for "emergency supplies" and then others could follow with less urgent needs. Eventually open visits could follow without much fuss. In this fashion the ban that existed since the abortive visit of the aircraft carrier *Franklin Delano Roosevelt* in 1967 could be broken. At the same time a low-key "private" visit by the South African chief of staff for meetings with top Pentagon officials could be arranged, breaking the ban on such high-level exchanges. This, it was felt, could lead to regular and open association between the two commands and even to joint maneuvers. The goals were seen as a "modest but meaningful" start to dismantling barriers between the two countries.[7]

One direct result of the meeting between Mulder and soon-to-be president Ford was the arrival of South African chief of staff, Admiral H. H. Biermann, at Washington's Dulles Airport on the last day of April 1974. This "private visit" marked the first time that a high-ranking South African military man was received in the United States in fourteen years. In the next few days he met with his counterpart, Admiral Thomas Moorer, chief of the US Joint Chiefs of Staff, and Acting Secretary of the Navy William Middendorf. It seemed at the time as if South Africa was indeed succeeding in its strategy to re-establish military cooperation despite the arms embargo.

In Washington Biermann frequently found himself discussing not South Africa but neighboring Angola and Mozambique. On 25 April 1974, only days before his arrival in Washington a coup had taken place in Portugal. The Portuguese authoritarian government of Marcello Caetano was replaced by a group of young left-wing military officers intent on ending White rule in Mozambique and Angola. While the imminent handover of these territories to Marxist Black liberation movements increased the importance of South Africa as the last bastion of the West, there were also negative implications. Both in Pretoria and Salisbury it added to the sense of isolation, while in Washington the imminent disappearance of White rule in the Portuguese territories removed one of the pillars that held the Tar Baby Option in place.

On 7 September 1974 the new Portuguese rulers signed a cease-fire agreement with the Frelimo movement and on 25 June 1975, its leader, Samora Machel, became the president of newly independent Marxist Mozambique. Its harbor at Beira was effectively closed to Rhodesia, making the rebel colony totally dependent on South Africa for access to the sea. Machel also cut back Mozambique's trade with South Africa and allowed the banned ANC to use his territory as a springboard for guerrilla attacks. In Angola there were, however, three liberation movements vying for supremacy. The National Front for the Liberation of Angola (FNLA). the Popular Movement for the Liberation of Angola (MPLA) and the National Union for the Independence of Angola (UNITA).

Early in January 1975 the Portuguese managed to bring all three parties together to discuss the formation of a coalition government but in March, Holden Roberto's FNLA, emboldened by CIA support, and the Agostinho Neto's MPLA, bolstered by Soviet arms and the promise of Cuban troops, engaged in battle. From the south Jonas Savimbi's UNITA aligned itself with the FNLA. On 10 November 1975, Portugal transferred sovereignty to the Angolan people even though it did not recognize any of the three guerrilla factions as the sole legitimate government. The next day the Marxist MPLA proclaimed its leader, Agostinho Neto, president of the People's Republic of Angola. The self-declared pro-Soviet Angolan government offered bases in Angola to SWAPO guerrillas fighting against South African rule in Namibia and provided the Vorster government with a good reason to get involved in the south on UNITA's side.

On 27 November 1975, Defense Minister P. W. Botha revealed that South Africa was supporting UNITA and the FNLA and appealed to the United States and other Western nations to assist in preventing the Soviets from gaining a foothold in Angola. Prime Minister Vorster warned on 31 December 1975, that "only a bigger Western involvement, not only in the diplomatic but all other fields" could keep Angola from being "hounded into the Communist fold."[8] The South African government was reluctant to launch a full-scale war on the MPLA government in Angola without the active and open involvement of the United States, as it felt that without such support it would risk Soviet intervention and sure defeat. US intervention was necessary, Pretoria believed, to help ensure victory over Communism.

Ignoring opposition by Assistant Secretary for African Affairs Nathaniel Davis and CIA Director William Colby, Kissinger recommended, and President Ford approved, covert US involvement in Angola. Some $32 million in funds and $16 million in military equipment were earmarked to be funneled to Holden Roberto's troops by the CIA via friendly Zaire. Thus Angola, in Walter Isaacson's view, became another "vivid example of Kissinger's tendency to see complex local struggles in an East-West context." Kissinger, according to this biographer, "saw in Angola the first test of the new rules of détente" and "a way to feel out the limits on how far each superpower could go in seeking an advantage in the third world."[9]

Encouraged by positive signals from both Ford and Kissinger, the South Africans advanced further into Angola on 16 December 1975. On 17 December, Defense Minister P. W. Botha signaled long-term commitment in Angola by introducing a three-month service requirement for South African reservists in the border region between Angola and Namibia. On 29 December 1975, the British *Financial Times* reported a major South African offensive around the Angolan town of Cela, 400 miles inside Angola. Awaiting open American participation, however, the South African government tried to keep details of its involvement in Angola secret. No open support was forthcoming from the United States.

On 19 December 1975, the Senate adopted the Clark Amendment prohibiting any further US involvement without specific congressional authorization. Given the mood at Congress, where Angola was equated to Vietnam, the final rejection on 27 January 1976, of Kissinger's and Ford's request for $28 million in military aid to the anti-Marxist guerrilla groups fighting the MPLA came as no surprise. White House warnings that such denial would open the door for Angola to fall under Soviet influence made no impact. As Congress voted down Ford's request for funds to aid the fight against the Communists in Angola, the South Africans found themselves under heavy bombardment on the outskirts of Luanda. Without US political support and sufficient armaments the South Africans selected to deploy further south and in March 1976, under severe international pressure, Vorster withdrew all his troops from Angola.

"The question is whether America still maintains the resolve to act responsibly as a great power," Kissinger argued before the African Subcommittee of the Senate Foreign Relations Committee in support of his request for funds in January 1976. "If the US is seen to emasculate itself in the face of massive, unprecedented Soviet and Cuban intervention," he asked rhetorically, "what will be the perception of leaders around the world as they make decisions regarding their future security?"[10] Senator Dick Clark, who chaired the hearings and sponsored the Clark Amendment, accomplished more than simply "emasculating" the United States and denying Kissinger a role in Angola. Clark effectively, albeit unwittingly, convinced the Ford Administration to abandon the Tar Baby Option and opt for a "moral" approach that not only denied South Africa assistance in Angola but thrust it back into pariah status. During the Angola hearings early in 1976, Clark suggested to Kissinger that US interests in Africa would be better served by appealing to the values of human rights and racial equality that America shared with Black nations on the continent. By trying this approach, Clark believed, "our cold war interests in Africa may very well take care of themselves."[11]

Kissinger, the ultimate proponent of *realpolitik*, may once have balked at the mere thought of courting the same liberation movements that he used to dismiss as tools of Moscow. But no longer. A new policy had become necessary as White rule disappeared in the Portuguese regions and pressures increased on Rhodesia, Namibia, and South Africa to capitulate. President Ford himself spoke in favor of a "new Africa policy in 1976" that "reflected my own sympathies." After having looked at regimes "that would not survive," Ford said, he felt that the US "ought to move toward a more humane point of view."[12] Writing in the *New York Times* on 23 June 1976,

Black former US Ambassador to Ghana Franklin Williams ascribed this switch in a "critical election year" to the realization that there were over 25 million Blacks in America "and that many of them vote."

In April 1976, barely two months after his spirited defense of the Tar Baby approach before the Senate African Affairs Subcommittee, Kissinger adopted Clark's approach as if it were his own. In analyzing Kissinger's African policy switch former Harvard colleague Stanley Hoffmann concluded that "he showed a remarkable talent for undercutting his adversaries by annexing their ideas." Hoffmann felt that this "chameleon-like ability" to embrace views that first seem alien to him testified to Kissinger's cleverness.[13]

At a luncheon in Lusaka hosted by Zambian President Kenneth Kaunda, Kissinger put this ability on display as he announced sweeping policy changes incorporating the moral approach enunciated by Clark only two months earlier. In this address on 27 April 1976, during a thirteen-day tour of African nations, Kissinger begged his Black African audience to put aside feelings about past American attitudes and to find "common ground." Racial justice, he declared, is the "dominant issue of our age." American support for this principle, he added, was "not simply a matter of foreign policy but an imperative of our own moral heritage." The United States, he assured his listeners, "is totally dedicated to seeing to it that the majority becomes the ruling power in Rhodesia." He also cautioned Pretoria that although it still had time to abandon apartheid peacefully, there was "a limit to that time—a limit of far shorter duration than was generally perceived even a few years ago." The United States, he said, was "prepared to work with the international community, and especially with African leaders, to determine what further steps would improve prospects for a rapid and acceptable transition to Namibian independence."[14]

"In the immediate future," Kissinger said, "the Republic of South Africa can show its dedication to Africa—and its potential contribution to Africa—by using its influence in Salisbury to promote a rapid negotiated settlement for majority rule in Rhodesia. This, we are sure, would be viewed positively by the community of nations, as well as by the rest of Africa." President Kaunda welcomed this speech as "an important turning point." One elated Kissinger aide said: "It's the first time in a long time that we are doing the moral thing."[15] The response in South Africa and Rhodesia was understandably less enthusiastic. In the matter of one luncheon speech the American Secretary of State had thrown the Tar Baby out with the bath water and set a whole new course where Whites were no longer regarded as the sole key to change. Rhodesian Prime Minister Ian Smith responded that same evening, indicating in "the strongest terms" that he had no intention to "surrender" as part of a policy of "appeasing" the Communists.[16]

New York Times correspondent Michael Kaufman was one of many journalists who followed Kissinger on his African tour as he laid the foundation for a concerted shuttle diplomacy effort in Africa to terminate

White rule in Rhodesia and Namibia. To speed the process, he reported, South Africa's cooperation was crucial. The question was, what "inducement" was needed to have South Africa tighten the screws on Rhodesia and also loosen its grip on Namibia?[17] Would Kissinger go as far as conceding to Black African demands for US support of tougher sanctions? While South Africans pondered this possibility, US conservatives were using the Lusaka speech to undercut President Ford in the Texas primary for the upcoming presidential race. Speaking at a symbol-laden rally in front of the Alamo, his rival for the Republican candidacy, Ronald Reagan, charged that Kissinger's speech could lead to "a massacre" in Rhodesia and "undercut the possibility of an orderly settlement."[18] Ford's crushing defeat by Reagan in this Texas primary a few days later was largely attributed to the unpopularity of Kissinger's African pronouncements.

Although Kissinger's decision to embark on a shuttle diplomacy mission to settle the Rhodesian dispute might also have had the appearance of outright interference in British affairs, it was tolerated in those quarters. Kissinger could rationalize this intrusion by arguing that he was simply trying to prevent the Soviets from scoring the same success in Rhodesia as they did in Angola and Mozambique. At this time Rhodesia was already deeply embroiled in border clashes with Joshua Nkomo's Zimbabwe-Africa Political Union (ZAPU) and the rival Marxist-inspired Zimbabwe-Africa National Union (ZANU) under Robert Mugabe.

Although similar to his efforts in the Middle East, Kissinger's African shuttle mission started with a major drawback. While in the Middle East both sides wished to reach agreement, the Rhodesian Whites were not craving for a settlement and the response of Black liberation movements was lukewarm. Kissinger had, however, the support of newly won friends among Black heads of state and the ready, if somewhat reluctant assistance of the Vorster government. The latter was obtained with a certain measure of coercion, as Vorster was warned that he too would be facing punitive sanctions unless he helped to bring Rhodesian Premier Ian Smith to the negotiating table. South Africa was already under growing sanctions threat at the UN over Namibia.

At their first meeting on 24 June 1976, in the Bavarian resort village of Grafenau, Kissinger repeated to Prime Minister Vorster the promise made in Lusaka that South Africa could count on wider acceptance and more patience if it jettisoned Rhodesia. Reporters traveling with Kissinger got the impression that Vorster was "amenable" to working out a formula for Black rule in Rhodesia even though he was primarily interested in discussing South Africa's isolation and the need for American cooperation against Communist encroachment in Southern Africa. Events in South Africa as the two men met further forced Vorster's hand. On 16 June 1976, only days before the South African Prime Minister departed for Europe, the worst racial violence in South African history had broken out in the black township of Soweto, causing the whole world to focus attention once again on that country and its unpopular racial policies. "The explosion of Soweto on June 16 added urgency to Vorster's mission and gave Kissinger another stick to apply to South Africa," observed a US expert panel a few years afterward.[19] In a television appearance shortly before his departure for Grafenau, Vorster charged that the riots were timed to "sabotage" the meeting. He blamed it on "Communists and other agitators." While the Johannesburg *Sunday Times* agreed that it "may have been deliberately ignited by people who will not hesitate to employ even children to attain political ends," it claimed that "this week's dynamite had a long fuse."[20]

First, the sudden collapse of White rule in the Portuguese territories created doubts and now Soweto and its bloody aftermath finally destroyed the premise of White permanency on which the Tar Baby Option was based. The South African officials tried their utmost to present the meeting on 24 June 1976, between Vorster and Kissinger as a "major diplomatic achievement." This first high-level meeting with the United States since World War II was, according to the South African spin doctors, an important step closer toward ending international ostracism. Kissinger, on the other hand, now driven by his new moral mission in Africa, made it clear that this meeting was not intended to make concessions or to lend approval to the system of government in South Africa. Before leaving Washington he told Congress that his goal was to determine whether South Africa was prepared to "separate its destiny" from that of Rhodesia so that additional international pressure could be brought on Rhodesia to enter into meaningful negotiations.[21]

As with Sharpeville sixteen years earlier, South Africa experienced a sudden drop in business confidence and capital flight. The price of gold plunged as a result of massive sales of US reserves. This action by Treasury Secretary William Simon helped depress the price from $126 to as low as $80 and forced South Africa to scramble for international credit to finance arms and petroleum purchases.

It was against this backdrop of fulmination, flames, and economic strain in South Africa, coupled with war and sanctions fatigue in Rhodesia, that Vorster undertook to assist Kissinger in forcing Smith to the negotiating table. When Kissinger and Vorster held their second meeting at Zurich on 4 September 1976, South Africa looked even more vulnerable. The Soweto riots had spread despite strong police and military action. In Black areas schools, offices, shops, and public buildings were destroyed in arson attacks. The death toll stood at around 500, many of them Black schoolchildren. The disturbances that started as a protest by 10,000 schoolchildren against the teaching of Afrikaans at schools in Soweto had taken on a wider focus. The Vorster government kept insisting that the unrest was not spontaneous but the work of Communist agitators, Black Power activists, and organized subversives. Harsh police action to put down the violence led to calls at the United Nations for punitive action against South Africa. There was growing pressure on the United States to do something beyond rhetorical retribution.

In an address on the eve of his departure for the parley in Zurich, before a predominantly Black audience at Philadelphia's Convention Hall, Kissinger pleaded for support in his endeavors to settle the Rhodesian and Namibian disputes. He promised also to exert pressure "to bring about change" in South Africa itself. Apartheid must come to an end and majority rule must come, he said.[22] This drew an immediate irate response from Vorster. "Moral lessons and threats" from other countries" made no impression in South Africa, he retorted. Without specifically naming Kissinger, he asserted that "South Africa's internal and external policy is determined by itself and not prescribed to her by any persons or country from outside."[23]

Despite these differences in public both Kissinger and Vorster had ample though vastly different reasons to find common ground in Zurich. Although Kissinger had set progress toward independence in Namibia as a minimum goal and regarded the Rhodesian settlement as more remote, the latter was reported to be his ultimate aim. This would not only enhance Kissinger's status as a super-diplomat but also count in President Ford's favor in his upcoming re-election bid. Vorster, on the other hand, could improve South Africa's deteriorating international position by urging the White minorities that governed Rhodesia and South West Africa to accept Black majority rule.

No major breakthroughs were announced at the conclusion of the three-day Kissinger-Vorster summit in Zurich, but the talks were promising enough for Kissinger to proceed with another round of shuttle diplomacy in Africa—even though he complained that time was running out. With the prospect of being replaced as Secretary of State after the November 1976 presidential election regardless of whether Ford or challenger Jimmy Carter won, Kissinger's efforts had assumed a new sense of urgency. As details of the discussions in Zurich were leaked on a piecemeal basis, it became evident that Vorster had accepted the British-American plan that provided financial guarantees of between $1.5 billion to $2 billion to Rhodesia's Whites in return for their surrender to majority Black rule. If the White Rhodesian leadership proved intransigent, Vorster promised in Zurich, he would cut off Rhodesia's rail links with the vital South African ports.

Addressing a National Party rally in Bloemfontein on 8 September 1976, Prime Minister Vorster drew a standing ovation from the more than 10,000 present when he declared his government totally opposed to "sharing of power" with Blacks in South Africa. But he vowed to help bring about peaceful transition to majority rule in both Rhodesia and Namibia. The principal reason for his cooperation with Kissinger on this score, Vorster explained, was the defeat of Communism, which he believed to be the main force behind the black guerrilla movements operating in this territories. "You can say what you like about the United States," Vorster added, "but I will continue to support them because they are anti-Communistic."[24]

Heartened by this breakthrough, Kissinger departed for Africa on 14 September 1976, for the next phase of his African shuttle diplomacy.

Starting at a meeting in Tanzania with President Julius Nyerere, representing the Frontline states (FLS), Kissinger developed a plan providing for interim Black and White power-sharing in Rhodesia that would lead to Black rule in two years. The FLS—consisting of Angola, Botswana, Mozambique, Tanzania, and Zambia—was formed to help resolve the conflict in Rhodesia. Eventually, after this rebel colony gained its independence as Zimbabwe, it too joined the FLS and the focus shifted to Namibia and South Africa.

On Friday afternoon, 24 September 1976, Kissinger and his entourage arrived in Pretoria—the highest-ranking American official ever to visit South Africa. The purpose of Kissinger's visit was not, however, to enhance South Africa's status but his own as a deal maker. Ian Smith was scheduled to arrive the next day, ostensibly to watch a rugby game. First Kissinger met with Smith at the residence of the American ambassador where he told the rebel White leader that according to American estimates, the Rhodesian economy would be crippled in a year and that the Black liberation movements were gaining strength. Communism, Kissinger argued, would take hold of Rhodesia unless there was a settlement. That same evening Smith was confronted by Kissinger and Vorster at Libertas, the South African prime minister's official residence in Pretoria, with a five-point plan for transition toward Black rule. Diplomatic persuasion was accompanied by a blunt warning from Vorster that South Africa was no longer prepared to underwrite Rhodesia's war effort. What the South African leader later described as "pointing out the realities" to Smith was the decisive factor. Without continued South African support, Smith had little choice. He signed what he called "a suicide note." It was, according to Robert Blake, an "astonishing *volte-face*" by Smith, "who had declared that black majority rule would not occur within a thousand years."[25] What made the difference this time, according to American officials, was that Smith found himself not only under strong pressure from the United States and Britain, but also from South Africa, which had been Rhodesia's economic lifeline.

In the ensuing months Kissinger continued pressing for progress on both the Rhodesian and Namibian issues. Although he eventually failed to bring the South Africans and SWAPO together in discussions regarding Namibia, Kissinger did manage to lure the Rhodesian warring parties to Geneva in November 1976. Throughout that month and deep into December 1976 Smith parleyed with Robert Mugabe, Joshua Nkomo, and other Black contenders. In the end the talks broke down.

On 17 December 1976, while Ford was in the process of handing over the White House keys to Carter, the Kissinger team finally conceded defeat on both issues. But even though Kissinger's shuttle diplomacy did not produce a solution in Rhodesia, it did, according to biographer Walter Isaacson, succeed in its "larger aims." The nations of Black Africa had begun to trust Washington as a force for majority rule and the outlines of the Kissinger agreement "would serve as a basis when his successor, Cyrus Vance, took up the cause."[26] But while Kissinger's conversion to human rights in foreign policy on the road to Lusaka in 1976 was considered to be one of convenience, the Carter administration's preoccupation with morality in foreign lands was much more serious.

Although initial expectations of a closer strategic and military relationship between the United States and South Africa and a roll-back of existing strictures did not materialize during Kissinger's tenure, there was little for Pretoria to complain about on the sanctions front. Despite US support of a few additional calls at the UN Security Council for stricter application of the arms embargo, the *status quo* remained. The United States had continued to refuse support for UN resolutions calling for severe economic and trade sanctions and an oil embargo. It also protested, unsuccessfully, against South Africa's suspension from the UN General Assembly and agencies such as the World Meteorological Organization, the International Civil Aviation Organization (ICAO), and the Universal Postal Union (UPU).

Nevertheless, South Africa had become a nation under siege in the early 1970s. In response to an Arab oil embargo introduced against it in November 1973, in the midst of the so-called OPEC crisis, it was forced to adopt stringent conservation measures and consider oil rationing. In December 1974 the Vorster government announced plans for the construction of a second multibillion rand oil-from-coal complex, ten times larger than the original Sasol plant. Fluor Corporation, the main US bidder for this project, sought Ex-Im Bank loan financing of $1 billion for the major components. Despite the support of Secretary of State Kissinger and more than twenty conservative Congressmen, it was eventually turned down.

During April 1975 an uranium enrichment plant went into operation at Valindaba, near Pretoria, using, according to an announcement by Prime Minister Vorster, an entirely new method of upgrading natural uranium into nuclear fuel. Repeated assurances that this operation was solely intended for peaceful purposes and designed to help South Africa become less energy dependent were met with skepticism from abroad. Fears that South Africa intended to develop a nuclear weapon were fueled by reports such as the one that appeared in the *Washington Post* on 14 April 1975, claiming that the US Nuclear Corporation of Oak Ridge, Tennessee, had sold South Africa 97 pounds of the kind of highly enriched uranium used in the construction of atomic bombs. In June 1976 South Africa was ousted as a board member of the International Atomic Energy Agency (IAEA) and replaced by Egypt.

On the military front, South Africa assumed the posture of a country on battle alert, saving no expense to obtain and develop the latest in armor and equipment under the guidance of Defense Minister P. W. Botha. While much of this military build-up was shrouded in secrecy, increased spending figures were not. During his budget speech on 26 March 1975, Finance Minister Owen Horwood announced a hike of 36 percent in defense spending and the following year another 42 percent increase to a figure of $1.6 billion out of total budget of $9.1 billion.

In the 1970s there were new forces at work that would eventually play a crucial role in the sanctions arena. Both in South Africa and the United States, labor started pressuring American business to either join the battle against apartheid or leave South Africa altogether. Labor had become an ally of the American anti-apartheid movement that started modestly with the establishment of the ACOA in the 1950s and grown into an extensive pro-sanctions lobby consisting of a plethora of church, academic, and political pressure groups.[27]

The Vorster government found "job reservation" as introduced into law by Malan, and refined by his successors, impractical and irreconcilable with economic growth. So ways were devised to facilitate exceptions—to turn a blind eye to Blacks filling positions reserved by law for Whites. Businesses had the best of both worlds. They got the labor they needed and they paid considerably less for non-unionized Blacks than they would for unionized whites. Black trade unions were prohibited by the White regime in fear that they might be exploited for political purposes. But illegal strikes were becoming commonplace despite this official ban on Black trade unions and work stoppages. A government report issued on 25 April 1973, revealed that in the preceding three months 61,410 Blacks were involved in 160 "illegal" strikes, resulting in a wage increase for 700,000 of the country's 6.5 million Black workers. In response the Vorster government took the first small step by passing the Bantu Labor Relations Regulation Act, giving Black workers the right to strike.

On 3 October 1973, Prime Minister Vorster announced that his government would no longer stand in the way of changes in South Africa's traditional work patterns, signifying a growing realization that Black labor was essential for further economic growth, and on 20 November 1974, the Master and Servants Act and portions of the Bantu Labor Act were repealed. Strikes mushroomed and some turned violent but most remained, according to government observers, wage-oriented and non-political. This assessment would soon prove to be wrong.

In the United States a small event of big significance took place on the labor front at the end of 1970. The manufacturer of photographic equipment, Polaroid, was picketed at its Boston headquarters by the so-called Polaroid Revolutionary Workers' Movement (PRWM) for selling its product to South Africa. The PRWM, consisting of only a handful of Black employees, received wide publicity for its claim that Polaroid cameras and film were being used in the manufacture of "passbooks" for Blacks. In an effort to reduce the negative impact, Polaroid's management sent a multiracial "fact-finding mission" to South Africa. On a basis of this mission's report, the company decided to place restrictions on all sales to the South African government and, on 13 January 1971, announced what became known as the "Polaroid experiment." This "one-year experiment" required Polaroid's South African distributor, Frank & Hirsch, and its retailers, to dramatically improve the salaries and other benefits of their non-White employees and to train them for important jobs.

The response to the Polaroid "experiment" was mixed. The South African government accused the company of being hypocritical, while those who favored sanctions dismissed it as a "rationale to business to stay in South Africa under the comfortable but false assumption that they could help end racism while making a tidy profit."[28] Appearing at a UN hearing together with the two Polaroid militants who master-minded the protest—Caroline Hunter and Kenneth Williams—ACOA Director George Houser insisted that Polaroid should leave South Africa altogether.[29]

Polaroid's "experiment" in 1971 was as revolutionary and trend-setting as the instant camera on which it built its fortune. It introduced a measure of morality in the American business presence in South Africa that would serve as a model for other American corporations eager to defend their presence in South Africa. Also the South Africa experts at the State Department found the "Polaroid experiment" useful in their attempts to justify the Nixon administration's stand against disinvestment. No longer did they have to rely on the somewhat negative argument that American business would suffer great losses if forced to leave. Instead of following the Johnson policy of neither encouraging nor discouraging investment in South Africa, the Nixon administration could now encourage involvement, claiming that American business was a force for political change—especially after General Motors, Chrysler, and American Metal Climax adopted programs similar to Polaroid's.

Guided by Assistant Secretary for Africa David Newsom, the State Department embraced the Polaroid concept as a catalyst for political change in South Africa. Polaroid, according to Newsom's deputy, Robert Smith, proved that change was feasible "even within the system" in South Africa.[30] Initially reticent to sound too enthusiastic about this "Polaroid experiment," in fear that it might offend the South African government, the Nixon administration by the end of 1971 openly advised American enterprises in South Africa to pressure Pretoria wherever legally possible. As 1971 drew to a close the US Consulate General in Johannesburg published guidelines for reform to promote the same equal terms of contract, equal pay, and equal opportunities for promotion prescribed by Polaroid.[31] In November 1971 a US delegate proudly told a UN committee that seventeen American corporations had already promoted Blacks to their boards of directors and that others had indicated their intention to follow suit.[32] The Nixon administration found a useful alternative to sanctions against South Africa. "There is an imbalance between the needs of South Africa's active economy and her adherence to racial problems which deprive her of the growing pool of human talent which that economy requires," Nixon reported to Congress in 1972. "There is some hope in that anomaly."[33]

On the surface at least it seemed as if the Nixon administration—and afterward the Ford White House—succeeded in sowing disarray among the disinvestors by exploiting the Polaroid experiment to its fullest. At a grassroots level, however, the sanctions movement continued to gain strength. The demonstration by the PRWM was not an isolated incident. It was but a ripple in a sea of protest against business involvement in South Africa that had developed in the 1970s on campuses and in church circles— in some cases launched independently by anti-apartheid pressure groups and in others as part of the prevailing anti-Vietnam, anti-establishment sentiments of the time. PRWM was only another acronymic blip on the crowded anti-apartheid radar screen.

In December 1976 the City Council of Madison, the capital of Wisconsin, was pressured into becoming the first local authority to introduce sanctions against South Africa. A new ordinance entitled the city to give preferential treatment to American firms without South African ties over others with such links when purchasing products or services. Contracts, it was decreed, could be terminated if it were discovered that an American company had any business links with South Africa. Just as Polaroid set a trend in corporate America, so did Madison among local governments. In years to come, many cities and states across the United States followed suit, putting in place their own local sanctions and boycotts.

But this event in Wisconsin went almost unnoticed in Pretoria where concerns were focused instead on the Carter transitional government in Washington, readying itself to take over the reins early in 1977 and introducing "morality" into foreign policymaking. This approach, it was feared, was bound to lead to a head-on collision and South Africa was bracing itself for tough economic sanctions.

NOTES

1. El-Khawas, Mohammed, and Cohen, Barry, eds., *The Kissinger Study of Southern Africa National Security Study Memorandum 39*, pp. 24-25.

2. Ibid.

3. Davis, Hunt, "US Policy Toward South Africa: A Dissenting View," *American Policy in Southern Africa,* ed. Rene Lemarchand, pp. 314-315.

4. *Die Burger* and *Cape Times*, 3 May 1969.

5. Martin, Patrick H., *American Views on South Africa, 1948-1972,* p. 174.

6. De Villiers, Les, *Secret Information,* pp. 64-70.

7. Ibid.

8. *The Star,* Johannesburg, and *Cape Times,* 28 November 1975.

9. Isaacson, Walter, *Kissinger: A Biography,* p. 675.

10. Henry Kissinger testimony before the Subcommittee on African Affairs, Senate Foreign Relations Committee, 29 January 1976.

11. Dick Clark statement at Hearings on Angola by the African Affairs Subcommittee of the Senate Foreign Relations Committee, 6 February 1976.

12. Isaacson, op. cit. p. 686.

13. Hoffman, Stanley, *Primacy or World Order,* p. 34.

14. Kissinger, Henry, "Southern Africa and the United States: An Agenda for Cooperation," Speech by Secretary Henry A. Kissinger delivered at a luncheon in his honor hosted by President Kenneth Kaunda in Lusaka, Zambia, April 27, 1976. (US Department of State, Bureau of Public Affairs, Washington, DC, 27 April 1976 (PR 205).

15. Isaacson, op. cit., p. 687.

16. *New York Times,* 28 April 1976.

17. Kaufman, Michael, "The Kissinger Mission in Africa," *New York Times,* 30 April 1976.

18. Isaacson, op. cit., p. 688.

19. Thomas, Franklin, ed., *South Africa: Time Running Out,* p. 354.

20. *Sunday Times,* Johannesburg, 20 June 1976.

21. *New York Times,* 25 June 1976.

22. *New York Times,* 1 September 1976.

23. *New York Times,* 2 September 1976.

24. *New York Times,* 9 September 1976.

25. Blake, Robert, *A History of Rhodesia,* pp. 406-407.

26. Isaacson, op. cit.

27. George Houser interview, May 1993.

28. Houser, George, *No One Can Stop the Rain,* p. 271.

29. *New York Times,* 7 February 1971.

30. Smith, Robert, "The Dilemma of Foreign Investment in South Africa," Address before the American Society of International Law, 30 April 1971, Department of State Bulletin, 64:1670, 28 June 1971, p. 827.

31. Coker, Christopher, *The United States and South Africa 1968-1985: Constructive Engagement and its Critics,* p. 81.

32. John Fletcher statement before the UN Committee of Three:Social, Humanitarian, and Cultural, UN General Assembly, 3 November 1971, Department of State Bulletin 65:1692, 29 November 1971, p. 637.

33. Nixon, Richard, "U.S. Foreign Policy for the 1970s: The Emerging Structure of Peace," State of the World Address, 9 February 1972, *Department of State Bulletin 66:1707*, p. 335.

5

The Threat of Sanctions

The greatest utility of sanctions is in the threat of its application rather than its actual use.

Cyrus Vance, US Secretary of State[1]

Human rights became a basic tenet of American foreign policy during the Carter presidency. Secretary of State Cyrus Vance felt that human freedoms should be promoted around the world if needed, through sanctions or, preferably, the threat of sanctions. The latter, he felt, was a more effective weapon than sanctions itself. South Africa, considered by many as one of the most serious human rights violators, became a top candidate for such pressure.

"We are supporting sanctions against South Africa," Jimmy Carter announced in 28 October 1977, nine months into his one-term presidency. The United States had decided to vote in favor of mandatory sanctions in the UN Security Council in the hope that this action would convince the South Africans to "take more constructive action in the future."[2] Carter was prodded into action by the sweeping curbs introduced by the Vorster government on 19 October 1977, to curtail a new wave of unrest following the death in detention of Black Consciousness leader Steve Biko. The banning of 18 anti-apartheid organizations, the closing down of two Black newspapers, and the arrest of some fifty protest leaders were greeted with new and stronger demands for sanctions in the United Nations. Like Kennedy in the early 1960s, Carter opted for an embargo on arms and on 4 November 1977, steered through the UN Security Council a resolution imposing a mandatory embargo. This gave South Africa the unenviable distinction of being the first member state against whom mandatory sanctions were introduced by the world organization.[3]

At a press conference shortly before the votes were cast in the Security Council, Secretary of State Cyrus Vance let it be known that the United States would not only withdraw its naval attaché in Pretoria but also recall its commercial officer in Johannesburg "in connection with our review of our economic relationships with South Africa."[4] This announcement had an ominous ring to it. Following on the heels of National Security Adviser Zbigniew Brzezinski's description of America's support for the UN mandatory arms embargo as only "the beginning of the reaction to the problem that we have been facing," it sent shock waves to Pretoria.[5] Stronger measures to enforce an arms embargo came as no surprise to South Africa. On New Year's Day 1977, several weeks before Carter took over, Prime Minister Vorster had warned in a radio address that in the event of a Communist attack, South Africa should be ready to face it alone as "certain countries who profess to be anti-communist will even refuse to sell arms to South Africa to beat off the attack."[6] But the threat of economic review added an unexpected and most unpleasant dimension.

As Nixon did before him, Carter also initiated a broad reassessment of African policy. He had brought with him a new generation of bureaucrats and advisers concerned over what they perceived as a blatant disregard for human rights and too much of a preoccupation with the Communist threat by previous administrations. This would set the Carter administration on a collision course with South Africa from the outset. In his first major foreign policy speech at Notre Dame on 22 May 1977, Carter stressed his new "affirmative action" human rights approach. Alluding to South Africa and a few others, he warned: "We are now free of that inordinate fear of Communism which once led us to embrace any dictator who joined us in our fear."[7]

It was Secretary of State Cyrus Vance who gave form and substance to the Carter's foreign policy. Vance faulted the Kissinger approach during the Nixon and Ford administrations as being too narrowly rooted in terms of the US-Soviet "geopolitical struggle." He believed the time had come to shift toward a new set of relationships in which power was more diffuse. "A nation that saw itself as a 'beacon on the hill' for the rest of mankind could not content itself with power politics alone," Vance felt. "It could not properly ignore the growing demands of individuals around the world for the fulfillment of their rights."[8] Put in simpler terms, it meant that "human rights" was to become one of the basic tenets of American foreign policy. South Africa was considered one of the most serious human rights violators and therefore a top candidate for such pressure.[9]

In May 1977 Vice President Walter Mondale traveled to Vienna to meet personally with Vorster and register his administration's "basic and fundamental disagreement" with apartheid. He insisted that South Africa take steps toward "full political participation by all the citizens of South Africa."

Asked by a journalist whether "full participation" differed from "one man, one vote," Mondale replied: "No, no. It's the same thing."[10] At about the same time newly appointed UN Ambassador Andrew Young arrived in Johannesburg. He received a warm welcome in Soweto, where he told Blacks that they might well consider adopting the same economic boycott tactics as the American civil rights movement used to accomplish its goals. This approach led to criticism by, among others, George Ball, former undersecretary of state under both Presidents Kennedy and Johnson, who accused Young of thinking that South Africa could be transformed into a "happy multiracial state" by applying the lessons of America's civil rights movement. Unfortunately, Ball pointed out in an article published in the *Atlantic Monthly* in October 1977, South Africa "is not the American South of the 1960s, or even of the 1860s; its problems are of a special kind."

During an appearance before a group of White South African businessmen in Johannesburg, Young reminded them that they held the key to the change needed to forestall their country's economic deterioration. "The good thing about South Africa is that nobody has anywhere to go and you have no choice but to work it out or fight it out and I hope you work it out," Young cautioned.[11] But business hardly needed any further prodding to "work it out." The debate in business circles over what to do about apartheid had been going on ever since Polaroid announced its "experiment" in 1971. Still, with Carter apparently more inclined to use official sanctions against South Africa to promote human rights, this debate had assumed a new sense of urgency. Two months before Young's arrival in Johannesburg, the Rev. Leon Sullivan, a Black director of General Motors, had adopted a six-point program setting conditions for American businesses to stay in South Africa. Carrying as they did, the imprimatur of a Black activist who only a few years earlier had confronted Congress with a five-point plan advocating total US government and business disengagement from South Africa, the Sullivan Principles, promulgated on 1 March 1977, had credibility. They called for:

1. Non-segregation of the races in all eating, comfort, and work facilities.
2. Equal and fair employment practices for all employees.
3. Equal pay for all employees doing equal or comparable work for the same period of time.
4. Initiation and development of training programs to prepare Blacks for supervisory, administrative, clerical, and technical jobs in substantial numbers.
5. Increasing the number of Blacks in management and supervisory positions.
6. Improving the quality of employees' lives outside the work environment in such areas as housing, transportation, schooling, recreation, and health facilities.[12]

Twelve companies immediately adopted the Sullivan Principles: American Cyanamid, Burroughs, Caltex Petroleum, Citicorp, Ford, General Motors, IBM, International Harvester, 3M, Mobil, Otis Elevator and Union Carbide.

They agreed to be monitored by an auditing firm, Arthur D. Little Company in Cambridge, Massachusetts, which, in turn, undertook to publish an annual report summarizing the progress of these companies for public scrutiny.

The South African government, through its Information Minister Connie Mulder, felt compelled to welcome the Sullivan Principles, noting that it was in line with its own desire to see higher wages and better working conditions for all workers. Still, the South African government and the White workers were not quite ready yet for aggressive integration at the workplace. So, corporations had to develop interesting techniques to break down race barriers. In one instance a US company started off with a flower box, trellis and vines dividing Black and White in the cafeteria. When the vines reached the ceiling the trellis was removed. Then the company stopped watering the vines and when they died, removed them. Eventually the flower box was taken away, quietly.[13]

Not only corporations practiced integration by stealth. The South African government, as fearful of the reaction of White trade unions as it was concerned about the threat of sanctions, followed the route of surreptitious surrender. Realizing that it had to go beyond the few cosmetic changes in the labor laws introduced in response to serious strikes in 1973, the government granted Black workers "White" jobs on a piecemeal basis. "In practice the Government has granted so many thousands of exemptions to allow Blacks to do White jobs, only about one in every one hundred [White] jobs is racially reserved," reported the Johannesburg *Sunday Times*.

The Sullivan code was, of course, not the first of its kind. As early as 1974 the British government had issued its own code of conduct for British firms in South Africa and even appointed a special attaché at its Pretoria Embassy to help monitor its performance. In 1976 the South African business community founded the Urban Foundation in response to the Soweto riots to help address the plight of urban Blacks and produced its own code of conduct to promote equality at the workplace. Eventually the British code was somewhat tightened and adopted by all the member countries of the European Economic Community (EEC). Australia and Canada introduced their own codes which set "voluntary guidelines" for their nationals doing business in South Africa.

While quite a few of the larger US corporations became signatories of the Sullivan Principles, many refused to allow what they regarded as "meddling" in their business. By the middle of 1985, when there were serious calls in Washington to make adherence to the Sullivan Principles compulsory, about half or 170 out of 350 American corporations with South African links, had signed up. Still, the Sullivan Principles helped "legitimize" a corporation's presence out there. Noted by its absence among the signatories was Polaroid, which had started it all in the early 1970s with its very own code of conduct for South Africa, presented to the public as the "Polaroid experiment." On 22 November 1977, instead of endorsing Sullivan, Polaroid became the first US company to withdraw its business from South Africa altogether. Polaroid's announcement was tied to a revelation by the ACOA that it continued to sell materials to the South African police but the company itself gave it opposition to apartheid as the reason for its pull-out.

The real reason was, indeed, more complex. The cost in time, money, and energy dealing with protesting Black and other pressure groups in the United States was, as Philip White pointed out, "far greater than the limited anticipated profits the company expected to derive from its South African operations."[14] While Polaroid's annual sales in South Africa of $4 million represented barely 1 percent of the company's world-wide trade, it required considerable boardroom time. The "hassle factor," as it became known, had taken its first victim.

In its 1980 confidential report, the South African Foundation conceded that the "hassle factor" was potentially one of the most dangerous strategies used to force American corporations out of South Africa. Through seemingly endless demands and attacks, anti-apartheid pressure groups forced these corporations to devote considerable time, energy, manpower, and other resources to justify their continued links with that country. Once too much time was spent on dealing with requests for information, on meetings, replies to correspondence, and on dealing with anti-apartheid shareholder resolutions, management would finally reach the point of exasperation and cave in. The South Africa Foundation was told by 65 percent of all American corporations interviewed that executives responsible for South African operations were spending between 30 and 35 percent of their time fighting sanctions pressures. While in none of these cases the South African holdings represented more than 2 percent of a company's total portfolio, several had to hire new personnel to deal exclusively with the disinvestment issue. The foundation cited in 1980 the experience of "one of the largest US companies in South Africa and a signatory of the Sullivan principles" that had to cope with anti-apartheid shareholder resolutions at every single annual general meeting since 1974.[15]

Out of the "bank campaign" launched by Houser's American Committee on Africa (ACOA) in the 1960s grew the idea to pressure all major American corporations into disinvesting from South Africa. Together with the Interfaith Center of Corporate Responsibility (ICCR), formed under the directorship of one of Houser's adjutants, Dr. Timothy Smith, the ACOA could rely on the support of more than a hundred Protestant and Roman Catholic groups with well over $25 million in US corporate stock. This gave them access to the annual general meetings of most major American corporations with South African links. Even though they were usually rejected, anti-apartheid disinvestment shareholder resolutions had a debilitating and disruptive effect on these meetings. At a 1975 IBM annual general meeting (AGM) anti-apartheid shareholder resolutions submitted by fourteen Protestant churches under ICCR guidance consumed one hour, or one-third of the discussion time.

In February 1978 the ICCR scored a major victory when Citicorp, as the holding company of Citibank, the second largest commercial bank in the

United States and a signatory of the Sullivan Principles, succumbed to the "hassle factor" by announcing that it would not make any further loans to the South African government or government-owned enterprises. This breakthrough at Citicorp followed a spate of announcements by university trustees—finally buckling under severe pressure from the ACOA, ICCR and *ad hoc* student groups—that they were disinvesting from corporations with South African business ties. Between 1977 and 1978 ten American universities withdrew investments from US firms with South African connections. While the sums, ranging from $40,000 at Hampshire College to $11 million at New York University's Law School, were relatively modest compared with the billions in holdings represented by these corporations, a beachhead had been established for further conquests. East Lansing, Michigan, became the second city after Madison, Wisconsin, to announce that it would give preference to corporations without South African links both in purchasing and assigning contracts.

The ACOA filed legal suits against companies doing business in South Africa on the grounds that they discriminated in their hiring and promotion policies. Court actions were also used to try terminating South African Airways' landing rights at New York's JFK Airport. The ACOA actually managed to stop the *New York Times* from carrying advertisements for jobs in South Africa on the grounds that they were not open to Black Americans and therefore violated New York City's anti-discrimination laws. Working with local groups in cities across the country, the ACOA distributed anti-Krugerrand literature and helped organize protest movements. Nationwide the offices of Merrill, Lynch, Pierce, Fenner & Smith, were picketed in 1978, forcing the nation's largest brokerage house to stop sales of the South African gold coin in 1978. Similar pressures caused television stations in Chicago, Boston, and New York to discontinue Krugerrand advertising.[16]

But most major US corporations either stood firm on their involvement in South Africa throughout the Carter era or expanded their operations. The *New York Times* reported on 4 December 1977, the presence of 350 US firms in South Africa with a combined direct investment of $1.7 billion. While it represented only 1.2 percent of the total US foreign investment, it constituted 17 percent of all foreign investment in South Africa. In 1982 American private direct investment in that country was estimated at $2.8 billion, an increase of 6.5 percent over 1981 and of 20.6 percent over 1980. Even though this increase was in large part derived from retained earnings by American companies in South Africa, a net capital inflow of $100 million was recorded over the two year period between 1980 and 1982. The main reason for the continued presence and expansion of American business in South Africa, despite intensifying disinvestment pressures at home, was profitability. According to 1983 estimates, US firms obtained an average return of 18 percent on manufacturing investment in South Africa in comparison with 12.6 percent in other parts of the world. In mining the return was 25 percent in South Africa compared with 13.7 percent elsewhere.

Four years later on 20 October 1980, however, *Business Week* quoted the general manager of Caterpillar in South Africa as saying: "We are secure here for five years. Up to 10 years it is a matter of caution. After that it is anybody's guess." In a special report the magzine cautioned potential investors in South Africa to balance "the appeal of high profits and fast growth" against "the hassle factor," which it described as "a blend of South African constraints, polemics back home from anti-apartheid spokesmen, and pressure from stockholding churches, universities, and other institutions on US companies to divest themselves of their South African operations." American companies, *Business Week* concluded, are now taking money out of South Africa at almost the same rate that they are putting it in. Martin Spring quoted a "man with direct responsibility for one of the largest single American investments" as complaining that "we cannot go on indefinitely supporting the South African Government." Another executive voiced a similar opinion: "Unless we see signs of radical change, it won't be the [Carter] Administration, it will be US business that will have to consider economic sanctions."[17]

The "hassle factor," as *Business Week* pointed out on 25 February 1980, was not only felt in America but also increasingly in South Africa, where Blacks were starting to channel their political aspirations through labor organizations. "American companies may be hardest hit" by the resulting tensions, predicted the business journal. By then the tentative labor reforms introduced by Prime Minister Vorster in response to serious strikes in the early 1970s, had been taken another step forward. The new Botha government had adopted the recommendations of the Wiehahn and Riekert Commissions, giving Black South Africa the ability for the first time to flex its muscle at the work place not only for economic but political gain.

Ever since the abrasive encounter with Vice President Walter Mondale in Vienna in May 1977, Prime Minister Vorster had used the "threat from America" to rally support in South Africa. Addressing a Pretoria audience, Mr. Vorster accused the US government of backing an international pressure campaign against South Africa that could result in chaos and anarchy. What Carter intended, he claimed, was the "strangulation [of South Africa] with finesse." The Carter administration, Vorster charged, having won the election with the support of America's Blacks, was now under pressure from both the Black Caucus and from other organizations.[18]

Asked on television by Walter Cronkite of CBS about South Africa's banning of Black leaders, organizations, and newspapers, which prompted Carter's support of mandatory UN arms sanctions, South African Foreign Minister R. F. Pik Botha said the government had to act when the safety of innocent people was threatened. His country, he said, would not be held hostage by threats of sanctions.[19] Referring to the Mondale prescription during another American television interview, Foreign Minister Botha claimed that to foist Black majority rule on South Africa would mean nothing less than suicide for the Whites. He described the call for "one-man-one-vote" as the "height of immorality" and added: "You want us to accept this new commitment—a commitment to suicide. Forget it. No way. We shall not accept that; not now, not tomorrow, never, ever."[20]

"Do your damnedest," Vorster challenged. In a speech before the American Businessmen's Luncheon Club in Johannesburg he said: "We are a small people and we know just how far our limitations go and we are a proud people. Even a small people must stand up for its rights."[21] The 600 in attendance gave him a standing ovation and so, more importantly, did the White South African electorate. Carter's support in early November 1977 for the UN mandatory arms embargo and threats of further punitive measures further helped to fuel the war psychosis. The National Party scored its biggest election victory ever by winning a record 66 percent of the White vote—ending up with 135 of the 165 seats in the House of Assembly.

Despite Vorster's successful exploitation of what he pictured as the US threat, there was considerable dissent within Carter's ranks over how to approach South African policy. During a discussion with the British about Rhodesia it had, according to Brzezinski, become clear that there was in fact no clear or basic concept of what it was that the Carter administration wished to achieve on Africa.[22] Diametrically opposed to Vice President Mondale with his "one man, one vote" demand, National Security Adviser Brzezinski had hoped, in much the same way Kissinger did, for "the modification of apartheid short of majority rule."[23] Anthony Lake, newly appointed director of Policy Planning in the State Department, also argued against a "blindly interventionist" approach.[24] It is unlikely that either Brzezinski or Lake endorsed Ambassador Andrew Young's brash interference during his April 1977 visit to South Africa. In between all these cross-currents stood Secretary of State Cyrus Vance, who favored the pursuit of human rights through more conventional diplomatic pressure and, if necessary, the threat of sanctions. Assistant Secretary for African Affairs William Schaufele, a holdover from the Kissinger-Ford era, soon to be replaced by a Carter appointee, found Brzezinski remarkably close to his own views. His replacement, Black American career diplomat Richard Moose, however, started out favoring the harder interventionist line.

Despite Carter's dismissal of the Communist threat in his Notre Dame speech, National Security Adviser Brzezinski continued to take the role of Communism in Africa seriously. He felt that both Vance and Young, along with most of those at State, took an "excessively benign view of the Soviet and Cuban penetration of Africa, underestimating its strategic implications."[25] Vance, on the other hand, insisted on an "even-handed" approach to these "difficult issues" instead of Brzezinski's hard line—"greatly influenced by his Polish background."[26] In his memoirs Brzezinski recalled how he argued against "anything radical" and became the only adviser to challenge the desirability of a direct confrontation between Vorster and Mondale so soon into the new administration's tenure. There was no point in "plunging the Vice President into the South African problem" until and unless a coherent plan of action was developed.[27] After "some very rough discussions" in the first few months of the Carter term, the Vance position was adopted by Carter.[28] It prevailed until the dying days of the Carter administration. After both Young and Vance left, when Brzezinski finally had things his way, it was too late to make much difference.

On entering office, writes Christopher Coker, "Carter looked forward to immediate progress on the political front, perhaps because he was misled by the Soweto disturbances, as Kennedy had been misled by Sharpeville, into thinking that progress could not long be delayed."[29] Early in his presidency, on 30 April 1977, Carter received from his National Security Council a position paper of forty-three pages listing as one of the ten foreign policy priorities the achievement of majority rule in Rhodesia and dismantling apartheid in South Africa. Curiously, there was no mention of Namibia in this "blueprint for the next four years." Despite this oversight, Namibia turned out to be one of the Southern African issues that occupied much time and effort in the Carter White House.

Soon after it took office, the Carter administration informed Pretoria that unless it accepted the UN plan for Namibian independence and scuttled the Turnhalle option, the Western nations would find it hard to resist growing African demands for mandatory sanctions. As in Kennedy's time, there was once again considerable agonizing over the issue of sanctions. "If there were no credible negotiating initiative, the Africans would be able to force a Security Council vote," Vance argued. "We would either damage our relations with black Africa by vetoing the resolution, which would be at odds with the Carter administration's Africa policy, or by approving it, destroy the negotiating process and harm important Western economic interests in South Africa, as well as set an undesirable precedent that might be used against our friends, such as Israel, in the future."[30]

The mere threat of sanctions, the Carter administration believed, might well coerce South Africa into complying with the UN's wishes. Barely two months into the Carter presidency, on April 7, 1977, Prime Minister Vorster was confronted in Cape Town with an *aide-memoire* by the ambassadors representing the Western contact group under American leadership, warning him that his internal settlement for Namibia was unacceptable and that if South Africa did not agree to UN-sponsored negotiations, the Western five would have to reconsider their stance in the Security Council. "This signified, as Vorster readily understood," Vance later explained, "that the five would no longer oppose mandatory UN sanctions against South Africa."[31]

Although Vorster reacted sharply, refusing to interfere with the Turnhalle process and branding this "threat of sanctions" as an "obnoxious" act, he agreed to receive the contact group, consisting of representatives from the United States, Britain, France, West Germany, and Canada. Toward the end of April, when they arrived in South Africa under leadership of US delegate Donald McHenry, the Western group found Prime Minister Vorster and his Foreign Minister Pik Botha ready to compromise. In a complete about face, the South Africans agreed not only to abandon the Turnhalle program but also accepted the main elements of UN Resolution 385. "The South African's changed attitude was, in the judgment of many, due to the united Western assertion that we would no longer prevent sanctions unless they began seriously negotiating for Namibian independence under international supervision," Vance noted.[32]

On 10 June 1977, South Africa formally agreed to abandon plans for an ethnically based interim government in Namibia and to accept a transitional government that would include SWAPO. It also agreed to UN-sponsored elections and announced the appointment of an administrator to govern in the interim. Justice Martinus Steyn arrived in Windhoek on 1 September 1977, to assume the position of administrator-general with SWAPO approval. This was seen as the first step toward implementation of the Western group's independence plan for the territory. The repeal of a law prohibiting mixed marriages in the territory signaled South Africa's serious intent to eliminate apartheid altogether. But in November 1977 SWAPO's demand that South African troops be withdrawn from Namibia before elections were held met with a blunt refusal from Vorster who insisted on a military presence until SWAPO stopped its guerrilla war.

South Africa did not abandon the Turnhalle option altogether. While continuing its negotiations with the contact group in June and again in September 1977, Pretoria allowed the Turnhalle discussions to develop. A stalemate was reached between the Western five and the Vorster government at the end of 1977 and South Africa scheduled its own Turnhalle elections for June 1978. In February 1978, however, contact resumed once again with the United States and its Western partners as South Africa accepted an invitation to join "proximity talks" in New York. These talks involved both SWAPO and the South African government in separate discussions with the contact group. Foreign Minister Botha left abruptly when his German counterpart, Hans-Dietrich Genscher, warned that Western-supported sanctions would become necessary should Pretoria refuse to cooperate. Despite the walkout in New York by his minister of foreign affairs, Prime Minister Vorster decided to accept in principle a new Western proposal designed to allay South African concerns about military control during the transition, the size of the UN monitoring group, and the status of Walvis Bay. While the Western contact group tried to enlist SWAPO's support for the new plan, South African troops penetrated deep into Angola in a strike aimed at eliminating the Black liberation movement's bases. Over UN objections, Vorster on 24 May 1978, finally announced plans for a Turnhalle-style election to be held in December.

Just as the chances of an agreement with the Western five looked at its slimmest, further negotiations took place, leading to Pretoria's conditional acceptance of the UN position and the arrival in Windhoek of an advance team of UN experts. They reported back to UN Secretary General Waldheim that 7,500 troops would be required to implement the UN independence plan—to the dismay of the South Africans who felt that 2,000 UN personnel would be more than sufficient. This objection against too large a UN presence resulted from South Africa's belief that the United Nations favored SWAPO. On 20 September 1978, hours before he resigned, Prime Minister Vorster formally rejected the Waldheim recommendation.

Nine days later, the United Nations Security Council retaliated with Resolution 435. This was adopted just as Vorster's successor, P. W. Botha, completed his first full day in office. The new resolution endorsed the Waldheim plan for Namibian independence. It authorized the Secretary General to proceed with the necessary arrangements despite South African objections. Resolution 435 would leave the responsibility for law and order during the transition period in South African hands, subject to monitoring and supervision by the UN Transitional Assistance Group (UNTAG) consisting of up to 10,000 civilian and military personnel. The plan also authorized the United Nations to organize and supervise "free and fair elections" while preventing infiltration across the Angolan border and monitoring the South African forces.

Before leaving for South Africa to confront the new South Africa prime minister with the latest UN plan, Secretary of State Vance sought guidance during a policy review meeting at the White House on 6 October 1978, chaired by President Carter. Vance, it was decided, should seek a private meeting with Prime Minister Botha and give him a personal handwritten letter from Carter, inviting him to Washington for discussions on how South Africa's international standing can be improved, providing Pretoria reversed its negative September 20 decision. As a further inducement, the foreign ministers would undertake to seek SWAPO's cooperation for UN-supervised elections in the spring of 1979 and the reduction of the UN peacekeeping force to 3,500 combat troops plus 1,500 support personnel. If Botha did not respond positively, the United States would be prepared to support sanctions, but only after a proper assessment of the results of the Pretoria talks. To avoid a confrontational atmosphere, it was decided not to reveal in advance the intention to apply sanctions if deemed necessary.[33]

Subsequently the Western five "contact group" met in New York and assembled a group of experts under the supervision of the US representative, Don McHenry, to prepare a list of possible sanctions that could be implemented if necessary. No one favored a total UN economic embargo. Considered instead were limited measures such as restrictions on landing rights for South African civil aircraft and on South Africa's access to Western export financing. In the end, neither Carter's letter nor the unannounced but implied pressure of further sanctions could move Prime Minister Botha to denounce the Turnhalle option. He merely offered to intercede with the winners of the December 1978 elections in Namibia to have them agree to another UN-sponsored election that included SWAPO. The new South African leader had called Carter and the Western contact group's bluff and escaped unharmed.

On 13 November 1978, the African nations forced the UN Security Council to vote on sanctions against South Africa as punishment for its prevarication on the Namibian issue. The Western five abstained. In the eyes of Black Americans and the African nations, Carter's subsequent signing of congressional legislation adding further restrictions on Export-Import Bank financing of trade with South Africa hardly compensated for its refusal to respond to the renewed call for Security Council sanctions. To add insult to injury, Prime Minister Botha confidently dismissed the oil embargo favored by some African nations as unlikely to have more impact than the weapons embargo already in force. "If an arms embargo is not feasible, I don't think an oil embargo is feasible either," Botha was quoted as saying. While he now publicly expressed interest in visiting the United States, as suggested by President Carter in the letter handed to him by Vance, he gave no indication of trying to meet its conditions.[34]

During a visit to New York on 27 November 1978, Foreign Minister Botha was once again cautioned by the Americans that mandatory sanctions could well be in the offing unless his government complied with UN Resolution 435. He proceeded to Washington, where he obtained an audience with President Carter, only to be told that failure to cooperate with the United Nations on Namibia could lead to sanctions. To soften the blow, the American president repeated his offer to meet with Prime Minister Botha as soon as he showed willingness to comply with the UN's demands on Namibia. Before he left, Botha sought a meeting with UN Secretary General Waldheim and assured him that South Africa would strongly recommend to the winners of the December Turnhalle elections that they adopt Resolution 435 and participate in new elections under United Nations supervision. In the absence of SWAPO, the Democratic Turnhalle Alliance (DTA) won almost every seat in the newly established Namibian Constituent Assembly. Although the DTA agreed in principle to UN-sponsored elections, it was opposed to the idea of reducing the South African military presence prior to a complete cease-fire.

At a meeting with the Western five in New York during March 1979, now attended by Foreign Minister Botha and a delegation from the Turnhalle parties, further objections were raised to the UN plan. If South Africa intended to keep the UN at bay while proceeding with its own agenda, the strategy seemed to have worked—for a while at least. Pik Botha was applying his talent for skillful equivocation, high drama, and posturing to provide the necessary maneuvering space in Namibia despite the looming threat of sanctions. Hawkish P. W. Botha needed time to implement his military option—an all-out effort to neutralize SWAPO and its Marxist allies on the battlefield and give the DTA a chance to win its battle for the hearts and minds of Namibians without interference from the Black liberation movement.

While Carter concluded his term in frustration over the stalemate on Namibia, he could at least claim credit for helping to resolve the Rhodesian issue. America added weight to the British effort by tightening sanctions against Ian Smith's Rhodesia. It also convinced the South Africans that it would ultimately support further UN sanctions unless they refrained from aiding and abetting the Smith regime.

Since its unilateral declaration of independence (UDI) from Britain in November 1965, Ian Smith's white-ruled Rhodesia not only managed to survive economically but to prosper despite extensive sanctions by the United Nations and all the major Western powers. Even though Smith's sanctions-busters were artful, the real secret for survival lay immediately south of the Zambesi river. By refusing to support sanctions, South Africa provided the maverick British colony with valuable access to harbors, oil supplies, weaponry, and the like.

One of the first actions by President Carter after he was sworn in early in 1977 was to ask Congress to repeal the Byrd Amendment, which permitted American importation of Rhodesian chrome despite America's adherence to mandatory UN sanctions against Rhodesia. In March 1977 Congress granted him his wish. Next the United States started pressuring South Africa into isolating Rhodesia as well. According to Vance, President Carter had decided that the United States would support sanctions against South Africa if necessary. In discussions between the British and the Americans during September 1977, it was, however, decided that while Smith had not accepted the Anglo-American settlement proposals, he still seemed willing to negotiate. Therefore the time had not yet arrived to seek sanctions against South Africa.

On 3 March 1978, Rhodesian Prime Minister Ian Smith, Bishop Abel Muzorewa, the Rev. Ndabaningi Sithole, and Chief Jeremiah Chirau reached their own internal agreement providing for the transfer of power to the Black majority after "free elections" supervised by a transitional government under Smith. On 29 September 1978, however, Smith indicated a delay "for purely mechanical reasons" and ruled out the transfer of power to a Black majority before 31 December. When the four Rhodesian leaders visited Pretoria on 15 November for talks with the newly installed Prime Minister P. W. Botha, they were cautioned against any further delays. Botha warned that he would not support the Rhodesian interim government unless elections were held by April 1979. Coming from a man who as defense minister was on occasion reprimanded by Vorster for getting too deeply and too enthusiastically involved on the side of the White Rhodesians, Smith had no choice but to take the threat seriously.

The internal Salisbury agreement was boycotted by the Patriotic Front alliance, consisting of Joshua Nkomo's Zimbabwe-Africa Political Union (ZAPU) and the Marxist Zimbabwe-Africa National Union (ZANU) led by Robert Mugabe. It was also rejected by the Organization of African Unity (OAU), the United Nations, the United States, and Britain. Despite this opposition, Smith proceeded with the elections under the internal agreement and on 29 May 1979, Bishop Abel Muzorewa was installed as Rhodesia's new prime minister.

Even though Carter acceded to Senator Jesse Helms' request and met with the newly elected Muzorewa at Camp David in July 1979, he remained firm on sanctions, forcing Rhodesia, now no longer able to draw on South African assistance, back to the negotiating table. In September 1979 all the parties finally gathered for discussions at Lancaster House and in December of that year agreement was reached. Before year's end, Britain, the United States, and the United Nations lifted the sanctions. In March 1980 ZANU leader Robert Mugabe won UN-supervised elections and on 18 April he was installed as prime minister of newly independent Zimbabwe.

Reviewing the events of that time, Secretary of State Vance has no doubts that the threat of sanctions obliged South Africa to withdraw vital support from its northern neighbor and hastened the final settlement. In this case, he believed "the greatest utility of sanctions power" proved to be "in the threat of its application rather than its actual use" against South Africa.[35] Although he found fault with most of the Carter's foreign policy assumptions, Chester Crocker, who later became the chief Southern African policy planner for Reagan, concurred on this score. As director of African Studies at Georgetown University, Crocker wrote that "the threat is more valuable than the deed" when it came to sanctions against South Africa.[36]

For the Carter administration, "undoing apartheid" and "breaking the stalemate on Namibia" proved more difficult than achieving majority rule in Rhodesia.[37] While the threat of sanctions seemed to have played an important role in enlisting South Africa to help pressure Smith of Rhodesia to capitulate, it had little success in forcing South Africa to abdicate in Namibia and dismantle apartheid. If anything, the threat proved to be counter-productive as the South Africans responded by withdrawing into the proverbial "laager."

On 28 September 1978, Pieter Willem (P. W.) Botha was chosen with a slim majority of seven by the National Party caucus over front-runner Cornelius (Connie) Mulder to succeed Vorster after his resignation as premier for "health reasons." Botha promised reform and "clean" government. The latter was in reference to what had by then become known as Infogate or Muldergate. As in the United States during the early 1970s when important matters of state were sidelined while the Nixon White House and the nation agonized over Watergate, South Africa now became preoccupied with Infogate. Initial charges of misuse of secret government funds by Mulder's Information Department soon led to an endless spate of sensational revelations. As the story unraveled it became evident that the South African Information Department's well-publicized, open but unorthodox diplomatic successes in the United States and elsewhere, were only the tip of an iceberg. In 1978 this iceberg of secrets sank Vorster's ship of state. It was a disaster that had a profound effect on South Africa, both domestically and internationally. It basically eliminated South Africa's covert counter-offensive against sanctions.

While South Africa had long been flooding the United States with "propaganda" literature under the "new direction" at the Department of Information, "most of the effort has been going into activities which are much more sophisticated and subtle than the distribution of literature," concluded Barbara Rogers in *The Great White Hoax*.[38] Eventually as the inner core of this multilayered propaganda effort became known, the scope and depth of its sophistication and subtlety far exceeded even Rogers' worst fears. South Africa had managed to infiltrate and manipulate business, labor, church, academic, and political circles in the United States and elsewhere in a mass-scale counter-offensive against sanctions and disinvestment.

Understandably, even the Botha government, which rode into power on the demise of Mulder and his Department of Information, seemed reluctant to part with these practices. On 7 December 1978, when Foreign Minister Botha rose in parliament to speak during a heated debate about Infogate, the Department of Information had already been disbanded and the propaganda task assigned to his department. He insisted that it was still necessary to conduct secret or covert projects in the face of "a great number of organizations that are active in the field against South Africa." In the United States alone, he claimed, there were eighty that "in sophisticated, virulent, subtle and underhand ways" were operating against South Africa. "They are not being investigated. Their funds and activities remain secret. If we are to stand here defenseless and helpless with our hands behind our backs and everything we do has to be done in sight of our enemies we shall never attain our goal."[39]

On the surface, however, it seemed as if covert propaganda and anti-sanctions campaigns came to an end with the departure of both Information Minister Connie Mulder and former Prime Minister Vorster. Mulder was pressured by P. W. Botha into resigning, first as cabinet minister and in January 1979 as a member of parliament. On 4 June 1979, after a few months in the largely ceremonial post of state president, Vorster was obliged to make an unceremonial exit from Tuynhuys in Cape Town.

Having purged the South African government, P. W. Botha now embarked on the road of reform. "We are moving in a changing world. We must adapt, otherwise we shall die," he cautioned. He questioned the need for the Mixed Marriages and the Immorality Acts. In May 1979 Botha accepted the recommendations of two labor commissions appointed by predecessor Vorster, removing constraints on Black labor unions and the movement of workers. One commission, consisting of labor leaders and businessmen under chairmanship of Professor Nic Wiehahn, suggested the total scrapping of job apartheid and recognition of Black trade unions. The other, headed by economic adviser Pieter Riekert, recommended unrestricted migration of Black workers to the cities. With these reforms in hand, the Botha government arranged a special road show for Wiehahn in the United States and Europe to try to counter mounting pressures for sanctions.

On 31 August 1979, Prime Minister Botha became the first White South African leader to visit the Black township of Soweto, where he was warmly received by some 5,000 residents. "This is not just a courtesy call," Botha assured them. "This is one of the highlights of my career."[40] The visit played well abroad. In October 1979, however, when Botha unveiled his twelve-point plan for the future of South Africa, it fell far short of demands on the left for one man, one vote. Although it subscribed to the principle of power-sharing as far as Colored and Indians were concerned, it offered nothing new for Blacks, but simply restated the old Bantu homelands or "grand apartheid" policy. While he promised to do away with "humiliating and unnecessary discriminatory laws," Botha also vowed never to compromise the "self-determination" of his own people.[41] It was a plan that satisfied neither the left nor the right wing and Botha drew fire from both sides.

On 18 January 1980, the price of gold jumped to an all-time high of $835 an ounce, igniting an economic boom in South Africa—the world's premier producer. That year gold averaged $600 per ounce—double the 1979 figure. Increased overseas investor confidence enabled Finance Minister Owen Horwood to introduce tax cuts and higher entitlements for Blacks in his budget of 26 March 1980. In the midst of all this unprecedented prosperity, however, political tension continued to mount in the Black townships as Prime Minister Botha stalled on the road of reform in the face of growing right-wing opposition.

In June 1980 South African air and ground troops mounted "Operation Smoke Shell," a large-scale conventional assault on SWAPO guerrilla bases deep inside Angola. Botha's forces claimed 350 guerrillas killed as opposed to only seventeen casualties among their own. It was an operation intended not only to impress the UN and SWAPO but also to serve as a warning to the outlawed ANC not to use its bases in neighboring Black states for continuing acts of sabotage in South Africa. But the problem posed by sporadic internal uprisings proved to be more difficult. Unrest among Coloreds, sparked off by a student boycott in April 1980 in protest against inferior educational standards, continued for months. On 16 June 1980, Soweto Day, violence engulfed Cape Town as Coloreds defied a ban on demonstrations and political meetings and resorted to looting and burning. The police fired into the crowd, killing thirty and injuring 175.[42] Despite the booming economy, Botha's promises of reform, and the unlikelihood of further sanctions in 1980, dark clouds continued to gather on the horizon.

The immediate threat of further sanctions by the United States against South African apartheid had, however, subsided as Carter's advisers applauded Botha's words "adapt or die" and acknowledged his first tentative steps toward domestic reform. On 30 April 1980, in testimony before Congress, Assistant Secretary Richard Moose, who once favored punitive measures as a foreign policy tool against South Africa, cautioned against letting "our desire to help obscure other facts." No amount of political action from overseas "can overshadow the solution to be worked out by South Africa's own people."[43] Towards the end of his tenure, in October 1980, Moose was asked by the African Studies Symposium in Pennsylvania to assess Carter's accomplishments in relation to South Africa. "Within the framework of our policy, we have taken a series of actions which speak to the seriousness of our intent," he said and proceeded to chalk up the following as examples of punitive measures introduced by the Carter administration:

- Support for the mandatory arms embargo by the UN Security Council;
- suspension of all nuclear cooperation, pending South Africa's adherence to the non-proliferation treaty;
- unilateral expansion of the UN arms embargo to cut off any and all exports to the South African military and police, including non-military or arms-related items;
- and the limiting of Ex-Im Bank and Commodity Credit Corporation facilities for South African trade.[44]

Moose refrained from mentioning that President Carter originally opposed the limits placed on Ex-Im Bank financing when it was proposed in Congress in 1978. He also failed to note that since 1977, the Carter administration had opposed every congressional bill seeking to impose economic sanctions against South Africa. By instructing his Commerce Department during February 1978 to restrict the sales of US products and technology to the South African police and military, Carter actually tried to preempt stronger measures proposed by Congress in angry response to the October 1977 arrests and bannings in South Africa. The Carter administration also opposed legislation aimed at tying investment in South Africa to labor practices, arguing that it would not only be ineffective but run counter to US policy on foreign investment elsewhere.

Throughout 1978, with American indignation still running high over the death of Black activist Steve Biko and the punitive detention of Black South African opposition leaders, more than twenty bills were introduced by Congress. None passed. Only one resolution introduced by Black Congresswoman Cardiss Collins that expressed concern "about the recent acts of repression by the South African government" made it through the

House of Representatives on 31 October 1977, by a vote of 347 to 54, with five voting "present." During 1979 and 1980, the last two years of the Carter administration, congressional interest in South Africa reached rock bottom.

On 28 June 1980, the influential Black newspaper, New York's *Amsterdam News,* complained that the American administration had offered only a "limp-wrist response" to the excesses of the Botha government—"a bit like trying to tame a man-eating tiger by spraying it with rose water." Later Brzezinski would concede that "we were failing to deliver enough to satisfy the Black Africans and yet at the same time we were frightening the Whites into unshakable intransigence."[45]

In November 1980, after Carter was defeated by the more amenable Reagan, Foreign Minister Pik Botha—to the puzzlement of observers—charged that "our fear of sanctions is being used to wring concessions from us." South Africa, he said, must no longer allow itself "to be pushed around by this fear, and [must] accept that sanctions will come." Later that month, Prime Minister P. W. Botha expressed the same sentiments. "If sanctions in one form or another are applied against us, we shall fight them tooth and nail," he declared. "We have experience in fighting sanctions. An arms embargo was applied against us for a number of years, and I happened to be in the thick of that fight. We not only withstood it but we are now in a position where we are exporting arms of sophisticated types."[46]

Picking up on this untimely economic war psychosis, the Johannesburg *Financial Mail* concluded on 21 November 1980: "As Pretoria sees it, it is necessary once and for all to lay the ghost of sanctions. Foreign Minister Pik Botha believed, it would seem, that now was the time to head the sanctions threat off at the pass. If he succeeds, that threat will become an empty one. He will have robbed it of currency by the device of inviting its execution."[47] John Barratt, director of the Johannesburg-based South African Institute of International Affairs, wondered if the Bothas were simply calling the international community's bluff. "Previously," he noted, "it appeared that South Africa was trying to avoid the imposition of sanctions, the assumption being that by at least keeping the door open to a United Nations sponsored independence settlement in SWA/Namibia, South Africa would be able to count on the Western powers to oppose sanctions," But now official statements gave "the impression that South Africa is not only ready for sanctions, but implicitly that the country in some ways even would welcome the challenge of sanctions."[48]

The Carter administration never quite fulfilled the dire prophecies of tough action against South Africa for its human rights violations. Barring its support for a stronger version of the UN arms embargo already in place, it did very little in the field of sanctions. Instead it invoked the threat of sanctions to accomplish its goals. But early in 1981 the Carter administration departed, leaving this threat hanging over South Africa like the sword of Damocles. Despite repeated efforts by the incoming friendlier Reagan administration to remove this sword, it remained in place because Congress wished it so. Sanctions in the late 1970s had become an integral part of policy toward South Africa, not merely because of Carter but through the efforts of a growing army of volunteer and professional anti-apartheid activists. These were people and organizations imbued with a desire to topple the White South African regime at any cost. Emboldened by the demise of the South African propaganda machine and signs of weakening resolve among American business, these pro-sanctions activists were preparing for the final onslaught—despite Reagan and "constructive engagement."

NOTES

1. Cyrus Vance interview.

2. Reply by President Carter to a question asked over the telephone by a member of the National Newspaper Association, 28 October 1977, during the NNA's annual convention in Houston. *Public Papers of the Presidents: Jimmy Carter,* 1977, pp. 1922-1923.

3. Although mandatory sanctions against Rhodesia were introduced earlier, the rebel colony was not a member state.

4. *Department of State Press Release* 497, 2 November 1977; *Department of State Bulletin,* 21 November 1977, pp. 715-716.

5. Zbigniew Brzezinski assistant to President Carter for National Security Affairs. Interviewed on *Face the Nation,* CBS-TV, 30 October, 1977. Department of State Bulletin, 5 December 1977.

6. *The Citizen,* Johannesburg, 3 January 1977.

7. *New York Times,* 23 May 1977.

8. Vance, Cyrus, *Hard Choices,* p. 29.

9. Cyrus Vance interview.

10. Statement and replies to questions at a press conference in Vienna, 20 May 1977, by Vice President Walter Mondale. *Department of State Bulletin,* 20 June 1977, pp. 661-666.

11. *New York Times,* 22 May 1977.

12. Bissell, Richard, *South Africa and the United States,* p. 86.

13. Spring, Martin, *Confrontation,* p. 97.

14. White, Philip V., "The Black American Constituency for Southern Africa, 1940-1980," *The American People and South Africa,* eds., Alfred Hero and John Barratt, p. 91.

15. "The Disinvestment Movement in the US: A Strategic Analysis," confidential South Africa Foundation report, 3 March 1980.

16. Houser, George, *No One Can Stop the Rain,* p. 270.

17. Ibid.

18. *South African Digest,* 12 August 1977.

19. *The Citizen,* Johannesburg, 29 October 1977.

20. Nagan, Winston, "The US and South Africa: The Limits of Peaceful Change," *American Policy in Southern Africa: The Stakes and the Stance,* ed., Rene Lemarchand, p.238.

21. *South African Digest,* 30 September 1977.

22. Brzezinski, Zbigniew, *Power and Principle,* p. 140.

23. Coker, Christopher, *The United States and South Africa 1968-1985: Constructive Engagement and its Critics,* p.118.

24. Lake, Anthony, "Africa in Global Perspective," Christian Herter Lecture, Johns Hopkins University, *Department of State Bulletin,* 12 December 1977, p. 844.

25. Brzezinski, op. cit., p. 143.

26. Cyrus Vance interview, May 1993.

27. Brzezinski, op. cit., pp. 140-141.

28. Cyrus Vance interview.

29. Coker, op. cit., p. 139.

30. Vance, Cyrus, *Hard Choices,* p. 275.

31. Ibid., p. 277.

32. Ibid.

33. Ibid., p. 308

34. *New York Times,* 20 November 1978.

35. Cyrus Vance interview.

36. Koenderman, Tony, *Sanctions,* pp. 31-32.

37. Brzezinski, op. cit., p. 143.

38. Burgess, J., and Rogers, B., *The Great White Hoax—South Africa's International Propaganda Machine,* p. 64.

39. *Debates of the House of Assembly,* Second Session, Sixth Parliament, Special Session, 7-8 December 1978, cols. 75-76.

40. *The Citizen,* Johannesburg, 1 September 1979.

41. P.W. Botha address before the National Party Congress, Durban, 15 October 1979.

42. *Cape Times,* Cape Town, 17 June 1980.

43. Moose, Richard, "US Policy Towards South Africa," hearings before the Sub-committee on Africa of the Committee on Foreign Affairs, House of Representatives, 96th Congress, 2nd Session, 30 April 1980, pp. 3-8.

44. Richard Moose speech before the African Studies Symposium at Pennsylvania State University, *Department of State Bulletin,* 13 October 1980.

45. Brzezinski, op. cit., p. 143.

46. Koenderman, op. cit., pp. 31-32.

47. *Financial Mail,* Johannesburg, 21 November 1980.

48. Koenderman, op. cit., p. 31.

6

Constructive Engagement

Under constructive engagement, we would continue our adherence to the arms embargo, our refusal to make use of South African defense facilities, our categorical rejection of apartheid policies and institutions—as well as our rejection of trade and investment sanctions and all forms of economic warfare against South Africa.

Chester Crocker
US Assistant Secretary of State for African Affairs[1]

Under constructive engagement as espoused by Chester Crocker, President Reagan's assistant secretary for African affairs, anti-Communism once again became a virtue. The new president lauded South Africa as an ally and a friend. In sharp contrast to the Carter years when the threat of sanctions was often invoked to try to force South Africa's hand, the Reagan administration was totally opposed to further punitive measures. While reluctantly adhering to existing embargoes, new sanctions were completely ruled out.

"We are not enthusiastic about economic sanctions," UN Ambassador Jeanne Kirkpatrick told the Overseas Press Club in New York on 29 April 1981. "The Reagan administration holds the view that economic sanctions are not a very useful instrument of policy." The Kirkpatrick speech played well in official circles in Pretoria, already buoyed by positive signs from President Reagan himself. Barely weeks into his first term, Ronald Reagan had extended the hand of friendship to South Africa on national television. "Can we abandon a country that has stood beside us in every war we've ever fought?" he asked in rhetorical fashion during a CBS television interview with Walter Cronkite on 3 March 1981. "A country that strategically is essential to the free world in its production of minerals we all must have and so forth?" On 29 March 1981 Reagan was quoted by the *Washington Post* as believing in "continued friendship" with South Africa rather than staying "aloof and distant."

Two days later, during a dinner appearance before the Trilateral Commission in Washington, newly appointed Secretary of State Alexander Haig reaffirmed this new, gentler approach toward South Africa. The Reagan administration, he said, had already completed the first part of its policy review and was now poised for the second phase. This involved a visit to the African Frontline states and South Africa by a special emissary, Haig said.[2] The man assigned this task was Assistant Secretary of State-designate for African Affairs Chester A. Crocker.

Since graduation Crocker had moved through a number of academic and research positions, including American University, the National Security Council (NSC), and finally Georgetown University. From 1978 he focused almost exclusively on African affairs, writing extensively in books and journals about the continent, and more specifically, South Africa. He testified at least four times before congressional committees on US African policies between 1978 and 1980, criticizing the Carter approach. In 1980 Crocker was appointed coordinator for Africa on the Republican National Committee and subsequently chairman of the Africa Working Group for the 1980 Ronald Reagan campaign. With such credentials it came as no surprise when he was nominated to be Reagan's point man for Africa at the State Department. Crocker elevated the post beyond its normal limited functions as he gave form and substance to a new approach to South Africa. He described this direction as "constructive engagement."

The term "constructive engagement" was not a Crocker original. As early as 1974, Anthony Lake, in his doctoral dissertation at Princeton University, talked about US policy toward South Africa at the time as one of "active and constructive engagement."[3] In a speech before a San Francisco audience in October 1978, Lake, then director of policy planning under Carter, saw the approach toward South Africa as one of promoting "constructive and peaceful change."[4] Crocker himself conceded that his policy of "constructive engagement" was not "a dramatic departure from the last twenty years of American policy." Under constructive engagement, as seen by Crocker, the United States would continue apply the arms embargo and refuse to make use of South African defense facilities. While categorically rejecting apartheid it would, however, refrain from applying trade and investment sanctions or any other form of economic warfare against South Africa.[5]

In 1978 Lake argued against isolation of South Africa and proposed instead working together with Pretoria "toward resolution of all three of the region's critical problems: Rhodesia, Namibia and apartheid in South Africa itself."[6] Crocker's insistence on working toward regional settlements, instead of dealing with South African apartheid in isolation, was therefore not original either. As Lake before him, Crocker also insisted that constructive engagement "made no sense except as a regional strategy."[7] The unresolved issue of Namibia still featured high on Crocker's list of priorities, while the war in Angola had now replaced Rhodesia as the other regional concern. Crocker did, however, introduce a significant shift by insisting that the Communist threat in Southern Africa once again be taken seriously. Soviet-Cuban adventurism had to be answered to restore the Western world's credibility in the region.[8]

The only real difference between the Carter approach as formulated by Anthony Lake, and Reagan's, as explained by Crocker, was one of nuance and emphasis, pace and perception. In both cases the ultimate goal remained the same: a South Africa acceptable to the United States and the world. In both administrations there was insistence on universal franchise in a unified South Africa as the ultimate acceptable solution. Independence for Namibia and peace in the region were simply milestones toward this goal.

Pretoria preferred to ignore these similarities in approach between the Carter and Reagan State Departments and proceeded in the belief that they had a friend in the White House—one that would not only oppose sanctions but be more sympathetic to South Africa as a bulwark against Communist aggression. Dismissing part of Crocker's credo as typical of the "liberal" State Department, South African State Prime Minister P. W. Botha and his securocrats (as Botha's security-conscious bureaucrats became known) chose to take their cue from far more partisan pronouncements by President Reagan himself.

But buoyancy in Pretoria early in the 1980s was not merely a matter of a perceived diminished threat of sanctions after Reagan came to power. Gold price rises brought an unparalleled bonanza and South Africa had managed to beat both the oil and arms embargo. The economy was booming. The violence that had erupted in 1980 was apparently under control. Seen from the viewpoint of the left, however, constructive engagement as applied during the Reagan presidency helped Pretoria "gain time to consolidate its grip on power within South Africa." By "fending off international pressure for sanctions for five years," the Reagan administration was seen to have given Pretoria a breathing space "to pummel its neighbors with a wide variety of economic and military aggression, and modernize the system of control within South Africa."[9]

The Reagan administration inherited the problem of Namibia. Barely days before Reagan was sworn in, yet another attempt to find agreement among SWAPO, South Africa, and the Frontline states, failed. The South Africans, apparently emboldened by the imminent departure of Carter and his replacement by the friendlier Reagan, was not particularly cooperative during this conference in Geneva. This abortive attempt led to renewed calls by the African states for mandatory UN sanctions against South Africa. Shortly after he took office, from April through September 1981 Crocker concentrated his efforts on trying to get Pretoria interested and by October re-engaged the other nations of the Western contact group as well as the Frontline states. It took another year to resolve Namibian issues dating back to the 1978-80 period, and in mid-1982, Crocker was finally able to introduce what he termed the Angola "track" of his strategy—making Cuban troop withdrawal from Angola a precondition for Namibian independence.

Even though the South Africans expected Reagan to be a committed ally in the battle against the "total onslaught" posed by Marxist forces in Southern Africa, Crocker's insistence on Cuban disengagement from Angolan soil came as a pleasant surprise. By linking Cuban troop withdrawal with the implementation of UN Security Council Resolution 435, Crocker provided South Africa with a further pretext to play for time. The Americans, however, did not introduce linkage of Cuban troop withdrawal to the implementation of Resolution 435 and Namibian independence as a favor to Pretoria. Crocker saw it as "the bait or flypaper" needed to obtain South Africa's cooperation.[10] It was not an easy task, as the South Africans objected to the UN security provisions relating to the military component of the UN Transitional Assistance Group (UNTAG) and found UN civilian election monitoring unacceptable because of what they perceived as a bias toward SWAPO. It was, Crocker complained, like trying to "nail Jell-O to a tree."[11] Ultimately, the South Africans still seemed to hope that Ronald Reagan himself would scrap the UN plan and join in a counter-offensive against the "total Marxist onslaught."

The Botha government used the valuable breathing space afforded by its foreign minister's delaying tactics to get on with its military destabilization plan. This was done with the knowledge that mandatory UN sanctions were unlikely to be supported by the Reagan administration or its allies in the Western contact group. The South African Defense Force (SADF) stepped up its clandestine activity in adjacent states, including Angola and Mozambique. The ultimate aim was to take the heat off Namibia and enlist the West as allies in support of an all-out anti-Communist regional strategy. Time was needed to create the right climate and conditions for a free election in which the other factions and parties would have a reasonable chance to win against SWAPO. Since 1978 Prime Minister P. W. Botha had been trying to consolidate these non-SWAPO forces in Namibia, transforming the DTA into a more inclusive Multi-Party Conference (MPC). This welcome break was also used to try to strengthen South Africa's standing in a subcontinent where power, not political prowess, seemed to be the answer .

In his 1980 New Year's message, Prime Minister Botha made another appeal to South Africa's neighboring states to join in his proposed Constellation of States, cautioning that while "we are prepared to strive for such peace, we are also prepared to fight for that peace and protect it."[12] In April 1980 Zambia, Botswana, Lesotho, Swaziland, Zimbabwe, Tanzania, Malawi, Mozambique, and Angola established their own constellation—the Southern African Development Coordinating Council (SADCC)—aimed specifically at reducing their economic dependence on South Africa. All the signatories, with the exception of Malawi, were at one stage or another involved in aiding and abetting either the African National Congress or SWAPO and were therefore perceived by Pretoria as part of the "total onslaught" against South Africa.

By supporting and nurturing proxy forces in neighboring Black states, the South African Defense Force (SADF) tried to force them into denying sanctuary and succor to the African National Congress and SWAPO. In Lesotho South Africa assisted the Lesotho Liberation Army in toppling the anti-South African Chief Leabua Jonathan.

In Mozambique Renamo, or MNR, with the help of the SADF became a thorn in the side of the Marxist government of Samora Machel. In Angola the South Africans assisted UNITA to pressure the Marxist MPLA government into denying bases to SWAPO and to restrict the war to Angola so as to leave the Namibian population in the north untouched by the ravages of war and free from SWAPO intimidation and influence.

Toward the end of 1983, the Mozambican government sought talks with the South Africans, and in March 1984 the Nkomati Accord was signed. Formalized at a highly publicized meeting on the steamy banks of the Nkomati River, which separates Mozambique and South Africa, P. W. Botha and his Marxist adversary, President Samora Machel, undertook to prevent "irregular forces or armed bands, including mercenaries" from using their countries for action against one another.

In December 1983 the SADF launched a massive conventional strike into Angola and demanded assurances that SWAPO would not take advantage of the situation, if South Africa withdrew. The MPLA agreed to this condition. With the help of the United States and other interested parties, including the Frontline states, the Lusaka Agreement was thrashed out to establish a frame-work for this withdrawal. This agreement excluded both the Cubans and SWAPO from the southern portion of Angola and established a joint monitoring commission to supervise the situation. South Africa committed itself to UN Resolution 435 on the condition that the Cuban troops be withdrawn within a twelve week period and not replaced by other forces.

The military option apparently succeeded, and the time had come to bring Pik Botha's diplomats back into play. In May 1984 the two Bothas and their wives departed on an eight-nation European visit. Despite a cool reception in France, where Prime Minister Botha laid the foundation stone for a monument dedicated to the many South African soldiers who died in World War I, the tour was a resounding success.

In November 1984 Foreign Minister Botha proudly told a German audience that "South Africa is an increasingly confident regional power which had the will, the power and the resources to play a role it has been invited to fulfill in the search for peace in this region."[13] This assessment, however, turned out to be a trifle too optimistic. As the foreign minister spoke, widespread unrest and violence had engulfed the townships and begun to put the will and power of the South African government to its ultimate test.

NOTES

1. Crocker, Chester, *High Noon in Southern Africa: Making Peace in a Rough Neighborhood,* p. 77.

2. Alexander Haig answer to a question after a speech before the Trilateral Commission Dinner Meeting, Washington, 31 March 1981, State Department files.

3. Lake, A., *Caution and Concern: The Making of American Policy Toward South Africa 1946-1970,* doctoral dissertation, Princeton, 1974.

4. Lake, A., "To Promote Peaceful Change in South Africa," address delivered at a conference on US Foreign Policy in Africa, San Francisco, 31 October 1978, *Department of State Bulletin,* January 1979, pp. 18-20.

5. Crocker, op. cit., p. 77.

6. Lake, op. cit.

7. Crocker, op. cit., pp. 76-77.

8. Ibid.

9. Danaher, K. "The US Struggle Over Sanctions Against Apartheid," *Sanctions Against Apartheid,* ed. Mark Orkin, p. 135.

10. Crocker, op. cit., p. 85.

11. Ibid., p. 92.

12. P. W. Botha New Year's Message, South African Broadcasting Corporation, 1 January 1980.

13. R.F. Botha address before the Hans Seidel Stiftung, 9 November 1984, Department of Foreign Affairs, Pretoria.

7

Storm Clouds

> The atmosphere in the target country is critical to the outcome of a sanctions episode. If storm clouds are overhead, rain may fall without man's help. If moisture-laden clouds are in the sky, chemical seeding may bring forth rain. If the skies are clear and dry, no amount of human assistance will produce rain.
>
> G.C. Hufbauer and J. Schott[1]

Ultimately, the success of sanctions depends on the economic health and political stability of the target country, concluded G.C. Hufbauer and J. Schott in their study of 100 such episodes since World War I.

In 1964 the South African government could revel in the strength of its economy, which enabled it to resist successfully the clamor for sanctions after Sharpeville, but in 1984 a weak economy coupled with widespread violence had left it vulnerable.

In his budget speech on 16 March 1964, a confident South African Finance Minister Eben Dönges described his country's economy as "one of the most important bulwarks" against the "blatant aggressive aims of some states" that clamored for boycotts and sanctions.[2]

When he spoke, South Africa's economy indeed seemed invincible despite increasing demands for sanctions. Shortly after the Sharpeville shootings in 1960, the government had managed to restore order and business confidence. Once again, after the Soweto riots of 1976 the authorities clamped down decisively and swiftly and restored this economic bulwark that served it so well in the wake of Sharpeville.

In 1984, however, the Botha government seemed either unable or unwilling to put a prompt end to the violence. Eventually, when it did act, it was too late. The sky over South Africa was heavily overcast toward the end of 1984. Both politically and economically it found itself in deep trouble. The country that had appeared invincible to outside economic pressures for so many years suddenly seemed weak and vulnerable. On 28 March 1984, when Finance Minister Barend du Plessis delivered his budget speech he spoke about a much weaker economy. He blamed this on "unexpected external factors" such as a drop in the price of gold, slow recovery of world demand for South African products, and the drought, over which the government had no control.[3] These factors would soon be overshadowed by the loss of local and overseas business confidence as unrest and violence escalated.

Richard Hull saw the mid-1980s as crucial years in the history of US-South African economic relations. "Rivulets of protest suddenly merged into a torrent of outrage that forced a fundamental reassessment of the United States' stance and stakes," he wrote. "The events of late 1984 through August 1985 represented a turning point in the anti-apartheid movement. The turmoil in South Africa received extensive and unprecedented coverage in the American media at a time when other regions of the world were relatively quiet."[4]

The promises of reform that came with Botha's accession in 1978 were symbolized by a photograph taken during his visit to Soweto. Showing a black hand grabbing that of the new prime minister through the window of the official limousine, it signaled a new spirit of cooperation around South Africa and the world. Admonishing his people to "adapt or die," and scrapping a few irritating laws such as the Mixed Marriages and Immorality Acts and introducing a tricameral parliament including Coloreds and Indians, were, however, dismissed by the Black opposition as nothing more than cosmetics.

After lackluster participation by Coloreds and Indians in the elections for the new three-chamber parliament, Botha assumed the new post of state president, co-opting the leadership of both the new Colored House of Representatives and Indian House of Delegates into a multiracial executive dominated by his ruling National Party in the House of Assembly. In the process he not only sacrificed twenty seats in parliament as Andries Treurnicht led the right wing opposed to power sharing out of the National Party to form the Conservative Party, but also further alienated the left.

During a speech in Johannesburg early in 1983, Colored activist and president of the World Alliance of Reformed Churches, Dr. Allan Boesak, urged against acceptance of the tricameral idea. He made a plea to churches, civic organizations, trade unions, student organizations, and sports bodies to pool their resources and inform the people of "the fraud" perpetrated by the Botha government.[5] Boesak saw his wish come true on 20 August 1983, with the formation of the United Democratic Front (UDF) during a rally at the Rocklands Civic Hall in Cape Town addressed by himself and other local anti-apartheid luminaries. Several hundred protest organizations sent more than 10,000 delegates and a large marquee had to be erected to accommodate those who could not be seated in the hall because outdoor political meetings were still banned by government decree.

The UDF never claimed to be an organization. It saw itself as a front representing a broad spectrum of class interests. This loosely knit nature was both a strength and a weakness. On the one hand, it made it hard to pin down, as the frustrated authorities would soon discover, while on the other it also led to divisive struggles between its members. A picture of the Rev. Boesak leading a UDF march with his purple clerical robe in stark contrast to a red hammer and sickle flag symbolized the broad spectrum of its membership. The government would use this picture of Boesak in his "battle dress" marching with the forces of Communism to discredit the movement—without much success. Since his student days in Holland, Boesak had been involved in the anti-apartheid movement, participating in demonstrations at the South African Embassy in the Hague, and on his return to South Africa he rapidly rose in the ranks of the Dutch Reformed Missionary Church to a position of international influence. His compelling, high-pitched voice became as irritating to the authorities as it was inspiring to the ranks of the UDF.

Equally effective in rousing emotions at home and fostering outrage against apartheid abroad was another cleric and patron of the UDF, Desmond Tutu. As a bright young student in the townships of Johannesburg, he was handpicked by two seasoned anti-apartheid hands, Father Trevor Huddleston and Ambrose Reeves. After graduating from Kings College in England and obtaining his doctorate in divinity at Harvard University, he served as prelate of the Anglican Church in Lesotho and Johannesburg before his appointment as General Secretary of the highly politicized South African Council of Churches (SACC). In the wake of the 1976 Soweto riots, Tutu had his first clash with the South African government when he wrote a pastoral letter to Prime Minister Vorster protesting the treatment of Blacks. He gained in stature and influence in the 1980s through his appointment as Archbishop of Cape Town and as a recipient of the Nobel Peace prize. Throughout the 1980s this wiry, diminutive Black cleric loomed large in the public eye as a proponent of sanctions. Determined to walk and talk with everyone as long as it helped to publicize the plight of Black South Africa, Tutu also served as a patron of the UDF.

Within weeks of its founding the UDF comprised more than 600 organizations. They included numerous civic organizations formed in the late 1970s to oppose and intimidate the government-supported town councillors on issues such as rent and transportation. Boycotts were used with great effectiveness by these so-called civics at grass-roots level where town councils, rental boards, stores, and transportation services were targeted. On 3 September 1984, a group of civics gathered in the East Rand township of Sharpeville to protest against an increase in service fees by the Lekoa Town Council. The march led to the home of the deputy mayor of Lekoa, K. J. Dhlamini, who was first stoned, then soaked with gasoline and set on fire. Twenty-six other people lost their lives on that day, signaling the beginning of the longest and most costly insurrection in South African history.

The same Sharpeville where sixty-nine protesters were shot by the police in 1960 became the flash-point for a furor that spread across the land and outraged the world. September 1984 marked the beginning of a drawn-out period of instability and violence, ranging from school and consumer boycotts to street marches and fighting, petrol-bombing, sniping, "necklacing," and massacres. Before sunrise on 23 October 1984, a procession of military and police vehicles entered the townships of Sharpeville, Boipatong, and Sebokeng with a total of 7,000 men to restore law and order. But Operation Palmiet, as it was called, had only limited success. The strong-arm tactics that served the Verwoerd government so well in 1960 and enabled Vorster to regain control in 1976 when the youths of Soweto ran amok, did not work this time. In a little more than a year, between September 1984 and March 1985, more than 2,500 people died. As late as 1987 the government Bureau of Information was still busy putting out body counts from the raging war on the dusty streets of South Africa's Black townships.

Theories abound on why P. W. Botha was unable to deal as swiftly and efficiently with the township violence as his predecessors. For one, Verwoerd and Vorster did not have to contend with the UDF and its many-faceted, well-organized cadres. Barely two weeks after Operation Palmiet started, on 5 and 6 November 1984, the UDF responded with a mass stay-away to protest the "assault" on their townships. Twenty four more people died in mob violence and police shootings. In response to what he saw as an attempt by the UDF to mobilize the masses toward increased violence and revolution, Botha hit at the UDF with all his might, forcing several of its members to seek refuge in the British Embassy. In a period of two weeks, starting on 19 February 1985, sixteen leading members of the UDF were arrested and charged with treason. A few months later Popo Molefe, the general secretary of the movement, and Patrick "Terror" Lekota, its publicity secretary, were caught and tried for treason together with twenty others. Then, in an apparent effort to extend a hand of friendship, Botha offered to release Nelson Mandela on condition that he renounce violence. The reply came in the form of a statement read by Mandela's daughter Zinzi at a UDF gathering. Her father, she said, would only forswear violence if the government did so first.

The vision of a country helplessly out of control appeared in regular newscasts on American television screens and front-page reports in the major newspapers. It scared away potential investors, angered Americans and put pressure on Congress to "send a signal" by imposing sanctions. Meanwhile, the South African authorities not only allowed but encouraged the media to record the violence in the belief that the horrifying scenes in the townships would serve to justify its own increasingly desperate and drastic measures to restore law and order.

Initially, the violence was mostly "Black on Black" but this changed on 21 March 1985, during the anniversary of the 1960 Sharpeville killings, when a mob at the township of Langa, near Uitenhage, went on a rampage. After trying in vain to stop them by other means, the police opened fire, killing twenty. Whatever sympathy the outside world may have felt for Botha dissipated overnight. The message was that of Sharpeville 1960 all over again—of White policemen killing Black protesters. According to Richard Cohen, a senior producer of foreign news for CBS, American television coverage of South Africa during this period helped to build concern in America through repetitive footage of brutal repression. It was, Cohen said, "the image of the padded, faceless policeman, club raised, the image of a black youth with fear covering every inch of his face as he throws a brick."[6]

Funerals of "apartheid victims" were useful photo opportunities for foreign television news cameras. Following the burial, radical mourners often vented their anger in violence directed against "informers" and bystanders. Appearances by prominent personalities such as the Rev. Boesak and Bishop Desmond Tutu at these events added further publicity value. Both men had become regulars on American television screens, alternating township, funeral, and stage appearances with satellite television interviews. Controversial and confident, they made for good copy or sound-bites. Both Allan Boesak and Desmond Tutu understood the ways of the media and politics. It was a matter not only of words but images, of being controversial, being denied a passport and being arrested. They had a better feel than the authorities of the stuff that made headlines and the images that would incense America and the world.

The South African government appeared to be at a loss in its dealings with Tutu. First officials confiscated his passport. Then, under pressure from the Reagan administration, they issued travel documents for a specific trip on condition that he refrain from advocating sanctions. Then they introduced yet another travel ban, only to lift it once again under pressure. In the process Botha and his government were playing right into the hands of the bishop and his growing constituency abroad. They looked on helplessly as Desmond Tutu moved from obscurity to becoming a household word in America and other Western countries.

Conceding that "extravagant claims have been made for Tutu's contribution to the sanctions debate in America," biographer Shirley Du Boulay nevertheless insisted that "it is hard to overestimate his influence." The eminent Black Washington lawyer, Vernon Jordan, she says, "is probably right in saying that though Tutu alone has not swayed the American people, it could not have been done without him."[7]

By sacrificing the right wing of his own party for the sake of a reformed parliament that included Coloreds and Indians, P. W. Botha had accomplished nothing. He simply opened the door to a flood of Black anger and violence that further dampened any hopes of economic recovery. What the banned ANC together with South African Communist Party (SACP) or the outlawed PAC failed to accomplish by means of armed assaults and sabotage, now suddenly seemed within grasp as internal violence made South Africa look ungovernable and out of control. In June 1985 the ANC's Radio Freedom proudly proclaimed: "The upsurges that are taking place in our town, civic organizations, Asian communities, are acting in unison as one sort of broad formation which at the time is organized under the United Democratic Front. There can be no doubt these uprisings have shaken the very roots of the White minority domination in our country."[8]

South Africa is going through an extremely anxious time, lamented mining mogul Harry Oppenheimer in June 1985. There was a deep recession, and high and growing unemployment, particularly among the Black youth. Black resentment of White privilege was growing fiercer and turbulence and violence had become endemic in Black townships. According to Oppenheimer the idea was widely entertained, especially in America, that boycotts and sanctions were the only way short of force to induce South Africa to move fast enough toward a society free from racial discrimination.[9]

During December 1984, while in Washington, Tutu stopped at the South African Embassy, not to pay his respects to the ambassador, but to join the protesters that had the building under siege since Thanksgiving Day. On Thanksgiving Day 1984, a group of demonstrators assembled under the banner of the Free South Africa Movement (FSAM) in front of the South African Embassy in Washington. Even though this vigil outside the somber gray South African Mission rarely reached crowd proportions, it attracted attention in the media—not because of its size but its sizzle. Set against the forbidding granite edifice of South African racism it thrived on cameo appearances by anti-apartheid luminaries. Tutu's appearance followed that of Jesse Jackson, Senator Edward Kennedy, Harry Belafonte, and a whole array of other celebrities and politicians.

This siege provided the electronic media with a much-needed local angle for the daily feed of violent footage coming out of South Africa. Photo opportunities at the South African Embassy brought these remote events closer to home. The ultimate target was the imposing Capitol Building where Congress had been vacillating for many years on the issue of apartheid. On 4 December 1984, the day of Tutu's arrival in Washington, the sanctions lobby scored its first major breakthrough when a group of thirty-five Republican Congressmen caved in and sent to the beleaguered South African ambassador, Brand Fourie, a letter demanding an "immediate end to the violence in South Africa accompanied by a demonstrated sense of urgency about ending apartheid."[10]

Under leadership of Newt Gingrich (Georgia), Vin Weber (Minnesota), and Bob Walker (Pennsylvania), the Conservative Opportunity Society, as they called themselves, threatened to "recommend" curtailment of American investment in South Africa and economic and diplomatic sanctions. Coming from Republican conservatives who in the past vigorously defended South Africa as "a vital ally against Communism," this letter caused great dismay in official circles—both at the White House in Washington and in Tuynhuys in Cape Town. The reason for their precipitous action was based on the most basic of human instincts: survival. Up for re-election in constituencies with a large number of Black voters, they were not about to risk their political future defending apartheid. Soon their Republican colleagues in Senate followed suit, trying to prevent the Democrats from hoarding anti-apartheid for their own gain in the upcoming elections.

The siege at the South African Embassy was the brainchild of Randall Robinson, a lawyer born into a prominent Black family in Richmond, Virginia. A man with a penchant for public performance and a knack for reducing complex issues of race and discrimination to strikingly simple and effective sound-bites, he had organizational talents to match. The Free South Africa Movement (FSAM) was the umbrella specially created for the occasion. It accommodated a variety of groups interested in sanctions against South Africa. Still, the FSAM's cloth and colors were unmistakably those of TransAfrica, established by Robinson in July 1977 to take up Black African causes.

TransAfrica called the shots during the siege of 1984 but it was hardly the only show in town or the first predominantly Black group to devote all its energy towards the eradication of apartheid in South Africa. The American Society of African Culture (AMSAC) was the very first Black American group to raise concerns over apartheid, but of far greater significance was the American Negro Leadership Conference on Africa (ANLCA), initiated by George Houser of the American Committee on Africa (ACOA) as a vehicle for the mobilization of Black civil rights movements against apartheid. The ANLCA started out in 1962 with a "call committee" of the "big six" civil rights movements and eventually comprised twenty-eight national organizations. Its very first conference was attended by, among others, Martin Luther King, president of the Southern Christian Leadership Conference (SCLC); Roy Wilkins, executive secretary of the National Association for the Advancement of Colored People (NAACP); and Whitney Young, the executive director of the National Urban League.

In September 1964, at its second biennial meeting, the ANLCA called for US and UN sanctions against South Africa. It urged the United States government to prohibit future investment in South Africa, to discourage continuance of subsidiaries or plants owned by Americans, and to support economic sanctions and an oil embargo by the UN. It pleaded for strict adherence to a UN arms embargo and an end to the practice of excluding Black US diplomats from serving in South Africa. This auspicious gathering, attended by more than forty Black and multi-racial organizations, for the first time explicitly linked the civil rights struggle with American foreign policy decisions in Africa. The Johnson administration sent UN Ambassador Adlai E. Stevenson,

Mennen Williams, assistant secretary of state for African Affairs, and Averill Harriman, undersecretary of state for Political Affairs, to the conference. Secretary of State Dean Rusk delivered a luncheon address.[11] The ANLCA's third biennial meeting in January 1967 dealt almost exclusively with Southern African issues. Although the organization seemed destined to become the voice of Black America on South African affairs, it withered away after unsuccessful attempts in 1968 to mediate in the Nigerian civil war.[12]

In November 1984, as Robinson's "troops" assembled in front of the South African Embassy in Washington under the banner of the newly formed FSAM, South African officialdom made the mistake of counting heads and discounting as a nuisance the placard carriers whose numbers dwindled as the cold of winter set in. When asked by the media a few weeks into the FSAM demonstration how long he could put up with the siege, South African Ambassador Brand Fourie confidently quipped: "As long as they go on."[13] Many months later, however, when he handed over the keys to his successor Herbert Beukes and left for Pretoria, the protesters were there on the sidewalk to wave him good-bye. Beukes would put up with them for many months to come. Eventually when they dispersed, it was not in desperation but triumph after Congress had given them their wish—comprehensive sanctions.

NOTES

1. Hufbauer, G. C., and Schott, J., *Economic Sanctions in Support of Foreign Policy Goals,* pp. 39-40.

2. Eben Dönges budget speech, *Debates of the House of Assembly,* 17 January to 19 June 1964, Parts 9,10, 11, 12, Third Session, Second Parliament, cols. 3130 and 3148.

3. Barend du Plessis budget speech on 28 March 1984, *Debates of the House of Assembly,* Fourth Session, Seventh Parliament, 27 January to 12 July 1984, Vols. 112, 113, 114, 115, col. 3944.

4. Hull, Richard W., *American Enterprise in South Africa, Historical Dimensions of Engagement and Disengagement,* p. 276.

5. Lapping, Brian, *Apartheid: A History,* p. 71.

6. Cohen, Richard, Op Ed page article, *New York Times,* 31 August 1987.

7. Du Boulay, Shirley, *Tutu: Voice of the Voiceless,* p. 179.

8. Radio Freedom, monitored by BBC, 30 June 1985.

9. "Disinvestment," special issue of *Leadership,* South Africa, June 1985, p. 8.

10. *Facts-on-File—Weekly World News Digest,* 1984, p. 905.

11. George Houser interview.

12. White, Philip, "The Black American Constituency for Southern Africa, 1940-1980," *The American People and South Africa,* eds. Alfred Hero and John Barratt, p. 88.

13. Fourie, Brand, *Brandpunte,* p. 79.

8

Rubicon

President Botha stumbled on the banks of the Rubicon, completed
a turnabout, and led his followers in a headlong rush back into the
laager.

The Star, Johannesburg[1]

In August 1985 President P. W. Botha delivered what has since become
known, somewhat derisively, as "the Rubicon speech." Instead of announcing
the far-reaching reforms anticipated after an enormous buildup beforehand,
the South African leader opted for mild changes that would not endanger
White rule.

The speech was intended in part to diffuse the violence and unrest that
persisted despite a severe clampdown. It was aimed at restoring overseas
business confidence and precluding the adoption of tough sanctions against
South Africa by the United States and other leading industrial nations. It had
the opposite effect.

But it would be inaccurate to say that the Rubicon speech of August 1985
was the ultimate cause of it all. There were overseas financiers who tried as
early as March of that year to call in their loans. New York's Chase
Manhattan was one of the first major ones to do so.

A banker, so the saying goes, is someone who offers you an umbrella when
the sun is shining and wants it back again when it starts raining. That is exactly what Chase Manhattan Bank decided to do in 1985 as the storm clouds
persisted over the political landscape in South Africa. In March 1985 it went
to the South African Reserve Bank and asked for its money back. Word got
around that one of the largest lenders to South Africa was trying to pull out.
Soon other American banks were making approaches as well. Eventually the

Europeans followed suit. Chase Manhattan started a run that turned into a rout.

Many years later a relaxed, semi-retired Willard Butcher, in the comfort of his well-appointed Manhattan office, spoke about this momentous decision in 1985. He was chief executive of Chase Manhattan Bank at the time and takes full responsibility for the action that resulted in South Africa's worst financial crisis—one that dealt it a blow from which it never quite recovered. It was an action, in the opinion of many observers, more devastating than any official sanctions applied against South Africa.

"Was your decision politically motivated or purely an economic one?" Butcher was asked in 1991. "When you say political in a broader sense and economical in a broader sense, I would rather say it was a combination," he responded. "Obviously, I and the bank here had deep concerns about the morality of apartheid and in the 1980s I saw the situation deteriorating both politically and economically. Both sides on the fight of apartheid seem to be getting more strident and therefore the chance of a political compromise that would maintain political stability in the country, was getting less and less. That had very strong economic implications."[2]

The crisis in Latin America, said Butcher, had shown that it is very hard to separate economic and political considerations. He was referring to the disaster that began to unfold in 1982 when Mexico first admitted that it was unable to meet its repayment obligations to Chase. Mexico was only one of several so-called less developed countries (LDCs) to which Chase and other American banks had made extensive loans in the 1970s. What initially seemed a smart way to recycle petrodollars turned into a banker's nightmare. Chase alone was exposed to more than $11 billion in such loans. As the violence persisted there was a growing concern that South Africa would soon join the ranks of these defaulters.

A crisis in confidence developed when other American banks got word of Chase's intention to pull out of South Africa and joined the line at the teller's window. This turned into a full-blown financial firestorm when President P. W. Botha delivered his long-awaited so-called Rubicon speech of 15 August 1985.

As South Africa hobbled through the first half of 1985 from one bloody incident to another, with the unrest and violence that started in September 1984 showing no signs of abating, the Botha government realized that clamping down the lid was not going to work this time—as it did in 1960 after Sharpeville and again in 1976 after the Soweto riots. Declaring a state of emergency in July 1985 was at best a drastic short-term measure to prevent the smoldering fires in the townships from spreading. It was not a solution to the problem. Needed in the long term was a dramatic move toward Black participation in government. Having signaled during the opening of parliament in January 1985 an end to the homeland policy and acceptance of a common citizenship for all South Africans, it now became urgently necessary for President Botha to elaborate. Plans for future Black participation had been under serious discussion since January 1983 in a Special Cabinet Committee (SCC), chaired by Chris Heunis, minister of Constitutional Development and Planning. Consensus seemed impossible with its membership almost evenly divided between liberals such as Foreign Minister Botha, Bantu Administration Minister Gerrit Viljoen, and Finance Minister Barend du Plessis, and conservatives such as National Education Minister and Transvaal leader F. W. de Klerk, and Law and Order Minister Louis le Grange—with Justice Minister Kobie Coetsee somewhere in between. After more than two years of deliberations the SCC still found itself unable to agree over detail or direction.

During 1985 the pressures for a dramatic reform announcement grew as the Department of Foreign Affairs and organized business became increasingly concerned about the mounting sanctions campaign. Two weeks before President Botha's keynote address before the Natal National Party Congress in Durban on 15 August 1985, Foreign Minister Botha called a few of his trusted advisers into his office to brief them on reforms expected to be announced by President Botha during the four upcoming provincial National Party congresses. While the foreign minister intended to carry these tidings of new reforms to Europe where he was also to meet with Reagan's emmissasries, former UN Ambassador Carl von Hirschberg was assigned to do the same in Japan and Taiwan. Pik Botha left for Europe while von Hirschberg stayed behind, waiting several days for a flight to the Far East. It was during this wait that von Hirschberg decided to prepare a draft speech for President Botha's Durban appearance on 15 August. Setting out to incorporate the "expected announcements couched in language designed to make an impact overseas rather than at home," this experienced wordsmith wrote a ten-page draft.[3]

The foreign minister's trip had assumed the character of a last-minute rescue mission. British Prime Minister Margaret Thatcher was expected to face further pressures for sanctions at the upcoming August 1985 Commonwealth conference, while in Washington the Reagan administration needed urgent relief as several punitive bills reached the floor of both the House and the Senate. At least one was destined to reach the desk of the president.

National Security Adviser Bud McFarlane and Assistant Secretary of State Chester Crocker flew to Vienna to meet with South African Foreign Minister Botha. Pik Botha, Crocker recalls, was at his "thespian best," going to great lengths in trying to convince the Americans of momentous announcements in the offing. In what appeared to be a "diplomatic act of last resort" Botha revealed "plans for bold reform steps, new formulas on constitutional moves, and further thinking relative to the release of Mandela."[4]   Highly visible, the meeting in itself raised expectations. Both parties had to return home with something. McFarlane needed positive signals from South Africa to enable his president to stave off congressional sanctions. For his part, Foreign

Minister Botha had to be able to convince his beleaguered president back in Pretoria that foreign rewards for reforms were worth the risk of right-wing revolt.

On Friday morning, 9 August 1985, when he arrived back in South Africa, Pik Botha was met by von Hirschberg, and his deputy minister, Louis Nel. Together they proceeded to the VIP lounge at Jan Smuts Airport and reviewed the speech draft drawn up by von Hirschberg and approved by Nel. Botha made only a few changes.[5] Over coffee that morning the South African foreign minister inserted the following line of his own: "I believe that we are today crossing the Rubicon. There can be no turning back."[6] This, he felt, would help dramatize what was bound to be a momentous and dramatic break with the past and the beginning of a new era of race relations. Von Hirschberg proceeded to the departure lounge for a long journey to Japan, where he was assigned to do what Botha had just done in Europe—promise major reforms. Pik Botha got into his limousine and sped to Pretoria, where he was scheduled to report back to President Botha and give him the speech draft.

In the last few days before P. W. Botha's speech on 15 August 1985, a fierce storm ensued as the right wing responded to rumors and press leaks of far-reaching promises allegedly made by Minister Pik Botha in various encounters with foreigners. The rumors started on the eve of Foreign Minister Botha's departure for Vienna when US Congressman Stephen Solarz emerged from a three-hour meeting with him, ecstatic over what he had heard. He had gained new insights, Solarz told the press on Wednesday, 7 August. If the government's intentions for reform were carried out, he said, these would be considered quite significant in America. The South African press, although not privy to the discussion, read into this dramatic switch on the part of one of the prime sanctions movers in Congress imminent far-reaching reforms by South Africa.[7]

Although the role of F. W. de Klerk was never clearly established, rumors persisted that he had indeed played a key role in diluting the original text of the Durban speech. "De Klerk is said to have pressed Botha into drafting his so-called Rubicon speech in 1985, a defiant warning that he would not change the white minority's hold on the country," wrote Allister Sparks in an article published in the *Washington Post* on 19 August 1989.[8] In 1985 de Klerk was seen by political scientist Robert Shrire as the "main conservative obstacle in the cabinet."[9]

But it was not only Foreign Minister Botha who raised hopes with far-reaching promises of reform. "Black people may be included in a new President's Council as part of the Government's plan to defuse racial conflict in South Africa—and even in the Cabinet," reported political correspondent Tos Wentzel in the lead story on the front page of the *Weekend Argus* on Saturday, 10 August 1985. Quoting inside sources, Wentzel described this as one of the major reform initiatives to be announced by President P. W. Botha at the coming round of National Party congresses starting in Durban on Thursday.[10] Wentzel did not identify his sources but it soon became apparent that it was a former member of Heunis' Department of Constitutional Development and Planning. When Heunis presented a draft in similar vein, Botha informed him that he was "not willing to be pressured into making announcemens by speculative reports" and intended to "give his own content to the speech."[11]

On Monday, 12 August, the local press carried reports of an interview that the London *Financial Times* conducted with Anglo-American Chairman Gavin Relly in which he called for the release of Nelson Mandela, the removal of influx control, and a commitment to talks involving all races on the future political shape of the country. That same day Congressman Stephen Solarz turned up at President Botha's office in Pretoria's Union Buildings for a meeting to get confirmation at the highest level of the "significant" reforms promised by Foreign Minister Pik Botha. When the American legislator spoke approvingly about what he understood from Pik Botha to be government's planned commitment to a concept of South Africa as a unitary state, President Botha reacted indignantly, recalled Prinsloo, who attended the meeting. Botha told Solarz: "No, no, he could not have said it, not a unitary state. He could not have said it and I will not accept that he said it."[12] It was a disappointed, dressed-down American legislator who emerged from a tongue-lashing by the thoroughly unhappy South African leader. The one-hour meeting, Solarz told the press, was such that it could have "made a cold shower feel warm."[13] Before departing to Zimbabwe that same evening, Solarz vowed to continue pressing for sanctions against Pretoria.

On the evening of Thursday, 15 August 1985, President P. W. Botha stepped out on the podium in front of a capacity crowd in Durban's Town Hall and onto the screens of millions of viewers around the world. He delivered his long-awaited message to the nation and the world between finger-stabbing exchanges with a few hecklers in the audience. It was vintage P. W. Botha—the ultimate hard-line hustings speech intended to regain lost ground at home instead of giving the Reagans and the Thatchers much-needed ammunition in their embattled stand against sanctions. "I am not prepared to lead White South Africans and other minority groups on a road of abdication and suicide," Botha declared. "Destroy White South Africa and our influence, and this country will drift into factional strife, chaos and poverty." He presented a manifesto for peaceful negotiation and reform that fell far short of all the promises and predictions made in the preceding weeks.[14]

These were not words that the international community expected to hear. Instead of a drastic new direction Botha merely gave the assurance that he intended to move forward with current reforms—that there would be no turning back. He was, he claimed, "crossing the Rubicon." Critics contend that

Botha never reached the other side. Some jokingly referred to the speech as the "rubic's cube" because it puzzled the whole world.[15] Both von Hirschberg and Pik Botha would later claim that only one line of the original ten-page text submitted had remained. That was the reference to the crossing of the Rubicon. On 17 September 1992, long after P. W. Botha had been ousted, Pik Botha, then de Klerk's Foreign Minister and right-hand man, released to the Johannesburg daily, *The Star,* what he claimed to have been the original draft of the Rubicon speech which "he wrote." If it were delivered in that form, Botha claimed, ANC leader Nelson Mandela would have been released from prison five years sooner. Why did P. W. Botha reject the early draft in favor of a tougher speech? "That is a mystery which I cannot resolve," Pik Botha told *The Star.* "But at last I have my record." Asked the same question, von Hirschberg, the original author, had an explanation. "It was not in President P. W. Botha's nature," he contended, "to be seen as giving in to pressure. The build-up to the Durban speech simply evoked defiance."[16]

"While South Africa waited for the promised reforms," wrote *The Star* two years after the event, "the launching pad from which the country could approach the new century with hope and justice for all, President Botha stumbled on the banks of the Rubicon, completed a turnabout, and led his followers in a headlong rush back to the laager." But, Brian Pottinger pointed out, hidden "amid all that bombast" were "some nuggets of information" but "imparted with such patent ill-grace that they became lost in the overall impression of his delivery."[17] Carl von Hirschberg felt that taken together with his speeches at the three other provincial National Party congresses that followed the Rubicon speech in Natal, Botha "had in fact alluded to all the reforms which had been expected, but in language so veiled that that it was almost impossible to detect."[18]

In an effort to repair the damage, these "nuggets' were extracted afterward, neatly set out in a letter about current and future reforms under State President Botha's signature, and sent to Reagan, Thatcher, Kohl, and other world leaders. The same letter seemed to satisfy Swiss banker Fritz Leutwiler, who had become concerned about the apparent lack of progress on reform early in 1986 as he set out to convince foreign banks to reschedule their debt arrangements with South Africa.

In Washington, Reagan's men also went digging for these nuggets in the aftermath of the Rubicon speech in an effort to forestall congressional sanctions. Privately disappointed, they attempted to appear positive in public. "The South African President has made an important statement, and we are studying it carefully," McFarlane told the press on 15 August 1985. In an address before the Commonwealth Club on the day after the Rubicon speech, Crocker tried to add his own positive spin. While the speech "was written in the code language of a foreign culture within a polarized society" and therefore "not easily interpreted," Crocker assured his audience that it was "an important statement in that it discussed some issues" at the core of the problem of apartheid. America should, he implored, "develop rather than with-draw" its influence in South Africa and not "walk away."[19]

But the die was cast. Try as they might, Reagan and his advisers knew that they would soon be confronted with a *fait accompli* on sanctions from Congress. A veto, it seemed, might well be overridden as many Republicans, including conservatives, joined Democrats in the clamor for punitive action. Rubicon provided the final push needed by the sanctions lobby in Congress. Now that this speech "dashed all real hope that the South African govern-ment is ready to change its racist ways," said Senator Kennedy, "let us send a clear and unmistakable message that the time for firm American action against apartheid has come."[20]

On 9 September 1985, before Congress could deliver its message, the Rea-gan administration decided to act in self-defense. Rather than risk defeat by Congress on sanctions, the White House imposed measures of its own through Executive Order 12532, which prohibited "trade and certain other transactions involving South Africa." The steps included a ban on computer exports to agencies involved in enforcing apartheid, an embargo on the ex-ports of nuclear goods or technology to South Africa, a possible ban on Krugerrands, and a ban on loans to the South African government. Apart from a ban on the importation of Krugerrands, these measures contained little in new sanctions, as confirmed during a press conference by Secretary of State George Shultz on 9 September 1985, when he explained that the president's order was merely a "codification and setting out of some things that are presently being done."

Compared with what happened on the private business and financial front in South Africa at the time, the presidential order seemed superfluous. Nothing that the president or even Congress could have decreed would have been able to match the impact of the devastating debt crisis caused by the panic among foreign banks after the Rubicon speech. After giving notice to the South African Reserve Bank in July 1985 that it wished to call up its loans to South Africa, Chase Manhattan held back for a while in anticipation of promised reforms to be announced in the much-heralded Durban speech. When President Botha failed to live up to these expectations, Chase refused to roll over South Africa's outstanding debts. Other American banks followed. Soon the panic spread to German and British institutions. In a matter of weeks more than 400 overseas banks were clamoring for immediate repay-ment of their loans.

Chase Manhattan Chairman Butcher did not like doing this. He had met with Reserve Bank Governor Gerhard de Kock, on several occasions and "was very fond of him."[21] But the fondness and respect that Dr. de Kock en-joyed among his peers abroad were to no avail as he embarked on a desper-ate salvaging trip abroad. It was a lonely voyage reminiscent of Smuts' mis-sion to the United Nations in 1946, when he found former friends and admirers sympathetic but unable to come to his assistance in the face of the attacks led by India.

On 27 August 1985, shortly before he left on his rescue mission to foreign financial capitals, de Kock delivered his annual address to the South African Reserve Bank stockholders. He described the steps taken by Chase and other overseas banks as unwarranted in view of South Africa's current account surplus, its tight monetary and fiscal policies, the low debt/service ratio and its 'perfect record' in meeting interest and loan repayments. This action, de Kock believed, was based on "distorted perceptions of the nature, extent and possible consequences of South Africa's domestic political problems."[22] South Africa, in contrast to Mexico and others, had never defaulted on loan repayments.

Unlike many LDCs where Chase and other major American banks were experiencing so-called non-performing loans, South Africa had never been an over-borrowed country in terms of conventional international lending ratios. At its highest in 1984, South Africa's short-term debt was only 1.7 times its exports, compared with the Western Hemisphere developing countries, whose debts on an average amounted to three times their exports. Its deficit on the current account of the balance of payments had been dramatically reversed in conformance with International Monetary Fund (IMF) requirements.

This was also the message conveyed by de Kock to long-standing international banking associates during a hectic trip abroad. But even the power of this logic and de Kock's reputation for reliability could not shake overseas bankers from their state of depression and a determination to lessen their exposure in South Africa. Like their governments, these foreign banks were gravely disturbed about the future of a South Africa, which seemed destined to self-destruct. What they read in their newspapers and saw on television seemed to confirm their worst fears.

The political crisis had such a dramatic impact on the foreign exchange rate of South Africa's currency that the rand tumbled from around 50 US cents to 35 cents within a day after the Rubicon speech, giving rise to wry humor in the Johannesburg financial community. There was banter in Hollard Street about a "Rubic rand" and the story circulated that P. W. Botha had now been invited to speak in Washington so that dollar could also take a plunge.

On 28 August 1985, the government was forced to step in and close the foreign exchange markets in South Africa and on 1 September 1985, shortly before the financial markets reopened and on the eve of Dr. de Kock's departure overseas, Finance Minister Barend du Plessis imposed a four-month freeze on all foreign loan repayments.

He also froze foreign investment in South Africa but promised that interest payments would still be met despite the moratorium. The minister blamed the debt crisis on "two or three" US banks and claimed that their motives were political rather than economic. To meet the "cash flow crisis" du Plessis announced a four-month standstill for foreign debt repayment. A "reputable and independent international financial expert" would assist in rescheduling these debt repayments and a dual exchange rate reintroduced. Initially South Africa's total overseas debt was estimated to be between $22 billion and $32 billion but after a survey the South African Reserve Bank confirmed on 7 October 1985, that country's total debt amounted to $23.7 billion, of which $14 billion was affected by these interim arrangements or caught "within the standstill net." This "net" applied to all South Africa's foreign loan obligations (mostly by private banks and institutions) but did not affect public sector debt—monies owed to foreign governments and their export credit agencies or debt commitments incurred by the Reserve Bank itself. The latter were considered as being outside the standstill net.

At the time South Africa owed US banks some $3.2 billion, most of it in the form of loans to private commercial banks. One of the major borrowers was Nedbank, which acted on behalf of parastatals or semi-governmental institutions such as the Electricity Supply Commissions (Escom). Table 1 indicates the extent of South Africa's official and private exposure to private American bank loans from 1981 until 1985.

Table 1
US Private Bank Loans to South Africa, 1981-1985 (millions of dollars)

Year	Total	To Private Banks	To Govt. Agencies	To Private Borrowers
1981	2,722.1	1,597.7	516.6	607.8
1982	3,676.4	2,319.1	285.5	1,071.8
1983	4,637.0	2,936.3	487.9	1,212.8
1984	4,704.4	3,228.6	353.1	1,122.7
1985	3,240.3	2,167.6	114.1	958.6

Source: Congressional Research Service, Washington.

While the $3.2 billion in US loans formed a substantial portion of South Africa's total foreign debt, it barely accounted for 1.1 percent of all outstanding US commercial loans to foreign customers.

On 23 October 1986, Dr. Fritz Leutwiler, a former president of the Swiss National Bank who had been selected by both sides to mediate, arranged the first meeting of foreign bankers with South Africa's newly formed Standstill Coordinating Committee (SCC). The SCC was headed by the South African director-general of finance, Dr. Chris Stals, who brought with him not only the authority of his current office but valuable experience in international banking as the former deputy governor of the Reserve Bank. As it was too unwieldy a task to bring together representatives of all the 430 overseas banks involved, the thirty largest ones were designated to speak and act on behalf of the rest.

Experts likened the predicament in which South Africa found itself to someone who, despite punctual and regular monthly payments, is suddenly required to pay a mortgage in full. Even though solvent and not in arrears, the borrower has no way of complying. Apart from the enmity that this step itself generated, politics and national pride also entered into the negotiations. The impartiality implied by Leutwiler's Swiss banking background was put to a severe test at the very first meeting of the interested parties on 23 October 1985. The South Africans arrived in London with a deliberate hard line—obviously intended as an opening gambit.

Just when the hostile response by the overseas banks threatened to break up the talks, positions on both sides softened. The South Africans were driven toward compromise by the risk of having their overseas assets attached should any individual creditor bank resort to legal action. They also did not want these outstanding loans to be classified as "non-performing" as it would spoil their perfect credit record. At the same token overseas banks, many of them already bruised by the bad debt experiences in South American and other Third World countries, preferred slow repayment to no payment at all.

On 20 February 1986, broad consensus was reached between South Africa and its major creditors on the basis of Leutwiler's "Outline Proposals." The specifics were left to be settled between South Africa's SCC and a newly formed, smaller Technical Committee, comprising twelve major overseas banks.

At the very first meeting in London, on 11 March 1986, between Stals' SCC team and the twelve designated foreign banks, disagreement soon developed into diatribe. An exasperated Leutwiler got up and walked out for a breather.

At this stage one of the senior American bank representatives reached across the table to Dr. Chris Stals. "Chris," he said, "we cannot go on like this. Let's settle it between ourselves."[23] Serious discussion ensued in a more relaxed atmosphere. When Leutwiler returned he found himself the happy recipient of an agreement which he could announce on 24 March 1986. Based on the original outline, it stipulated:

- Repayment by South Africa of 5 percent of the debt due before 30 June 1987, starting with 5 percent repayment in April 1986.

- Interest margins paid by South African debtors up to 1 percent above the 28 August 1985, levels.
- Interest rates paid by Public Investment Commissioners equal to LIBOR plus $^7/_8$ percent.[24]

"The banks have achieved what others in the United States had called for under the mantle of the disinvestment lobby," commented the *New York Times* on 2 December 1985. They gave "a graphic display" to South Africa's rulers of their "vulnerability to foreign economic pressures."

The Rubicon debt fiasco dealt South Africa a more severe blow than official trade sanctions could ever accomplish. On 8 September 1986, about a year after these "financial sanctions" were introduced, Reserve Bank Governor de Kock warned a Cape Town audience that they were having "a serious adverse impact on the South African economy." The "politically induced pressure" on the capital account posed a greater threat to the South African economy than any kinds of trade sanctions likely to be imposed, de Kock cautioned.[25]

Still, at one time it actually seemed as if an improvement in the price of gold and other favorable economic signals would enable South Africa to ride out the heavy burden placed on it by the overseas debt repayment schedule. In September 1987, Finance Minister du Plessis returned from the IMF and World Bank gatherings with apparent optimism. "Foreign bankers," he told the press, "are much more relaxed about their remaining exposure in South Africa than a year or two ago." Since late 1985, he said, South Africa had made foreign debt repayments totaling $5 billion. The interest on its remaining debt of $20 billion, du Plessis announced, amounted to a bare 10.7% of its exports, compared with a world average of 27.6 percent. Just before Christmas 1987, Governor de Kock reported that South Africa had repaid in full a 2 billion rand loan received from the International Monetary Fund toward the end of 1982. This, he noted, made it one of very few debtor nations to have settled its debt with the IMF in full. Therefore, the outlook for South Africa to obtain money from banks abroad, should it need to do so in 1988, was promising. In August 1988 de Kock talked about a "much improved perception" of South Africa among bankers abroad.

But by November 1988 Finance Minister du Plessis returned from the MF and World Bank meetings in West Berlin much sobered by what he had encountered. South Africa, he cautioned, would have to proceed with the restructuring of its economy without much hope of getting foreign capital to help smooth these developments. This, he said, was made plain to him during his encounters in Berlin. The head of the SCC, Dr. Chris Stals, revealed that South Africa would seek extension of the payment limits on about $10 billion of its foreign debt when the existing arrangements expired. In December 1988 the governor of the Reserve Bank, de Kock, saw the old year out hinting at tighter monetary policy in the future to "reduce the downward pressure on the rand, gold and foreign exchange reserves, and to curb inflation." Three months later, in March 1989, Finance Minister du Plessis warned his audience at a financial seminar in Johannesburg that South Africa needed an austerity budget at all levels for the coming year.

In April 1989 there was no longer any point in denying the rapidly worsening economic situation in South Africa. "It is established history by now that the South African economy was buffeted during the years 1984 to 1989 by a unique combination of extraneous economic and political developments," observed Dr. de Kock. "But most devastating of all were the effects of the largely politically induced capital outflow of $11 billion [about 25 billion rand] during the four years from 1985 to 1988.

This outflow, of which one half constituted identifiable debt repayments, was equivalent to roughly 4 percent of gross domestic product." These adverse extraneous developments forced the South African economy to undertake a massive balance of payments adjustment, de Kock added. The political realities left the country with no soft options. It had to adjust the hard way.[26]

In June 1991, Dr. Chris Stals, who succeeded the late Dr. de Kock as governor of the Reserve Bank, mused over the events of 1985 and their long-term impact on South Africa.

Like de Kock, whose seat he now occupied on the imposing top floor of the black marble Reserve Bank skyscraper in downtown Pretoria, Stals conceded readily that these financial sanctions accomplished what trade sanctions or even disinvestment could not. While sanctions-busting was possible in the case of trade embargoes, and monies from the sales of overseas factories could be blocked, there was little that South Africa could do in response to the refusal of banks to roll over existing loans or grant new credit—except pay up.[27]

It took 5 billion rand in savings every year to fund the continued net capital outflow from the counry. South Africa, which was under normal circumstances unable to finance expansion and development from its own account, now had to export a large portion of its savings. In a matter of only five years since 1985, South Africa lost 25 billion rand that would otherwise have been available for housing, education, hospitals and other social programs. "We will never regain that 25 billion rand," Stals concluded.

"The post-Rubicon events of 1985 had a devastating effect on the South African economy and contributed largely to unemployment and unrest." The fact that South Africa's debt shrank from $24 billion to $16 billion over the past five years while that of Australia ballooned from $20 billion to $120 billion in the same period was indeed cold comfort.[28]

In her analysis Merle Lipton noted that South Africa was not the only nation with a debt crisis in the mid-1980s but in South Africa's case "the crisis gave a boost to the sanctions campaign by exposing an area of vulnerability and by leading some to believe that South Africa was on its knees and that a *coup de grace* might be delivered by the imposition of sanctions." The debt crisis was therefore quickly followed by the widespread adoption of sanctions.[29]

The year of the Rubicon would turn out to be a watershed one for those who have tried for so many years to bring South Africa to its knees through sanctions.

NOTES

1. *The Star,* Johannesburg, 3 January 1987.

2. Willard Butcher interview, July 1991.

3. Carl von Hirschberg interview, June 1993.

4. Crocker, Chester, *High Noon in Southern Africa: Making Peace in a Rough Neighborhood,* p. 275.

5. Carl von Hirschberg interview.

6. Ibid.

7. *The Argus,* Cape Town, 7-8 August 1985.

8. Sparks, Allister, *Washington Post,* 19 August 1989.

9. Ibid.

10. *The Argus,* 10 August 1985.

11. Daan Prinsloo interview, November 1992.

12. Ibid.

13. *The Argus,* 16 August 1985.

14. *The Argus,* 16 August 1985.

15. Geldenhuys, D., and Van Wyk, K., "South Africa in Crisis—A Comparison of the Vorster and Botha Era," *South Africa International,* January 1986.

16. Carl von Hirshberg interview.

17. Pottinger, B., *The Imperial Presidency: PW Botha—The First Ten Years,* p. 405.

18. Carl von Hirschberg interview.

19. Crocker, Chester, "US Policy and South Africa," Address before the Commonwealth Club, San Francisco, 16 August 1985, *Current Policy,* Department of State, No. 732.

20. *Washington Post,* 16 August 1985.

21. Willard Butcher interview.

22. Gerhard de Kock address before the annual general meeting of the South African Reserve Bank, August 1985.

23. Chris Stals interview, June 1991.

24. De Villiers, Kevin, *The South African Debt Accord,* Deloitte, Haskins & Sells, Johannesburg.

25. Gerhard de Kock speech before SABRITA, Cape Town, 8 September 1986.

26. De Kock, Gerhard, *Growth-Oriented Balance of Payments Adjustment Via Market-Oriented Economic Policy: South Africa—A Case Study,* April 1989.

27. Chris Stals interview.
28. Ibid.
29. Lipton, Merle, *The Challenge of Sanctions,* p. 10.

9

Congress Strikes Out

> Congress could strike out on its own only with an acute awareness
> of its uncertainties and inadequacies, and the risks to the national
> interest and its own institutional understanding.
>
> *Murphy Commission, 1975*[1]

Disregarding the risks as outlined by the Murphy Commission in its 1975 report, Congress in 1985 decided to strike out on its own and push for sanctions against South Africa. Instead of performing its traditional role of review in matters of foreign policy, Congress decided to act on its own.

In January 1985, Senator Edward Kennedy laid the groundwork for congressional sanctions when he returned from a "fact-finding" trip to South Africa. Punitive legislation was necessary, he argued, because South Africa had failed to make "meaningful progress" in dismantling apartheid.[2] His office drafted sanctions legislation and enlisted liberal Republican Lowell Weicker of Connecticut as a co-sponsor. Kennedy's Anti-Apartheid Act of 1985 proposed banning new bank loans to the South African government and private sector, new investments and the importation of gold Krugerrand coins. Congressional sanctions were necessary, Kennedy maintained, because Crocker's constructive engagement policy was a "catastrophic failure."[3] Black Congressman William H. Gray 3d, a Democrat from Pennsylvania, initiated similar legislation in the House of Representatives in a bill endorsed by Stephen Solarz from New York and Howard Wolpe of Michigan and 123 other cosponsors. As a prominent member of both the Black Caucus and the powerful Appropriations Committee, former Baptist Minister Gray was a natural choice to lead the fight against apartheid. The argument that sanctions would increase the suffering of Blacks in South Africa, Gray claimed, was tantamount to saying that "you cannot end slavery because you will have an unemployment problem." He cited Tutu and Boesak as saying that Blacks are already suffering and therefore "crying out" for economic sanctions. It was, Gray insisted, the moral duty of the United States to accommodate them.

While Gray and other pro-sanctions legislators based their arguments on Tutu and Boesak, those who opposed such punitive measures found equally prominent South Africans to buttress their viewpoint. One of the strongest and most effective voices against sanctions was the well-known and widely respected liberal author Alan Paton. "I do not understand how your Christian conscience allows you to advocate disinvestment," Paton wrote in an open letter to Tutu, published in the Johannesburg *Sunday Times* on 21 October 1984. "I do not understand how you can put a man out of work for a high moral principle. It would go against my own deepest principles to advocate anything that would put a man—especially a black man—out of a job." Tutu's morality, charged Paton, was just as "confused" as was "the morality of Dr. Verwoerd [the architect of apartheid] in his utopian dream."[4] Undeterred, Tutu continued to insist on sanctions as the only viable alternative to violence. He accused those who used the argument that Blacks would suffer most under sanctions of being hypocritical. "It is amazing how everybody has become so solicitous for Blacks and become such wonderful altruists," he said. "It is remarkable that in South Africa the most vehement in their concern for Blacks have been Whites."[5]

The argument that Blacks would suffer most if sanctions were imposed was also dismissed by exiled ANC leader Oliver Tambo. Sanctions will not kill as much as apartheid. "It is our lives that we are sacrificing," he said, "that we are ready to sacrifice."[6] Easy argument, responded Zulu Chief Mangosuthu Buthelezi, chief minister of KwaZulu, when you are comfortably far removed from the scene of starvation and in no danger of losing your job and livelihood. Other "traditional" Black leaders such as Lucas Mangope of Bophuthatswana, Kaiser Matanzima of the Transkei, and Dr. Cedric Phatudi of Lebowa sided with Buthelezi on the issue of sanctions. "Let us make efforts to kill apartheid and not kill a black man," Phatudi, chief minister of the homeland of Lebowa, pleaded.[7] Matanzima of the Transkei accused Tutu of "trotting the globe preaching disinvestment" knowing full well that his fellow Blacks would suffer.[8]

The leadership of the major Black trade union came out on the side of sanctions in this ongoing debate despite the potential loss of jobs to their membership. During a trip in Europe the general secretary of the Black National Union of Mineworkers (NUM), Cyril Ramaphosa, took British Prime Minister Margaret Thatcher and German Chancellor Helmut Kohl to task for refusing to impose sanctions out of "concern about black unemployment."[9] The South African Chamber of Mines in turn accused Ramaphosa's NUM of making contradictory statements "supporting sanctions, while in the same breath threatening to strike if men are retrenched as a result of the implementation of sanctions." If even a small percentage of the 600,000 Black workers with their three million dependents lost their jobs, the Chamber contended, it would have "a disastrous impact on black employment."[10]

Starting out in opposition not only to sanctions but the ANC as well, the Black National African Federated Chamber of Commerce (NAFCOC) ultimately changed its stand on both. In April 1985 NAFCOC Vice President P. G. Gumede declared that "if there is anything which should unite South Africans across the color line, it is the issue of sanctions." Disinvestment would be "disastrous."[11] A year later Gumede still felt that most Blacks rejected ANC dogma because of its opposition to capitalism as a means for Black self-improvement.[12] Soon afterward NAFCOC started wavering. In July 1986 the organization's president, Sam Motsuenyane, indicated that Black member organizations switched and were "advocating total disinvestment and the application of sanctions [after] a year of unabating conflict and violence."[13] Later that same month he cautioned visiting British Foreign Secretary Geoffrey Howe that unless there were drastic reforms, NAFCOC could no longer oppose sanctions even though its members would be the most likely losers. "We are losing anyway," Motsuenyane added.[14] Eventually NAFCOC's leadership aligned itself with the ANC in support of sanctions.

The leadership of several White-dominated churches expressed support for sanctions without consulting their congregations. But they often seemed to go through the motions simply for effect. "The measure of how bad you think apartheid is," explained Archbishop Denis Hurley, president of the South African Catholic Bishops Conference, "lies in whether you call for economic pressure. If you don't, it means you don't think the system is really evil. Of course, whether, having called for them, you actually want sanctions imposed is another story altogether."[15] In the mid-1980s Sheena Duncan, president of the Black Sash, turned up in the United States to voice her support for sanctions. Started in the 1950s and named after the black sash that members wore "in mourning" over apartheid, Duncan's organization represented an alliance of liberal English-speaking housewives and Black women. She expressed satisfaction over seeing businessmen "running around like scalded cats" because of the threat of sanctions.[16]

Most White liberals were, however, against sanctions. One of their most effective spokesmen was Dr. Frederik van Zyl Slabbert, an Afrikaner and former sociology professor who led the Progressive Federal Party (PFP) until February 1986. He resigned in protest over the government's failure to live up to reform promises and became the first White politician to make serious reconciliation overtures to the ANC. But he remained opposed to sanctions. A healthy South African economy was needed, he believed, to improve "the lot of those who have suffered as a result of the government's policies." He described as "tortuous logic" the argument by some sanctions supporters that the country "had to get worse before it gets better."[17]

Critics dismissed Slabbert and another prominent PFP member, Helen Suzman, as representative of a "predominantly urban-based, middle to upper middle class, English-speaking" constituency.[18] Although Suzman on occasion warned that she might change her stand unless the government "got off its butt and does away with apartheid," she never did.[19] Echoing an argument often used by the liberal corporate establishment in South Africa, she described disinvestment as "self-defeating because it blunts the one weapon that Blacks are able to use—the power to withdraw skilled labor."[20] Ultimately, Slabbert, Suzman, and other members of the PFP were accused of acting as mouthpieces of mining mogul Harry Oppenheimer who, it was alleged, paid their way.

With his vast fortune in South Africa at stake, Oppenheimer often did his own talking as well. In June 1985 he predicted disaster if the necessary level of investment and the skills associated with it were not made available. "Outside South Africa those who want to promote peace and fair play in this troubled land should join forces with South Africans," Oppenheimer proposed, "in an effort to build up our industry on a basis of racial equality; and from a basis of economic strength to press the government to implement without delay those reforms which are essential and to which they have already in vague terms committed themselves." This was a "much better, much more humane, more practical and more hopeful course than a retreat from the real field of action into a sterile policy of disinvestment and sanctions which, if they have any practical effect at all, could only bring about change through violence."[21]

In the great debate over sanctions in the mid-1980s Congress did not rely only on pronouncements by prominent South Africans. In an environment where the number of telephone calls, letters, telegrams or faxes often determines a congressman's stand on issues, there was a need for grass-roots opinions as well. Several polls were offered as conclusive evidence of how South Africa's Blacks felt about sanctions.

The original poll most frequently cited by those opposed to sanctions was the so-called Schlemmer Survey, funded in part by the US State Department. Bishop Tutu, in testimony before the House African Affairs Subcommittee, dismissed it as "completely worthless," not only because it was "paid for" by the US government, but because of government informants Blacks were afraid to "say what they feel."[22] The ANC organ, Sechaba, accused Schlemmer of having relied "on members of Buthelezi's increasingly terrorist organization, Inkatha, to conduct the survey."[23]

The Schlemmer Survey was conducted between June and August 1984 under the leadership of Professor Lawrence Schlemmer of the University of Natal and involved a total of 551 Black factory workers in South Africa's seven major industrial regions. The survey found 75 percent of the respondents opposed to sanctions. A second survey, undertaken by Market Research Africa among 1,000 Blacks in eight metropolitan areas, confirmed Schlemmer's findings by showing 79 percent against "divestment" as a method "to frighten the government into removing apartheid."[24] Further surveys conducted in July 1984 and February and May 1985, by South Africa's state-funded Human Sciences Research Council (HSRC), showed Black males in the Pretoria-Witwatersrand-Vereeniging (PWV) industrial area rejecting sanctions by 80.9 percent, 54.3 percent and 75.8 percent, respectively.[25]

In September 1985 pro-sanctions forces had a survey in hand that favored their position. Conducted by the Community Agency for Social Inquiry (CASE), together with the Institute for Black Research (IBR) among 800 Black South Africans in ten major metropolitan areas, the CASE/IBR Survey found 73 percent of the urban Blacks favoring some form of disinvestment. Critics assailed the questions (some as long as 225 words) as unscientific and misleading.

In the three years from 1984, the International Freedom Foundation in London recorded twelve "sanctions" polls in South Africa. As early as 1978 polls were also conducted in the United States to determine American public opinion toward sanctions and South Africa. In that year a Louis Harris survey found that by 46 percent against 26 percent Americans felt that the United States should put pressure on South Africa to give Blacks greater political freedom and participation in government. More than half (51 percent to 24 percent) were in favor of an arms embargo and 46 percent against 28 percent supported the idea of US companies putting pressure on Pretoria. A ban on new investment was supported by 42 percent against 33 percent. An end to the US corporate presence in South Africa was, however, rejected by 51 percent to 21 percent, and military action against South Africa opposed by 73 percent to 7 percent.[26] These results were largely repeated in another poll conducted by the Carnegie Endowment for International Peace in 1979.[27]

According to subsequent polls, however, some attitudes were changing in the mid-1980s. In February 1985 a joint *Business Week*/Harris poll found Americans three to one in favor of "putting pressure on the South African government to change its racial policies"—up from 46 percent that supported such action in 1978. Some 68 percent wanted the US to press Pretoria to give more freedom to Blacks—up from 46 percent in 1978. About 54 percent opposed the blocking of all new business investment—up from 33 percent in 1978. Some 51 percent were against the barring new bank loans and two-thirds opposed an end to all trade with South Africa. Those who wished to see US business forced to close down their South African operations were up to 76 percent in 1985 from 51 percent in 1978. Almost two thirds were "sympathetic" to protests at South African government offices in the United States. About 53 percent against 39 percent of the respondents considered it "immoral for the United States to support a government such as South Africa

that oppresses Blacks." About 64 percent, however, felt that the United
States "must stay on good terms" with Pretoria because of South Africa's
rich resources.[28] Toward the end of 1985 a Media General/Associated Press
poll found that 32 percent of all Americans were in favor of stopping US investment and American corporations from doing business with South Africa,
while 40 percent opposed such action and 28 percent were unsure. Half of the
respondents maintained that withdrawal would hurt Blacks and Whites while
28 percent considered it immoral to conduct business in South Africa.[29]

Commenting on the battle of the polls that accompanied the congressional
sanctions debate in the mid-1980s, Harvey Tyson, the editor of the *The Star*
in Johannesburg, felt that "the emotionalism aroused by the debate on disinvestment is matched only by the disinformation that accompanies it." There
were spokesmen, he pointed out, "who 'prove' that Blacks seek disinvestment, despite possible material suffering [and] there are polls to 'prove' that
the black majority rejects proposals for disinvestment." Neither claim was
relevant to the current debate, concluded Tyson. "For, in the United States
at least, the debate is concerned less about black South Africans and
apartheid than about US politics and the social conscience of America. The
disinvestment issue has adopted a life and character peculiar to the United
States."[30]

In the 1970s South Africa finally decided to hire professionals to help plead
its case against sanctions at Congress. As the battle heated up in the mid-
1980s, however, it soon became evident that paid lobbyists were no match
for the anti-apartheid activists led by Randall Robinson of TransAfrica. For
several years Robinson had been invoking the power of Black Americans to
prod Congress into action. Just as Jewish Americans used their influence in
the case of Israel, Robinson showed, African Americans could make their
presence felt when it came to voting on apartheid and sanctions.

TransAfrica was founded in 1977 on the premise that "foreign policy is not
made in a vacuum, but by people, by citizens." As Blacks constituted 12
percent of the citizenry of the United States, they had, according to
Robinson, "a responsibility and duty to participate in the foundation of
foreign policy."[31] In the mid-eighties he had managed to cobble together a
loose but lethal coalition of Democrats and Republicans, liberals, moderates,
and conservatives—all concerned about how their attitude toward South
Africa would influence the Black vote in their own constituencies in the
upcoming elections.

"Without impugning the sincerity of many of the participants in the current
protests, it is hardly unfair to point out that the South African issue is probably the one issue in American politics that comes closest to being cost-free,"
observed Herman Nickel, US ambassador to South Africa in 1985. "Within
the respectable spectrum of American politics, there is no significant pro-
South African constituency." There was strong political pressure on moderate
and conservative Republicans in Congress to come forward with their own

sanctions measures. Unless they wanted to be branded supporters of apartheid, they had to translate mere indignation into "doing something."[32]

On 9 April 1985, the *New York Times* reported a total of twenty separate sanctions bills pending in Congress. The Kennedy-Weicker Bill took center stage in the Senate while the Gray Bill dominated in the House of Representatives. Some bills amounted to little more than grandstanding, but others influenced the wording of the final sanctions legislation that emerged from both houses. Introducing legislation of his own, Congressman John Conyers Jr. (D-Michigan), claimed that the United States dominated 70 percent of South Africa's computer market and supplied 40 percent of its refined oil and 25 percent of its automobiles. It could therefore "tie the South African economy up in knots."[33]

The Republicans in the Senate Foreign Relations Committee, in an attempt to preempt harsher legislation proposed by the Democrats, introduced their own bill on 27 March 1985. The bill, sponsored by Senator Charles Mathias (R-Maryland), postponed action against South Africa until President Reagan had a chance to report to Congress in two years' time on South Africa's progress in ending apartheid. Preempting a much stronger sanctions bill introduced by Senator Alan Cranston (D-California) that would have banned bank loans to South Africa, the Mathias Bill was passed in the Foreign Relations Committee by sixteen votes to one, with conservative Republican Jesse Helms of North Carolina dissenting. Fully aware that it was no longer possible to shy away from the sanctions issue, the Republicans further fine-tuned the Mathias Bill, hoping that it would pass on the Senate floor and also replace the tough Kennedy-Weicker Bill. The revised bill— apart from the two-year grace period on sanctions—proposed financial support for Black-owned businesses in South Africa and making the Sullivan Principles compulsory for American businesses operating out there.

Another bill floating around at the time was one sponsored by Republican Senators William Roth (R-Delaware) and Mitch McConnell (R-Kentucky). It proposed cancellation of US landing rights to South African Airways and a ban on bank loans. It also instructed the president to coordinate US sanctions with the European governments and proposed closing down one South African Consulate in the United States.

Street protests proliferated as apartheid was selected as the theme for the 17th anniversary on 5 April 1985, of the assassination of the Rev. Martin Luther King Jr. A crowd of 4,000 demonstrators joined the siege at the South African Embassy in Washington. Fifty-eight demonstrators were arrested for crossing the police line at the embassy, bringing the total number of arrests since November 1984 to almost 2,000. These arrests in full view of the TV cameras included Connecticut Republican Senator Lowell Weicker, singer Stevie Wonder, the Rev. Jesse Jackson and Amy Carter, daughter of former President Carter. At New York's Columbia University several hundred students blockaded a campus building and demanded divestment of $32.5 million in stock from companies with South African business links. On the Berkeley campus of the University of California more than 4,000 students and residents participated in a protest demanding withdrawal of the university's $1.8 billion shareholding in firms operating in South Africa. Similar protests were held at Rutgers University in New Brunswick, New Jersey, and Cornell University at Ithaca, New York. This nationwide "National Anti-Apartheid Protest Day," marked by many rowdy incidents and arrests, ensured ample television and newspaper coverage and helped bring a new sense of urgency to the sanctions debate in Congress.

The Reagan administration deputized Assistant Secretary of State for African Affairs Chester Crocker to try to cut Congress off at the pass. Conceding that South Africa's reforms had fallen far short of Black aspirations, Crocker nonetheless tried to convince the Senate Foreign Relations Committee that "fundamental pillars of the apartheid system have eroded." Sanctions would not only prove "counterproductive" but accomplish nothing, he argued.[34] In a major speech on 16 April 1985, timed to coincide with the start of these congressional sanctions hearings, Secretary of State George Shultz, while conceding that "apartheid must go," reiterated the Reagan administration's belief that sanctions was not the way to achieve this goal. The South African government had "crossed the historical divide," he contended, and the United States should continue to encourage the reform process already underway. [35]

The US secretary of state cited ABC's *Nightline* program, which "set up shop for a week" out there to "probe and dissect the country's ills, film heated debates between government leaders and their most ardent critics," as an example of a new openness on Pretoria's part. Opinion polls by "reputable organizations" in South Africa revealed that the overwhelming majority of Black factory workers were opposed to disinvestment by American firms. "I do not understand why it is good for American investors to create jobs for black workers in Zimbabwe or Zaire but not in South Africa," Shultz said.[36]

Both Crocker and Shultz were fighting not only to stave off sanctions but to prevent Congress from scrapping constructive engagement and robbing them of their policymaking on South Africa. Crocker had worked hard and long to bring the recalcitrant Botha government to the edge of granting independence to Namibia. He dreaded the thought of seeing South Africans walk away in protest over sanctions. So Shultz and Crocker tried their utmost to stop sanctions. The administration, they declared, had "no intention of waging economic warfare on South Africa and its people."[37] They questioned the motives of those who supported sanctions merely for the sake of morality and to feel good. Congress should be "more interested in promoting real progress than in posturing, debating points, or grandiose schemes that are likely to prove ineffectual," Shultz cautioned. While the United States "should be indignant at injustice and bloodshed, indignation alone is not a strategy," he said.[38] "Moral indignation by itself is not a foreign policy," Crocker told Congress.[39]

These pleas by Reagan's deputies failed to stop Congress in its inexorable march toward tougher action. Leading Republicans told their president that stonewalling against sanctions was no longer an option. Congressional action was imminent, warned Senator John Heinz (R-Pennsylvania.), chairman of the International Finance and Monetary Policy Subcommittee. There was "a substantial amount of House and Senate bipartisan support for doing something more than we are doing now."[40] Senator Nancy Kassebaum, the Republican head of the Senate Foreign Affairs Subcommittee on African Affairs, was among the few in Congress who still tried to stave off sanctions. Congress, she pleaded, should refrain from taking steps that may "perpetuate the violence in such a way that any attempt for constructive involvement by the United States becomes irrelevant."[41]

On 5 June 1985, the Gray Bill was passed in the House of Representatives by an overwhelming 295 to 127 votes. Sixty-five Republicans sided with the Democratic majority against their own president. This sanctions package, banning new loans and investments, the sale of computers to the South African government, and the importation of Krugerrands, was somewhere between two milder bills proposed by Republicans and a more severe one proposed by Black Democrat Ron Dellums of California. The Republican bills sponsored by Rep. Mark Siljander (R-Michigan) and Rep. Steve Anderson (R-Wisconsin) tried to delay the implementation of sanctions for a few years while reform in South Africa was monitored, and the more drastic bill by Black Californian Rep. Ron Dellums called for total disinvestment.

The Gray Bill imposed penalties ranging from five years in jail and a $50,000 fine for individuals to $1 million in fines for organizations or businesses violating the sanctions. President Reagan would be permitted to waive for one year bans on new investment and importing of Krugerrands if he determined, and Congress agreed, that South Africa had met one of the eight conditions stipulated in the bill. For each additional condition met, the waiver could be extended for six months. The conditions required the elimination of influx control that restricted Blacks from seeking employment where they chose and an end to policies that give Black and White South Africans different types of citizenship. South Africa was also required to stop the forced removal of Blacks from certain locations because of race or ethnic origin, to eliminate residential restrictions based on race and ethnic origins, to start talks with Black leaders on a nondiscriminatory political system, to reach an internationally recognized agreement on Namibia, and to free all political prisoners. Conceding afterwards that it would not end apartheid, Congressman Gray felt it would at least stop its "future financing." House Speaker Thomas (Tip) O'Neill Jr. (D-Massachusetts) welcomed the Gray Bill as one that put an end to the "gentleman's agreement" with apartheid.

On 22 May 1985, the Senate Foreign Relations Committee under chairmanship of Senator Richard Lugar (R-Indiana) came forward with its own sanctions bill. All but one Republican on the seventeen-member committee, Senator Jesse Helms of North Carolina, voted for it. It called for an immediate ban on bank loans to the South African government, a prohibition on computer sales to any agency involved in enforcing apartheid, and an embargo on all nuclear technology to South Africa. It also proposed making the Sullivan Principles mandatory for all American corporations operating in South Africa and suggested legal and educational aid for Blacks. Provision was made for further sanctions if after eighteen months the president found that "significant progress has not been made toward ending the policy of apartheid." This new bill stood in stark contrast to the original Mathias version adopted by the Republican-dominated Senate Foreign Relations Committee a few months earlier.

The Lugar Bill, as it became known, tried to steer a middle course. It incorporated amendments by liberal Democrat Christopher Dodd of Connecticut and Republican Senators William Roth (Delaware) and Mitch McConnell (Kentucky). Critics, however, pointed out that its measures were hardly new and would simply sign into law existing practices. American banks, under heavy pressure from anti-apartheid groups and state and city institutions, had for some time been refusing loans to the South African government, while the administration had already clamped down on both the sales of computers and nuclear cooperation. Lugar managed, however, to dissuade Democratic Senators Edward Kennedy of Massachusetts and Alan Cranston of California from toughening his bill with further amendments by arguing that it had a better chance to be signed into law by President Reagan in its milder form. Last-minute efforts by a few conservatives to extend sanctions to the Soviet Union and other Communist countries were also staved off. On 11 July 1985, the Republican-dominated US Senate voted for the first time to impose sanctions against South Africa by passing the Lugar Bill by an overwhelming 80 to 12.

As is customary when the two houses of Congress pass different bills on the same subject, a conference committee went into action to work out a compromise between the Gray and Lugar bills. In the meantime the declaration of a state of emergency in South Africa further weakened the Reagan administration in its desperate efforts to prevent Congress from taking matters in its own hands. Faced not only with growing pressure from the Congress but also a demand to support UN sanctions, President Reagan presided over an hour-long meeting of his National Security Council (NSC) on 26 July 1985. In the end, however, the United States still decided to abstain together with Britain leaving the other thirteen members of the UN Security Council to pass a resolution introduced by France to suspend new investments in South Africa. While indicating through White House spokesman Larry Speakes that he wished to see South Africa lift the state of emergency, Reagan once again reiterated his opposition to sanctions. "Economic sanctions could lead to more bloodshed," Speakes said. "They could do harm to the very people we're trying to help." Instead, the administration preferred a policy of "quiet diplomacy" to end "the violence and repression" in South Africa.[42]

Senator Richard Lugar and other legislators pressed ahead, predicting confidently that they would have a compromise sanctions bill ready in matter of days and expected President Reagan to endorse it. On 31 July 1985, conferees drawn from the House and the Senate, without having to resort to a formal vote, reached consensus over a new joint bill to replace the Lugar and Gray bills. The Anti-Apartheid Act of 1985 contained most of the provisions of the Lugar Bill but also incorporated the Gray call for tougher sanctions if South Africa did not show progress toward ending apartheid within one year. On 1 August 1985, the House of Representatives approved this compromise bill by 340 to 48 votes. Explaining their vote in favor of the bill by letter to President Reagan, conservative Republicans Newt Gingrich of Georgia and Robert Walker of Pennsylvania described it as "a fair and reasonable compromise" with bipartisan backing. They also cautioned their own president that they would "actively work" to override his veto of this measure. Rep. Stephen Solarz, the Democrat from New York who had been in the forefront seeking punitive measures against South Africa, was elated: "We are saying *Kaddish* for the policy of constructive engagement."[43]

Senator Jesse Helms and his few remaining allies threatened with a filibuster to prevent the Senate from approving the compromise bill before its recess started on 2 August 1985. This gave the administration another month to come up with a strategy to prevent the now imminent sanctions legislation from reaching the president's desk. In a press conference on 5 August 1985, President Reagan, apparently mindful of the two-thirds majority that Lugar had in hand in the Senate to override such an action on his part, carefully skirted the question of whether he would resort to a veto. Instead he restated his belief that constructive engagement was working and that sanctions would hurt Blacks in South Africa as well as the neighboring territories. He even expressed understanding for the police crackdown and state of emergency in South Africa. "I think we have to recognize sometimes when actions are taken in an effort to curb violence," Reagan said. While the state-controlled South African Broadcasting Corporation afterward praised Reagan for being "a dependable ally," his remarks drove some of his own supporters in Washington to sheer desperation. Refusing to "cut and run," as Reagan was doing, was in the view of both Crocker and Shultz no longer a viable option. Another way had to be found to stop Congress in its tracks, to prevent sanctions and to save constructive engagement.

As early as March 1985 the State Department had started using harsher language in its condemnation of the developments in South Africa in an effort to regain the initiative on South Africa. Secretary Shultz abandoned the customary restraint by dubbing the violence within the townships as proof of the "evil and unacceptable" system of apartheid. In June 1985 when South Africa attacked ANC bases in Gaborone, Botswana, and in July 1985, when Botha declared a state of emergency in a desperate attempt to quell the violence, the State Department responded with a strongly worded condemnation. It blamed apartheid for being "largely responsible for the violence" and demanded an immediate lifting of the state of emergency, further reforms, and serious negotiations with the Black opposition.

All this posturing was to little avail. In the fall of 1985 it had become clear that deeds, not words, were needed to stop Congress from taking control and passing sanctions legislation. The Reagan Administration started turning the screws on the Botha government to provide palpable proof of further reform and to ease up on emergency measures. While President Botha found it impossible to comply with the latter demand as violence continued to plague the Black townships, he did indeed try to oblige in other ways. After threatening in late July 1985 to expel up to 1.5 million Black workers from neighboring southern African states if their countries applied punitive UN Security Council sanctions against South Africa, Botha changed his mind. First recalling Ambassador-designate Herbert Beukes from Washington in response to American criticism of its actions, the South African government in August 1985 softened its stance and requested a meeting with the Reagan administration to discuss future reforms.

So started the flurry of exchanges involving Assistant Secretary Crocker, National Security Adviser Robert McFarlane, South African Foreign Minister Botha, and Ambassadors Nickel and Beukes, which led to the Rubicon fiasco. President Botha's Durban speech, declared Senator Edward Kennedy, "dashed all real hope that the South African government is ready to change its racist ways." Congress, he insisted, should send a message that the time for "constructive engagement with racism is over." House Foreign Affairs Chairman Democrat Dante Fascell (D-Florida) branded the Rubicon speech as "tragically more of the same" and insisted that Reagan abandon his "ineffective" policy of constructive engagement. Senator Lowell Weicker (R-Connecticut) described the speech as "a vacuous attempt" to "take the world's eye off the ball." District of Columbia delegate, Black American Walter Fauntroy, left no doubt as to what "the ball" meant. "We now have no choice but to move ahead vigorously with sanctions," he insisted.[44]

Attempts by Crocker, Shultz, and McFarlane to put an optimistic face on the Botha speech were to no avail as the Senate moved resolutely toward acceptance of the Anti-Apartheid Act of 1985. In a last-ditch effort to prevent Congress from hijacking American foreign policy relating to South Africa, the Reagan administration was forced to impose its own sanctions. On 9 September 1985, President Reagan signed an executive order imposing limited sanctions against South Africa, thereby preempting congressional legislation and averting a foreign policy defeat. Although the presidential order incorporated most of the measures contained in the proposed Anti-

Apartheid Act of 1985, it did not mandate additional sanctions if South Africa failed to make progress. While the more militant House objected to further dilution by the administration of an already weakened sanctions bill, there was little it could do to at that late stage.

On 7 January 1986, a bipartisan group of six congressmen arrived in South Africa to determine the effect on South Africa of the sanctions imposed by presidential executive order. They were also there to "express solidarity with the [black] majority," explained tour leader and prominent member of the Black Caucus, William Gray. The American visitors were refused permission to meet with jailed ANC leader Nelson Mandela, but had meetings with Zulu Chief Mangosuthu Buthelezi and the Rev. Boesak of the UDF.

During the same month, Assistant Secretary Crocker arrived in South Africa, breaking with past practice by meeting not only with government officials but also with some Black activists. The American diplomat's reception by President Botha on 13 January 1986, was hardly friendlier than the chilly treatment meted out to the congressional group. In anticipation of future congressional pressures, despite Reagan's executive sanctions order of September 1985, the State Department had felt it necessary to nudge the South African president into adopting further reforms. Crocker turned up at Tuynhuys with a letter from Reagan urging the South African leader to step up the pace. Like Vance under Carter many years before in his encounter with P. W. Botha, Crocker was authorized to hold out the possibility of a meeting with the American president "if there was 'content' which we could support."[45]

From the outset Crocker felt unwelcome during what turned out to be his final meeting with P. W. Botha. Whereas Pik Botha, the foreign minister, welcomed him warmly ("You've been away too long"), President Botha stiffly enquired, "Why are you here?" He also wanted to know whether Crocker had met secretly with ANC leaders in Lusaka before coming to Cape Town.[46] During November and December 1985 the ANC had stepped up its campaign with a series of bomb blasts that killed several White and Black civilians. And while White House insiders rationalized the Reagan sanctions order as a victory in that it staved off much tougher congressional sanctions, this subtlety was lost on South Africans who felt that they were rebuffed despite all their politically costly concessions and reforms. The South African leader felt himself trapped and it was showing.

When he met again with Pik Botha in Geneva during February 1986, Crocker found the South African foreign minister a little more upbeat than during their encounter in Cape Town a month earlier. The reason for this new optimism was President Botha's parliamentary opening speech a few days before. The president had formally accepted "an undivided Republic of South Africa" with only "one citizenship." As part of this more conciliatory approach, the South African leader offered Blacks for the first time a limited advisory role in government. Through the establishment of a National

Council, he told parliament on 31 January 1986, Blacks would be able to play a role in shaping constitutional policy. He promised to scrap the hated pass laws and hinted that jailed ANC leader Nelson Mandela might be released on "humanitarian grounds."

Now in Geneva, Foreign Minister Botha proudly claimed hours of personal input in this speech, and pressed for a meeting between Reagan and P. W. Botha. Despite Pik Botha's attempts to dress up the latest reform announcement, the Americans remained skeptical. They had arrived "armed with an elaborate series of steps that they needed Pretoria to take—"sequenced with supporting moves we would be prepared to make." The demands, wrote Crocker, "carried all the way up to the beginning of black-white negotiations and the scrapping of all apartheid laws."[47] During a private dinner with Crocker on the outskirts of Geneva at the end of two days of deliberations, Pik Botha finally conceded: "We cannot meet your price."[48]

But the South African foreign minister and his diplomats continued trying to stave off further sanctions with the reforms in hand. Regular checklists were published by the South African Embassy in Washington in an apparent effort to convince Congress of Pretoria's honest intentions. In August 1986 the South African Embassy in Washington reminded readers in its official newsletter that "one year ago at his inauguration as the Anglican Bishop of Johannesburg, Bishop Desmond Tutu called on the South African Government to actively start dismantling apartheid by scrapping influx control, making massive investments in black education, cease the denationalization of Blacks and ending forced removals." Tutu, the embassy noted, had threatened that unless these conditions be met within 18 to 24 months he would for the first time call for punitive sanctions. Although South Africa had met all these demands, the embassy complained, Tutu still went aehad and called for economic sanctions in April 1986.[49]

By now every reform seemed cosmetic as Mandela remained in prison and President Botha refused to negotiate with the ANC. Botha had made it clear that one man, one vote or Black majority rule in a unified South Africa was not an option. He demanded also that the ANC renounce violence before any talks could take place. The ANC on the other hand, sought a clear undertaking by the White South African government that it would hand the reins over to the Black majority. Even when Botha eventually accepted the notion of South Africa as one undivided land with many minorities, he still voiced opposition to one man, one vote. "Our policy is to reform," Botha told parliament on 17 August 1987, "but we are not willing to abdicate." Addressing a passing-out parade at the South African Police College in Pretoria during June 1986, he criticized "leftist critics abroad" and "even radicals in this country" who spoke of "genuine reform" while they wanted nothing less than the "final transfer of power to the South African Communist Party and its front, the African National Congress."[50]

With words like these President Botha had set South Africa and himself on a collision course with Congress where renewed calls for sanctions were being debated. Once again the Reagan administration was desperately searching for ways to regain its initiative on South Africa—and to save constructive engagement.

NOTES

1. Franck, T. M, and Weisband, E., *Foreign Policy by Congress,* p. 9.

2. *New York Times,* January 13, 1985, p. 10.

3. The Anti-Apartheid Act of 1985, hearings before the Senate Committee on Banking, Housing and Urban Affairs, 99th Congress, 1st Session, April 16, May 24, and June 13, 1985, p. 7.

4. Paton, Alan, *Sunday Times,* 21 October 1984.

5. Reuter, 2 April 1986.

6. Radio Freedom, 7 August 1986.

7. *House of Commons: Sixth Report from the Foreign Affairs Committee,* Vol. II, HC 61-II, London, 1986, pp. 208-221.

8. South African Press Association (SAPA), 14 July 1986.

9. *Natal Witness,* Durban, 27 August 1986.

10. *The Argus,* Cape Town, 22 September 1986.

11. *Post,* Johannesburg, 27 April 1985.

12. *South African Digest,* 30 May 1986.

13. *Cape Times,* Cape Town, 9 July 1986.

14. *The Argus,* 24 July 1986.

15. *Weekly Mail,* 9 May 1986.

16. *The Star,* Johannesburg, 3 October 1985.

17. *House of Commons,* op. cit., pp. 12ff.

18. This is also how Slabbert himself described the PFP (Hanlon, J. and Omond R., *The Sanctions Handbook*, p. 61).

19. South African Press Association (SAPA), 9 April 1986.

20. *International Herald Tribune,* Paris, 4 June 1986.

21. *Disinvestment,* special issue of *Leadership,* South Africa, June 1985.

22. The Current Crisis in South Africa, hearing before the Subcommittee on Africa of the Committee on Foreign Affairs, 98th Congress, 2nd Session, House of Representatives, 4 December 4, 1984, p. 18.

23. *Sechaba,* September 1985.

24. *Disinvestment,* op. cit.

25. *Pretoria News*, 16 August 1985.

26. Hanlon and Omond, op. cit., pp. 165-166.

27. Myers, Desaix, *US Business in South Africa,* p. 135.

28. *Cape Times,* 6 February 1986.

29. *Business Day,* Johannesburg, 20 December 1985

30. *The Star,* Johannesburg, November 1985.

31. *The Disinvestment Movement in the US: A Strategic Analysis,* confidential South Africa Foundation Report, 3 March 1980.

32. *Disinvestment,* op. cit., p. 24.

33. *Wall Street Journal,* 30 April 1985.

34. Crocker, Chester, "The US and South Africa: A Framework for Progress," *Current Policy, No. 732,* Department of State, p. 38.

35. Shultz, George, "Toward an American Consensus on Southern Africa," speech before the National Press Club, 16 April 1985, *Current Policy, No. 685,* Department of State.

36. Ibid.

37. Crocker, Chester, "The US Response to Apartheid," statement before the Subcommittee on Africa of the House Foreign Affairs Committee, 17 April 1985, *Current Policy No. 688,* Department of State, 1985.

38. Shultz, op. cit.

39. Crocker, op. cit.

40. The Anti-Apartheid Act of 1985, hearings before the Senate Committee of Banking, Housing and Urban Affairs, 99th Congress, 1st Session, April 16, May 24, and June 13, 1985, p. 22.

41. US Policy Toward South Africa, Hearings before the Senate Committee on Foreign Relations, 99th Congress, 1st Session, April 24, May 2 and 22, 1985, p. 36.

42. Ibid.

43. *Kaddish* is a Jewish prayer for the dead. *Washington Post,* 2 August 1985.

44. *Washington Post,* 16 August 1985.

45. Crocker, Chester *High Noon in Southern Africa: Making Peace in a Rough Neighboirhood,* op. cit., p. 310.

46. Ibid.

47. Ibid.

48. Chester Crocker interview, August 1992.

49. *South Africa Facts,* South African Embassy Newsletter, Washington, September 1986.

50. *The Citizen,* Johannesburg, 21 June 1986.

10

The End of Quiet Diplomacy

We can no longer rely on talk and quiet diplomacy.
US Senator Claiborne Pell
(D-Rhode Island)[1]

Speaking on the floor of the US Senate on 12 August 1986, Senator Claiborne Pell declared an end to quiet diplomacy in regard to South Africa. As the ranking Democrat on the Senate Foreign Relations Committee, he expressed full support for bipartisan sanctions Bill S. 2701, which eventually, with few modifications, would pass in both houses of Congress and become the Comprehensive Anti-Apartheid Act of 1986—after President Reagan unsuccessfully tried to veto it.

As early as June 1986 it had become clear that the Reagan administration was in grave danger of losing its initiative and its ability to formulate its own policy toward South Africa. On Friday, 13 June 1986, Assistant Secretary Crocker received an urgent call from Republican Senator Nancy Kassebaum, chairwoman of the Senate Foreign Affairs Subcommittee on Africa. She warned him that the president had to "get out front" on the South African issue fast or the Republican-controlled Senate would march off in its own direction. Crocker urged Secretary of State George Shultz to confer with both Kassebaum and Senate Foreign Relations Committee Chairman Richard Lugar.[2]

Lugar told Reagan's State Department that they needed urgent relief. Over the next few months Crocker and company left no stone unturned trying to accommodate them, trying to stop the sanctions tidal wave that was threatening to engulf the Senate. But Lugar, who worked with the president in 1985, enabling him to stave off congressional sanctions with a watered-down executive order, "was not interested in last-minute maneuvers this time around." He bluntly informed the administration "that it had forfeited the opportunity to lead on South Africa."[3]

After a premature lifting of a limited state of emergency on 7 March 1986, in a move apparently intended to impress the outside world, President Botha had taken several steps that negated this ill-timed concession.[4] On 18 May 1986, the SADF launched a combined air and land attack on the capitals of three neighboring countries—Botswana, Zambia, and Zimbabwe—aimed at the ANC. None of the people killed in Gaborone, Lusaka, or Harare, it was alleged, were actually members of the ANC or even South Africans. The leaders of the three target countries were joined in their condemnation of the raids by the United Nations and the United States. There was even speculation at the time that the raids were designed to slow down the work of the Eminent Persons Group (EPG), launched by the Commonwealth in mid-February 1986 as a last-ditch effort to find a peaceful solution for South Africa instead of imposing sanctions. The raids were executed on the very day that the group, under leadership of former Australian Prime Minister Malcolm Fraser, returned to South Africa from discussions with the ANC leadership at Gaborone.

With these raids P. W. Botha had finally thrown down the gauntlet and abandoned attempts to satisfy the Commonwealth, the European Community, or the United States. On 12 June 1986, the EPG itself called for comprehensive and mandatory UN economic sanctions. On the same day, Botha imposed a nationwide state of emergency that gave the security forces virtually unlimited powers and placed restrictions on the media. Acknowledging that this step would "elicit strong criticism and even punitive measures from the outside world" and a negative reaction in "financial and economic spheres" abroad, he insisted that they were necessary because the security of South Africa was at stake. "The call for sanctions presently heard in the USA," Botha charged, "is a cynical political move to buy Black votes in the USA at the expense of job opportunities for Black people in the Republic of South Africa."[5]

On 13 June 1986, Reagan declared South Africa in "a state of outright war" and appealed to both sides to exercise restraint. Reiterating his opposition to sanctions, Reagan nevertheless urged Pretoria to lift the state of emergency and allow peaceful demonstrations on 16 June—the anniversary of the Soweto uprising. On that date, however, the State Department noted with regret that Botha had defiantly rejected Reagan's appeal.

Although some form of congressional sanctions legislation was now considered imminent, the adoption in the House by voice vote in June 1986 of the far-reaching Dellums bill caught everyone by surprise. The bill imposed a complete trade embargo (with the exception of strategic minerals) and required all US firms to leave the country within 180 days. It was timed to coincide with anticipated further unrest and violence in South Africa on the tenth anniversary of the Soweto uprising. With the 1986 mid-term elections drawing closer, conservative Republicans found it expedient to let this drastic measure pass in the belief that it had little chance of prevailing in the Senate. Rep. Mark Siljander dubbed the Dellums Bill "a lemon" and "a kiss of death." Its more ardent supporters, however, intended the bill as a rhetorical measure that would send a strong signal and spur the Senate into taking action of its own.   On both sides of the Atlantic anti-apartheid activists celebrated what they considered to be the first salvo in a new congressional drive for sanctions against South Africa.

On 21 July 1986, the *New York Times* reported Foreign Minister Botha during a speech before a rural White audience in South Africa as "very nearly" daring the United States and the Western world to impose economic sanctions. "Don't let them make you afraid," Botha was reported as saying. The sooner sanctions came the better, because that would be the opportunity to "show the world we are not soft." On another occasion he threatened that South Africa would reduce any unemployment resulting from sanctions by sending home some of the 400,000 foreign workers from neighboring Black countries such as Botswana, Lesotho, and Swaziland, crippling their economies. "At the moment," observed South African financial writer Tony Koenderman, "the [South African] government is giving the impression it would almost welcome sanctions as better than the current state of uncertainty."[6] This confidence seemed to be further bolstered by the belief that the "worst" sanctions had already been imposed, namely, the withdrawal of loans and investments by foreign banks in the wake of the Rubicon speech in 1985.

In an encounter with the press late in June 1986, National Security Council Adviser John Poindexter let it slip that a policy review on South Africa was underway. The US State Department was indeed at that time searching frantically for new ways to stave off the congressional sanctions drive and to regain the initiative on South Africa. Instead of having Secretary of State Shultz go on a high-profile diplomatic initiative, it was decided to await the outcome of a last-minute rescue mission to South Africa by British Foreign Secretary Geoffrey Howe, scheduled for late July 1986.

Soon, however, the focus shifted to a major speech scheduled to be delivered by President Reagan on 22 July 1986. The upcoming address was officially announced during a photo opportunity when Howe and Reagan met at the White House on 18 July. President Reagan, the press was told, would deliver "a major speech" on South African policy to forestall sanctions by Congress.

Work on this important address had already started toward the end of June 1986. "For over a month Chet Crocker and I struggled back and forth with the White House speech writers," Shultz recalls. "I wanted some fresh actions to go with the words: termination of South African Air landing rights in the

United States; establishment of visa procedures that would keep out of the country white extremists and people suspected of potential violation of US laws; the expulsion of South African military attaches from the United States and the withdrawal of ours from Pretoria; the prohibition of new investment in South Africa unless the company doing the investing adhered to the Sullivan Principles; expanded US support for regional development of transport links among South Africa's neighbors (Zimbabwe, Zambia, Mozambique, and Malawi) as a means of reducing South Africa's stranglehold over their economies; and expanding consultation with allies on stockpiling of strategic minerals in which South Africa had a commanding position. I wanted also to place the United States firmly behind negotiation, including talks with the ANC."[7]

It was felt that while Reagan could state his personal reservations about punitive economic sanctions, he should also make it clear that the United States did not oppose sanctions in principle and that it would be adopted as last resort when all else failed. Early 8 July, the State Department draft went to the White House and about a week later came back what Crocker called the "Buchanan/NSC" substitute. National Security Adviser Poindexter had apparently allowed Reagan's conservative Communications Director Pat Buchanan to "do what he wished with the speech." The result, Crocker felt, would "give no US senator apart from Jesse Helms and a few associates any ground to stand on." Buchanan's purpose, Crocker felt, was to discredit the concept of higher-level American contacts with the ANC and to undermine the argument for pressing Pretoria to unban and negotiate with it. To add to his dismay Crocker heard from South African Ambassador Herbert Beukes that he had received "assurances" from the White House that Pretoria "need not worry."[8]

The "battle of the speech drafts" lasted from 13 until 22 July, when Crocker and Shultz received Buchanan's final changes to the original draft— only minutes before Reagan delivered it. On the afternoon of 22 July 1986, US Ambassador Herman Nickel, who happened to be in Washington at the time, accompanied Secretary of State Shultz on a limousine ride to the White House where President Reagan was about to deliver his speech. Glancing over the final copy that came back from the White House, Secretary of State Shultz was "livid." Instead of his usual "Buddha-like" demeanor, Nickel recalled, the secretary of state was openly agitated over last-minute changes. On arrival he "stormed" into Admiral Poindexter's office saying: "What is this? I am supposed to brief the press about the speech as soon as it has been delivered by the President and here with a few deft changes a White House speech writer completely pulled all the teeth." Shultz, according to Nickel, was "absolutely furious" that Communications Director Pat Buchanan should have at the last moment "pulled a fast one, as it were, and given the President a text which he had not seen at that point."[9]

That same morning American newspapers carried reports and pictures of a meeting in Cape Town the day before between President Botha and Bishop Tutu. The topic was "the serious and deteriorating situation." The closest the two men got to each other was when they agreed to pose together for photographers. Tutu told the press words were not minced, while Botha related how he "told" Tutu that he expected him "to stand up against foreign intervention in the affairs of our country." In the wake of this apparent implacability President Reagan went on the air waves, addressing a select audience assembled at the White House for the occasion. Decrying apartheid as "the root cause" of South Africa's "disorder," he nevertheless firmly rejected sanctions. Instead he proceeded to set out six "necessary components" for progress toward political peace in South Africa:

- "First, a timetable for elimination of apartheid laws should be set.
- Second, all political prisoners should be released.
- Third, Nelson Mandela should be released to participate in the country's political process.
- Fourth, black political movements should be unbanned.
- Fifth, both the Government and its opponents should begin a dialogue about constructing a political system that rests on the consent of the governed.
- Sixth, if post-apartheid South Africa is to remain the economic locomotive of southern Africa, its strong and developed economy must not be crippled."

While the first five points were almost identical to those contained in bills before Congress, the legislators intended to accomplish this through tough economic sanctions, Reagan remained implacably opposed to such action. It would destroy America's flexibility and deepen the crisis in South Africa, Reagan felt. So he urged Congress to "resist the emotional clamor for punitive sanctions." Citing reforms introduced by President Botha as "dramatic change," Reagan insisted: "We must stay and work, not cut and run."

The speech evoked a bipartisan storm in Congress. Assigned by the Democrats in Congress to respond to Reagan's speech, Rep. William Gray in his broadcast assailed the American president for not wanting to impose sanctions against South Africa while supporting punitive measures against Libya, Nicaragua, Poland and Cuba and "some 20 nations throughout the world." Why not South Africa, Gray asked. Why the double standard? But it was the fierce criticism from fellow Republicans that hurt most. Senator Lugar, who visited the White House the day before the speech to warn President Reagan of the dire consequences if he did not go along with sanctions, expressed deep disappointment and promised to keep up the pressure. He joined Republican Majority Leader Bob Dole (R-Kansas) in accusing their own president of having shown "a lack of leadership."[10]

In a telephone interview with AP Network News on the morning after the speech, Bishop Tutu bristled. "Your president is the pits as far as Blacks are concerned," he fumed. In another interview with Britain's Independent Television News (ITN) Tutu declared: "I am quite angry. I think the West, for my part, can go to hell." He said he found the speech "nauseating." While "over 70 percent of our people in two surveys have shown that they want sanctions," he claimed, "President Reagan knows better—we will suffer." Reagan "sits there like the great, big white chief of old" telling "us black people that we don't know what is good for us."[11] Fellow anti-apartheid spokesman, the Rev. Boesak, claimed that the speech destroyed "the last bit of confidence that many people may have had in the United States." It was now "up to Congress and the people of the United States to show Ronald Reagan is wrong and does not speak for the whole of America," he said.[12] Chief Mangosuthu Buthelezi, leader of the Inkatha Freedom Party, was the only prominent Black leader to praise the Reagan speech.

On 22 July 1986, the day Reagan delivered his speech, President Botha received a letter from the American president stressing the urgency of creating a negotiating framework. The next day Botha was to receive British Foreign Secretary Sir Geoffrey Howe on a mission to resuscitate negotiations after the aborted EPG mission and to stave off calls in the European Community for sanctions against South Africa. What he was trying to achieve, Howe explained, was a situation where both sides, the South African government and the ANC, made each other an offer it could not refuse. President Botha was not in a mood to listen or deal. Sir Geoffrey returned empty-handed to London. On 5 August 1986, Britain proceeded with limited sanctions in response to a more extensive initiative by the six other Commonwealth countries, and on 16 September, it joined the other members of the European Economic Community (EEC) in imposing trade restrictions on South Africa. For the first time, on 19 September 1986, the British gave high-level recognition to the ANC when Sir Geoffrey Howe met officially with its exiled president, Oliver Tambo, in London.

These developments in Europe simply confirmed to Shultz and Crocker what they had already accepted as inevitable after the Reagan speech, namely, that they had lost the sanctions tug-of-war with Congress on July 22, 1986. But they kept trying, not for South Africa's sake, but their own, to prevent Congress from muscling into their domain and calling off constructive engagement. The day after Reagan's speech, on 23 July, Secretary of State Shultz turned up at Congress where he faced a barrage of angry questions during a four-hour session before the Senate Foreign Relations Committee. Shultz underlined the importance of continuing negotiations with South Africa and told about his plans to advance that process by meeting with exiled ANC leader Oliver Tambo. He urged the lawmakers to postpone action on the pending new sanctions legislation at least until September to give the Reagan administration the opportunity to complete a review of its South African policy.

By now the "White House line" was changing almost hourly. On 24 July 1986, White House spokesman Larry Speakes told reporters on Air Force One that while President Reagan opposed "broad economic sanctions" as counterproductive, "other sanctions" were a distinct possibility. Arriving in Miami, Reagan told reporters that he had not closed any doors. In further elaboration Speakes said the president had always ruled out "punitive economic sanctions" but that "there are other sanctions that are not punitive sanctions." Asked what type of sanctions the White House was considering, Speakes replied: "I would guess landing rights." Other officials cited visa restrictions, the freezing of certain bank assets, and some of the measures then under consideration by the European Community and the Commonwealth.[13]

An editorial on 30 July 1986, in the *Washington Post* accurately reflected the mood in the capital. "The United States must be heard and must be seen to be enthusiastically on the side of black freedom rather than white privilege," wrote the *Post*. "America is a multiracial society that strives to ensure equal rights for all its citizens, and this impresses a moral stance on American policy toward South Africa."

In the Senate the Republican leadership, now acutely aware of the upcoming elections, decided to defy their president and initiate sanctions of their own. Senate Foreign Relations Committee Chairman Richard Lugar (R-Indiana) circulated the outline for sanctions legislation that he felt could win bipartisan support and forestall the more drastic Dellums Bill passed by the House. It incorporated all of the measures proposed by the House of Representatives in the previous year and proposed making permanent the sanctions imposed the previous year by presidential executive order. On 1 August 1986, this Lugar Bill passed the Senate Foreign Relations Committee by a vote of 15 to 2, with Senators Jesse Helms (R-North Carolina) and Larry Pressler (R-South Dakota) voting against.

On Thursday, 14 August 1986, at 9:15 in the morning Richard Lugar rose in the Senate to introduce Bill 2701, the Comprehensive Anti-Apartheid Act of 1986, "to provide a comprehensive policy for the United States in opposition to the system of apartheid in South Africa, and for other purposes." The "other purposes" soon became evident as several lawmakers jumped in the fray to try to gain trade advantages for their own states by introducing additional strictures on the importation of South African products. In anticipating such action, the silver-haired, soft-spoken Republican senator from Indiana cautioned everyone "to keep the focus of this bill on the issue of apartheid" even though some may be "mightily tempted to offer amendments that ban products for South Africa that compete with the products of their states."[14]

His plea went unheeded as Senators Paul Simon and Edward Kennedy argued in favor of not only "sending a message we ought to be sending" but at the same time "helping our own economy."[15] The corn farmers of Illinois, Iowa, and Indiana, Simon said, did not want to see corn imported from South Africa, any more than rice growers, sugar growers, tobacco growers, or any

other growers wished to compete with that country's products. Kennedy interrupted Simon to add fruit, vegetables, and steel to the list of convenient and
beneficial targets. "We can produce some of the finest fruits in the world,"
Kennedy pointed out. "Let me give the senator a practical illustration,"
Simon continued. "In downtown Chicago, we have the State of Illinois
Center, built with South African steel. Just a few miles away, a steel works is
closed. In Gary, Indiana, the senator from Indiana knows this better than I do,
they are in terrible shape."[16]

Lugar intervened. He saw danger in the "colloquy" between Kennedy and
Simon. Although "congenial" and "appealing to the American people," it
called for "a protectionist trade bill by another name" and "demeaned" the
South African debate. The objective should not be "economic devastation"
but "persuasion," Lugar insisted—to little avail.[17] The Kennedy amendment
prevailed, adding to the list of prohibited imports from South Africa agricultural products, iron, and steel. It also barred US exports of crude and refined
petroleum products to South Africa. The Senate approved by 67 to 29 an
amendment to ban textile imports from South Africa, in clear rebuke of the
Reagan administration, which had just signed an agreement with that country
to increase its textile export quota with the United States to 4 percent.

Faced with certain defeat, Senators Pressler and Helms and a few others
who opposed the bill tried to rescue something out of the ashes by
introducing their own amendments. The Senate went along with Pressler's
suggestion that a clause authorizing the president to sell off US gold to lower
world prices and put pressure on Pretoria be deleted. He and others made the
point that it would not only hurt South Africa, but seriously damage the
economies of the gold-producing states in the United States as well. The
Senate also passed a watered-down version of an amendment proposed by
Helms that sought to bar the ANC from US-sponsored negotiations should it
refuse "to abandon violence." In its final version it merely excluded the
Black liberation movement from negotiations if it refused to follow the South
African government in suspending violence.

For two days the debate raged on the Senate floor and over C-Span, the
newly introduced gavel-to-gavel cable television coverage of congressional
proceedings. It made for high drama as a handful of dissenters tried to defeat
the sanctions bill. What "we are looking at is middle-class, comfortable
White senators playing up to the Black population of America and the liberal
population of America," complained conservative Senator Malcolm Wallop
(R-Wyoming).[18] But the day belonged to a confident Senator Edward
Kennedy, who now sensed victory as large numbers of Republicans defected
and joined his long -fought sanctions campaign in Congress. He conceded
that there might be some truth in the charge that South Africa had become
"the new civil rights issue in this country." But, he insisted "we care about
injustice."[19]

"The same coalitions that worked to pass the great bipartisan civil rights legislation of the sixties—the churches, the labor unions, the students and political leaders from both parties—have been mobilized again in support of sanctions against South Africa," Senator Kennedy proclaimed. He took the opportunity to thank "the millions of Americans who have worked tirelessly to place our country on the right side of freedom and justice in South Africa."[20] Senator Lowell Weicker (R-Connecticut) was more specific in expressing his gratitude. "If this measure is passed and if sanctions become law, the person most responsible for that is Randall Robinson, and those of his circle who, day after day after day, kept this matter before the American people, when the American people did not care at all," Weicker contended. Randall Robinson, he explained, was the man who organized the demonstrations in front of the South African Embassy in Washington and who, "with just a handful, when this was no issue at all, protested this policy of evil." It was not a congressman, a senator, or a president who brought the matter of South Africa to the attention of the American people but "citizen" Randall Robinson.[21]

In a last-ditch effort President Reagan conducted a nationally televised news conference from Chicago on 12 August 1986—barely three days before the Senate was due to cast its vote. Most of his remarks concerned South Africa and sanctions. He reaffirmed his belief that sanctions would not only hurt "the people we want to help" in South Africa but also be "disruptive to surrounding states."

In the evening of 15 August 1986, the Senate passed its final version of the Lugar Bill in response to the more strident Dellums House Bill. Now known as the Comprehensive Anti-Apartheid Act (CAAA), the Senate Bill was adopted by an overwhelming 84 votes against 14, with 37 Republicans joining 47 Democrats in a bipartisan rebuff of Reagan. Despite intensive lobbying, the Reagan administration barely mustered the support of 25 percent of its own Republican Party to vote against the measure. Senator Richard Lugar saw the adoption of his bill as "a very important shift." Congress, he believed, was "very clearly involved in reshaping foreign policy." The first official to react from South Africa was Deputy Finance Minister Kent Durr, who denounced the Senate sanctions bill as "protectionism dressed up in morality." It would, if it became law, make South Africa less able to finance reforms, Durr claimed.[22]

The time had come for the Reagan administration to try the same tactic that worked in 1985. On 4 September 1986, President Reagan renewed the executive sanctions order of 1985. His announcement, just as Congress returned from its brief summer recess, was accompanied by authorized leaks that the White House was about to appoint a Black foreign service officer, Edward Perkins, as ambassador to South Africa. Neither the House of Representatives nor the Senate was, however, in a mood to compromise. The executive order that served as a wrench in the wheel to stop the congressional sanctions cart in 1985 snapped this time as the legislators moved ahead at double speed to show results before the upcoming November elections. On 12 September 1986, the House adopted the Senate's Comprehensive Anti-Apartheid Act and sent it to President Reagan for his signature. He vetoed it.

In his 1,700-word veto message, Reagan once again implored Congress to "stay and build, not cut and run." Is America helping the Black people of South Africa—"the lifelong victims of apartheid"—by throwing them out of work and leaving them and their families jobless and hungry, Reagan asked. "Or are we simply assuming a moral posture at the expense of the people in whose name we presume to act?" The White House, according to the *New York Times,* purposely delayed the veto until after the House of Representatives had adjourned on Friday, 26 September 1986, and President Reagan left for a weekend at Camp David. By doing so, it bought time to seek additional votes to sustain the veto and to determine whether anything was to be gained by offering further concessions on the sanctions front.[23]

While the South African government refrained from praising Reagan's veto in an apparent fear that it might be counter-productive, Bishop Tutu showed little restraint in his response. Reagan gave the "ritual verbal condemnation" of apartheid, Tutu charged, but he "refuses steadfastly to take any effective action against one of the most vicious policies the world has known."[24] On Monday, 29 September 1986, the House overrode the President's veto by an overwhelming 313 votes against 83. After this rebuff by a House of Representatives firmly under control of the Democrats, the Reagan administration now directed all its powers of persuasion at the Senate, where the Republicans held a slim majority. To stave off another imminent defeat Reagan wrote a letter to Republican Senate Majority Leader Bob Dole on 29 September 1986, in which he promised to incorporate some of the proposed new sanctions contained in the CAAA in an executive order, if the Senate would allow his veto to prevail. This was rejected as a ploy by Rep. Stephen Solarz, who branded it a "counterfeit version" produced out of "incredible moral arrogance and supreme political cynicism." House Speaker Thomas O'Neill Jr. wrote to Reagan calling the executive order a "backward step."[25] Lugar, as a Republican, noted that the South African government "has made it clear that anything less than the congressional bill would be a victory" and that he was not about to grant Pretoria that satisfaction. Regardless of "how many executive orders are issued and diplomatic initiatives undertaken, the United States would be seen as apologists for apartheid," he contended.

On 30 September 1986, the appointment of Edward Perkins as America's first Black ambassador to South Africa was finally announced as Secretary of State Shultz turned up at Congress for another round of lobbying. Shultz also told a group of Republican senators that overriding Reagan's veto would undermine President Reagan's bargaining power at the upcoming mini-summit in Iceland with Soviet leader Mikhail Gorbachev. Some senators who leaned toward supporting Reagan claimed to have switched sides as a result of what they felt was a far-fetched linkage of two totally separate issues.

At this stage Foreign Minister Botha, frustrated by the failure of the White House, his own diplomats, and their hired lobbyists to make any headway at Congress, decided to try some long-distance arm-twisting of his own. On 1 October 1986, he telephoned a number of senators representing key Midwestern states, to inform them that the South African government would cut off all grain purchases from the United States if the Senate overrode Reagan's veto. On the other hand, he promised, if the veto were allowed and the bill defeated, South Africa would buy more grain. This last-minute effort, facilitated in part by Senate Agriculture Committee Chairman Jesse Helms (R-North Carolina), caused a furor among legislators. Lugar accused Botha's efforts at "intimidation and bribery" as "despicable" while Senator Edward Kennedy (D-Massachusetts) referred scornfully to "the bullies and thugs of Pretoria." Among those contacted by Botha, at least one, Senator Mark Andrews (R-North Dakota) stated that he was thinking of sustaining Reagan's veto until Botha's "cheap trick" convinced him to vote against it. Senator Edward Zorinsky, a Nebraska Democrat, who was one of the legislators contacted by Botha, described the effort as "tantamount to blackmail"—one that hurt the Reagan administration's cause.[26] On the very day that the Senate was scheduled to vote, Botha responded angrily to these charges, dismissing the criticism as "absolutely laughable." He described his warning to the senators as "normal diplomatic practice." It was "not interference" but "the conveyance of ideas on a given matter," Botha added.

On 2 October 1986, the Senate voted by 78 to 21—far exceeding the required two-thirds majority—to override the presidential veto, dealing Reagan an insulting blow. It was the first time since President Nixon had been overruled on his veto of the War Powers Resolution in 1973 that a president had suffered such a heavy loss on an important foreign policy issue. According to Shultz "it represented a true erosion of presidential control over foreign policy issues." Afterward, Senate Majority Leader Bob Dole, described the vote as a "litmus test" of legislators' feelings on civil rights. Crocker simply called it "daylight robbery."[27] The *New York Times* depicted Randall Robinson of TransAfrica and Congressman Ron Dellums in elated embrace.[28] It left no doubt as to who the winners were.

The CAAA contained the toughest and most far-reaching sanctions legislation introduced by any of South Africa's major trading partners. It mandated a wide-ranging trade embargo and banned new US loans to and investments in South Africa. These were the key provisions:

• A ban on all new public and private loans and investments in South Africa except for reinvesting profits from South African enterprises, short-term credits, and the rescheduling of existing debt. Also exempted were loans and credits for educa- tion, housing, or humanitarian projects and investments in firms owned by Black

South Africans. Unlike the earlier House version, the final Act did not require dis-investment or withdrawal of existing loans or investments from South Africa.

- A ban on exports to South Africa of petroleum products, crude oil, munitions, and nuclear technology or materials. It also prohibited the exporting of computers, software, and services to the South African military, police, or other agencies administering apartheid.
- A ban on US imports of South African iron, steel, arms, ammunition, military ve-hicles, and farm products. Imports of coal, uranium, and textiles would be prohib-ited within ninety days after passage of the Act, as of January 1987. A total ban on any direct or indirect imports from South African state-owned companies, and a permanent ban on the importation of Krugerrand gold coins.
- Termination of landing rights in the United States for South African Airways.
- A prohibition on US government purchases of South African goods and services, and a ban on the promotion of tourism to South Africa, the promotion or subsi-dization of trade with South Africa, or any cooperation with the South African military except for intelligence-gathering purposes.
- An allocation of $40 million in assistance to those "harmed" by apartheid.

The CAAA allowed the president, subject to congressional approval, to ei-ther suspend or modify any of its measures if the South African government complied with the first condition (the release of Mandela) plus three of the other four stipulations:

1. The release from prison of Nelson Mandela and other political prisoners.
2. The repeal of the state of emergency and the release of all persons detained un-der it.
3. The unbanning of "democratic political parties" and the permission of free polit-ical process.
4. The repeal of the Group Areas Act and the Population Registration Act.
5. Agreement "to enter into good faith negotiations with truly representative mem-bers of the black majority without preconditions."

The Act also required a report from the president after twelve months to in-dicate whether "substantial progress" had been made by Pretoria in disman-tling apartheid. If not, additional sanctions could be imposed, including:

- A prohibition on the importation of steel from South Africa.
- A prohibition on military assistance to countries that continue to circumvent the international arms embargo regarding South Africa.
- A prohibition on the importation of food, agricultural products, diamonds, and textiles from South Africa.
- A prohibition on US banks accepting, receiving, or holding deposit accounts from South African nationals.

- A prohibition on the importation into the United States of strategic materials from South Africa.

The CAAA severed most of South Africa's trade, technological, and financial links with the world's leading economic power and its single most important trading partner. But it had a much wider significance. It served notice on South Africa's other major trading and business partners to apply similarly severe measures or run the risk of jeopardizing their valuable marketing opportunities in the United States. The CAAA gave US nationals the "legal right" to "seek damages against any person who takes commercial advantage of a sanction or prohibition" under the Act. It also instructed the State Department to submit reports to Congress on the sanctions performance of other nations so that US could punish nations that dared to fill the void.

With the passing of the CAAA, Congress not only closed out all the remaining blank spaces in the American row on the South African sanctions "tic-tac-toe" board. (See Figure 2 on page 148). It caused other nations to cut back their trade with South Africa and to impose additional sanctions. Following on the heels of other official sanctions imposed by the Commonwealth, Britain, and the EEC toward the end of 1986, the CAAA finally brought the full weight of America's economic power and global influence to the sanctions campaign against South Africa.

The initial response in South Africa to the CAAA was predictable. In business circles there was considerable concern. President Botha, however, predicted that South Africa "will not just survive but come out stronger in the end." Absent from the government's rhetoric, however, was any mention of withholding its strategic minerals in retribution. Instead of following up on its often repeated threat to retaliate with an embargo on the sales of vital strategic minerals, there was relief in South Africa that Congress saw fit to exclude strategic minerals from the list of banned imports. On 3 January 1987, *The Star* welcomed the US decision to exempt ten minerals "of vital strategic importance to the country's economy from its sanctions list." It meant, the Johannesburg daily pointed out with no small measure of gratitude, that "many thousands of South African workers in these sectors are no longer living under a cloud." For South Africa, it estimated, a US import ban on these minerals would have meant the loss of an estimated 4 billion rand in foreign exchange—"not to mention the harmful effect it would have had on local manufacturing and equipment suppliers to the mining industry."

Assessing the potential loss for the United States as a result of the CAAA, the Economics Division of the Congressional Research Service (CRS) found US investment, trade, and loan exposure to South Africa insignificant. With a trade of $3 billion between the two countries in 1985, South Africa accounted for less than 1 percent of the total US trade. Buying $1.2 billion worth of American goods in that year, South Africa ranked thirty-first as a US export market. The level of US direct investment in South Africa stood at $1.3

billion in 1985, having already dropped considerably from its peak of $2.6 billion in 1981, and formed less than 1 percent of America's global total. Action prohibiting loans to South Africa would have little direct effect on US banks, as the $3.2 billion in loans to South Africa in 1985 accounted for only 1.1 percent of all outstanding US commercial loans to foreign customers.[29]

On the other hand, South Africa stood to lose much more in view of the important role that the United States played in its trade, investment, and financing. In 1985, sales to the United States accounted for 15 percent of all its exports, making the US its number one overseas market. Imports from the United States represented about 16 percent of South Africa's purchases from abroad, and consisted mainly of machinery and equipment vital to its manufacturing industry. While an estimated $1.3 billion in direct US investment in 1985 was only 1 percent in global American terms, it gave the United States more than a 70 percent share in that country's computer industry, half of its petroleum sector, and about one-third of its automobile industry.[30]

But the CRS conceded that South Africa, the world's principal producer of critical metals, including chromium, platinum-group metals (PGM), and manganese, was of utmost strategic importance to the United States. These were all minerals classified, along with cobalt, as "first-tier" strategic metals for which the quantity "required for essential civilian and military uses" exceeded reasonably secure domestic and foreign supplies. South Africa in 1985 accounted for 55 percent of America's PGM imports, 45 percent of its chromium, 55 percent of its manganese, and 40 percent of its ferromanganese. In all cases the only real alternative supplier was America's superpower competitor, the Soviet Union. "In sum," the CRS concluded, "while South Africa does not account for a significant portion of US trade, it is an important non-Soviet supplier of certain strategic materials on which the United States is import-dependent."[31]

Although South Africa did not intend to make good on past threats of withholding strategic minerals in retaliation, the United States seemed preoccupied with this possibility. On 10 February 1987, the Secretary of State's Advisory Committee, established in terms of President Reagan's preemptive executive sanctions order of 1985, expressed concern over US dependence on South African supplies of strategic metals and minerals. While Congress had originally threatened to prohibit imports of strategic minerals from South Africa if it failed to make satisfactory progress toward reform, it now felt obliged to ask in the CAAA for a report on the impact of "strategic minerals imported from South Africa."[32]

Sobered by the knowledge that an embargo on strategic mineral sales to the Americans would hurt itself as much if not more than the United States, South Africa's leaders had altered their message accordingly. Instead, they now issued dire warnings of what would happen should these mineral resources fall in the wrong hands. "If our enormous reserves and strategic minerals fall into Communist hands, they will have the potential to cripple the industries and defense capabilities of the Free World," President Botha warned at the 75th anniversary celebrations of the SADF in Cape Town during April 1987. Therefore America and the West needed to assist South Africa in fighting SWAPO and the ANC, whom "Communist countries financed, trained and supplied [with] weapons."[33]

"While the US sanctions are far from a complete trade embargo on South Africa, they have caused great concern within South Africa, giving rise to denunciations of US 'interference' by South African officials and extensive commentary in the South African press," reported the Congressional Research Service (CRS) to Congress in its 30 December 1986, report on the immediate impact of the CAAA.[34] The same view was echoed from within President Botha's ranks. "In many South African circles there seems to be an impression that sanctions, coupled with the unrest situation in South Africa, will bring the South African Government to its heels," wrote Dr. D. A. S. Herbst of the SADF in November 1986.[35]

In the mid-1980s while Shultz, Crocker, and the two Bothas were bandying about phrases like "crossing the historical divide" and "crossing the Rubicon" to convey promises of great reforms, Congress had built a bipartisan bridge that enabled it to cross another divide. It moved onto White House turf and took control of US foreign policy toward South Africa, passed sanctions, and signaled its determination to stay on the case until apartheid was gone. At a press conference on 2 October 1986, during his visit to United Nations headquarters in New York, Zimbabwe Prime Minister Robert Mugabe congratulated Congress: "I say, well done to the people of the United States. Leaders come and leaders go, but the people live forever."[36]

But did Congress really speak for the American people on this issue? A few days after Reagan's crushing defeat and the adoption of sanctions by Congress, US Secretary of State George Shultz received a telephone call from pollster Lou Harris, who informed him that by a margin of 60 percent to 30 percent the American people opposed sanctions "that would cause American companies to get out of South Africa." Harris told Shultz: "People seem to support what you are doing, but you're not presenting it right."[37]

NOTES

1. *Congressional Record, Proceedings and Debates of the 99th Congress, Second Session,* Vol. 132, Part 15, 12-15, August 1986.

2. Crocker, Chester, *High Noon in Southern Africa: Making Peace in a Rough Neighborhood,* pp. 323-324.

3. Ibid.

4. As violence had not subsided "there were no ostensible reasons for lifting the emergency," observed Pottinger (Pottinger, B, *The Imperial Presidency: PW Botha - The First Ten Years,* p. 323).

5. *Debates of the House of Assembly, Third Session, Eighth Parliament,* 9-13 June 1986, cols. 8111-8112 and 8118.

6. *New York Times,* 21 July1986.

7. Shultz, G. *Turmoil and Triumph: My Years as Secretary of State,* pp. 1121-1122.

8. Crocker, op. cit., pp. 320-322.

9. Herman Nickel interview, August 1993.

10. *New York Times,* 23 July 1986.

11. Ibid.

12. *New York Times,* 24 July 1986.

13. *New York Times,* 25 July 1986.

14. *Congressional Record, Proceedings and Debates of the 99th Congress, Second Session,* Vol. 132, Part 15, 12-15, August 1986.

15. Ibid.

16. Ibid.

17. Ibid.

18. Ibid.

19. Ibid.

20. Ibid.

21. Ibid.

22. *New York Times,* 17 August 1986.

23. *New York Times,* 27-28 September 1986.

24. *New York Times,* 28 September 1986.

25. *New York Times,* 30 September 1986.

26. *New York Times* and *Washington Post,* 2 and 3 October 1986.

27. Crocker, op. cit., p. 323.

28. *New York Times,* 3 October 1986.

29. Cooper, W. H., ed., *South Africa-US Economic Ties,* Congressional Research Service, Library of Congress, Economics Division, 23 December 1986.

30. Ibid.

31. Ibid.

32. Comprehensive Anti-Apartheid Act of 1986, Title V, Section 502-509.

33. *Beeld, Business Day* and *The Citizen,* Johannesburg, 7 April 1987.

34. Affelder, Jeanne S., and Copson., Raymond W., eds., *South Africa and International Sanctions,* Congressional Research Service, Library of Congress, Foreign Affairs and National Defense Division, 30 December 1986.

35. Herbst, D. A. S., *SA Forum Position Paper,* Vol 9 No 11/12, November 1986.

36. *New York Times,* 3 October 1986.

37. Shultz, op. cit., p. 1123.

11

The Sanctions of the Markets

> The economic pressures on South Africa were not so much
> exerted by the legislative sanctions as by the sanctions of the
> markets.
>
> *Herman Nickel,*
> *US Ambassador to South Africa, 1982-1986*[1]

The sanctions of the markets placed stronger pressures on US corporations
and banks with business links to South Africa than any legislation—or even
harassment by pressure groups. While the Comprehensive Anti-Apartheid Act
of October 1986 and the many city and state sanctions laws that preceded it
placed extra burdens and restrictions on doing business with South Africa, the
markets itself determined the degree and pace of America's corporate and financial disengagement.

As long as corporations stood to make good profits in a relatively sound
and stable South African market, they were willing to endure a large degree
of inconvenience and criticism.

Once, however, the hassle factor and perceived political risk exceeded
profitability, the exodus mounted. At the end of 1986 when the CAAA was
passed, major American corporations were already in the process of
diminishing their risk in South Africa—fearful of the continuing violence and
political instability.

On Friday, 7 November 1986, barely a month after the passing of the Comprehensive Anti-Apartheid Act, President P. W. Botha and his cabinet held
talks in Pretoria with 200 South African business leaders. The theme was:
"Forward in Confidence." It was a disappointing affair. While no executive in
the past would have passed up on an opportunity like this, several now found

convenient excuses to decline. What was supposed to be a celebration of the future turned out to be a subdued discussion—a wake of sorts. The pallor of sanctions showed. Some of those who attended felt that "Lost Confidence" might have been a more appropriate description.

It was very different when P. W. Botha held his first summit with South Africa's business leaders in November 1979, shortly after he became prime minister. In contrast to his predecessors, who cautioned business to stay out of politics, Botha actively sought input from the private sector. On 22 November 1979, Botha was host to a capacity crowd of more than 300 top business, labor, and agricultural leaders at a glittering reception at the Carlton Hotel in Johannesburg. There was an air of confidence and optimism. The purpose of the Carlton Conference was to plan the future together and to enlist business support for the concept of an economically interdependent "Constellation of States" in Southern Africa.

The captains of industry were all there: Harry Oppenheimer, Anton Rupert, Punch Barlow, Mike Rosholt, Gavin Relly, Fred du Plessis. An invitation was regarded as such an honor that busy businessmen eagerly set aside important previous commitments to hasten to the Carlton Hotel for this audience with the new South African leader. Speaking as the doyen of the business community, Oppenheimer saw "greater reason for real hope in the future of this country than in many, many years."[2] Prime Minister Botha responded by expressing solidarity with Oppenheimer's belief in a South Africa that "should not be an isolated stronghold, but a bastion of hope for the Free World."[3]

After the conference Botha's bureaucrats established a permanent secretariat to carry forth the idea of a constellation of Southern African states. But eventually all the working groups, regional liaison committees, and promises of assistance could not lure the neighboring Black states into joining. These independent states were under too much political pressure from their peers elsewhere on the African continent. The constellation turned out to be nothing more than a grouping of Black South African homelands, neither recognized nor condoned abroad—dismissed as children of apartheid. The same disappointment awaited those business leaders who expected Botha to move at deliberate speed toward far-reaching reform after his famous "adapt or die" speech. While he responded favorably to the Wiehahn and Riekert Commission reports and proceeded to scrap job reservation and other apartheid laws that inhibited economic growth, he tried at the same time to reassure the conservative wing of his party by applying the brakes in other important areas of reform.

On 12 November 1981, Botha was host to his second business summit at Cape Town's Good Hope Center. This conference was intended to narrow the widening gap that had developed between Botha and the business leaders since 1979. In February 1981 Harry Oppenheimer had sharply criticized Botha's lack of substantial progress toward "genuine political power sharing and social justice." He saw the country heading "towards armed revolution."[4] Another corporate executive, Chris Saunders, compared the pace of reform with that of an ox-wagon.[5] Botha, now acutely aware of the disquiet within the South African business community, called for a renewed spirit of cooperation in Cape Town. After a one hour briefing on government economic policy, regional development, new growth areas, stability, decentralization, and incentives, Botha took his seat among dignitaries on the lavishly decorated stage of the Good Hope Center to listen to comments and suggestions and to field questions. Afrikaner tobacco millionaire Anton Rupert, a man of metaphors, summed up for the rest: "I believe that if you want to jump across a large gap between two cliffs, it can't be done in stages." Obviously irritated, Botha responded: "Yes, but I would like to add that before you jump you should make certain that you are going to reach the other side."[6]

Addressing issues such as job color bars, Black access to education and training, Black mobility, and property rights was not sufficient. Concerned about increasing unrest and violence, business wished to see meaningful social and political reforms. In 1982, the Federated Chamber of Industries (FCI) and Associated Chambers of Commerce (ASSOCOM) jointly urged the government to consider questions of citizenship and political rights for all Blacks. They wanted him to jump, but he refused. "No National Party Government," Botha told the party faithful in Vryburg, "can accept the principle of majority rule in one state." Instead, he spoke vaguely about being "prepared to consult with the black leaders, to deal with them, to have the necessary discussions with them, to confer with them to carry out a system in South Africa that will make it possible for them to achieve their own independence."[7]

The rift between Botha and business continued to widen. In October 1983 he sent his minister of Constitutional Development and Planning, Chris Heunis, to address the South African Federated Chamber of Industries. "The current constitutional debate in South Africa is often heated and emotional," Heunis said. "As a result there is a tendency among certain participants in the debate to lose track of the realities of our situation."[8] The implication was clear.

With the rest of the world, South African business leaders waited for the Rubicon speech in August 1985 with bated breath. Among those impressed with the rumors of real reform was Tony Bloom of Premier Milling. The prospects of reform within South Africa seemed to be reaching "unprecedented heights," Bloom felt. If the government summoned the courage to choose a road carrying its bold statements about adaptation and the removal of discrimination into practice, "one could proceed with some confidence that the great potential of our great country can be realized," he said. But if the government chose the other road, "clinging to the obstinacies of the past, retreat into its heavily armed white stockade, and embark upon another disgraceful wave of arrests, bannings and detentions without trial," the future was not going to be a pleasant one.[9]

Botha's Durban speech proved to be a grave disappointment for Bloom and many of his peers. The business community decided that the time had come to take matters in its own hands. In September 1985, Gavin Relly of Anglo-American led a delegation to Lusaka to meet with the exiled leaders of the ANC, greatly enhancing the status and international standing of the outlawed organization. Afterward, in an apparent attempt to restore relations with an incensed Botha, Relly told the press that the South African president was "misunderstood by the world." He criticized the ANC for taking the view that all Blacks were the same instead of recognizing "that the Black community was not one group favoring majority rule, but tribal and urban groups who were existing power blocs which do not want to be swamped by simple universal suffrage."[10] But all this fence mending was to little avail.

Receiving a special citation at a ceremony in Johannesburg in October 1985, the chairman of the giant Barlows Group, Mike Rosholt, used the occasion to challenge Botha, who by then, "not unlike his predecessor," had called on "businessmen to stick to business and leave politics to the politicians." Business, Rosholt said, could not possibly comply. In South Africa there was no longer any clear distinction between political and socio-economic issues, Rosholt insisted. They were inextricably linked.[11] President Botha chose an appearance at the annual congress of the Afrikaanse Handelsinstituut (Afrikaans Chamber of Commerce) in Bloemfontein to reply. "Business leaders can safely leave the government in the hands of the people who are the chosen leaders of the country," he warned.

In 1987 Botha got his revenge when he charged Chris Ball, chief executive of South Africa's Barclays Bank, with financially assisting the ANC in the placement of an advertisement in several English language newspapers on the occasion of the outlawed organization's 75th anniversary. Following Ball's denial that he had any knowledge that the overdraft of 150,000 rand granted to a certain Yusuf Surtee was to be used for the ANC advertising campaign, Botha ordered an inquiry. To the embarrassment of Gavin Relly of Anglo-American, as the largest shareholder of the bank, Justice Munnik of the Cape Supreme Court found that Ball was fully informed beforehand. Not long afterward Ball resigned and emigrated to Britain. So did Tony Bloom of the Premier Group and Gordon Waddell, chief executive of Anglo-Vaal, and former son-in-law of Harry Oppenheimer.

In October 1985 Oppenheimer was trying his hand at damage control. At the age of seventy-six, still active behind the scenes in Anglo-American decision-making, Oppenheimer was obviously embarrassed and disappointed by the Relly trip to ANC headquarters, which, it is said, happened without his prior knowledge or approval. He informed a gathering of the American Chamber of Commerce in South Africa that the ANC sought "an economic system that would destroy everything that we in this room stand for" and urged business not to offer it either "moral support or material support." Oppenheimer's caution against lending moral or material support to the ANC seemed trite at a time when Amcham had its hands full trying to keep its overseas members from joining the exodus from South Africa. In 1985 alone forty American firms had sold out or closed down their operations and the pace was quickening as internal and external pressures kept mounting.

Concerned about increasing pressures in Washington for a total ban by Congress on American business in South Africa, Amcham in Johannesburg decided to do something drastic. On 3 June 1986, the chamber endorsed and distributed a document titled "Civil Disobedience" among its dwindling membership. Compiled by the Get Ahead Foundation, with Bishop Tutu and Dr. Nthato Motlana as its directors, the document provided tips on how to fight the system and disobey discriminatory laws. Blacks, it said, should be encouraged to gradually move into White residentiál areas, and if any of them encountered problems traveling on a train or bus reserved for Whites, Amcham would pay the legal expenses. Integration should be promoted in White government schools while private schools maintaining quotas for Black pupils should be boycotted. At the same time, private schools that forfeited government subsidies because they declared themselves completely "open" should be financially supported.

On 19 February 1986, General Motors stepped out in front as its American chief executive in South Africa, Robert White, promised financial and legal aid to Black employees who wished to violate Port Elizabeth's White beaches law. Extensive precautions by the local police in anticipation of hordes of law-breaking Black GM workers proved unnecessary as no one took White up on his offer. On 23 May, GM announced a ban on the sale of cars or trucks to South Africa's police or military forces—a decision prompted by pressures at shareholder meetings in America and tightening US regulations. One South African official was quoted as saying that the government "on the whole" preferred disinvestors to foreign corporations that remained in the country and lobbied against apartheid in the political arena.[12] This comment was made as both GM and IBM announced their departure shortly after the passage of the Comprehensive Anti-Apartheid Act (CAAA) by Congress in October 1986.

Other American disinvestors during 1986 included Proctor and Gamble, Coca-Cola, Prudential, General Electric, American Telephone and Telegraph, Sara Lee, Warner Communications, Eastman Kodak, Dun & Bradstreet, Revlon, and Exxon. Still standing firm were Mobil and Shell. Mobil, an active promoter of the Sullivan Principles, announced the establishment of a multimillion-dollar foundation for Black education and development as further proof of its good intentions. Shell vowed to remain as a positive force for change despite strong pressures from the powerful AFL-CIO trade unionists in America. At the close of 1986 an estimated 250 US companies were still operating in South Africa—down from 300 at the beginning of the year. They employed some 47,000 Blacks, or 0.8 percent of the country's total Black work force of 6.1 million.

In his announcement of GM's pull-out on 20 October 1986, Chairman Roger Smith cited as the main reason "the slowness of progress in ending apartheid." IBM Chairman John F. Akers, in his withdrawal announcement the very next day, listed both his corporation's opposition to apartheid and the deteriorating economy as reasons for its departure.

At the time, GM was the single largest American subsidiary in South Africa, with annual sales exceeding $300 million and a work force of 3,056, most of them Black. Port Elizabeth, the Detroit of South Africa, stood to lose not only jobs but considerable funds spent by the American automaker on welfare and social programs.

It was still reeling under the impact of Ford's disengagement the year before when it merged and transferred its operations to a local Pretoria-based company. Fearing large-scale lay-offs, GM's workers struck, demanding severance pay, refunds on pensions, and representation on the board of the new holding company headed by a buyout group under leadership of American Robert Price. Violence broke out and the police were called in to help usher GM out and the new entity in.

IBM did not experience the same turbulent transfer. It simply handed over operations to a new company called International Systems Management (ISM) and continued selling its product. Neither GM nor IBM received enthusiastic applause from activists at home. The Rev. Leon Sullivan expressed fears that the new companies under South African control would no longer conform to the Sullivan Principles. These fears were well-founded.

"The history of disinvestment is that as soon as a company becomes wholly South African-owned, it tends to cut its links with Sullivan," said Lionel Grewan, executive director of the Sullivan Signatory Association in South Africa.[13]

There were also charges that both GM and IBM were playing "corporate shell games" by still marketing their products and running their operations through "third parties." Especially IBM came in for heavy criticism from trade union leaders who claimed that the computer giant had withdrawn in name only to escape criticism and boycotts at home. Although IBM released very little information about its disinvestment, it boasted that all employees were to participate in a profit-sharing plan amounting to 3 percent of pretax earnings.[14]

The managing director of ISM, the South African unit that replaced IBM in South Africa, assured clients of uninterrupted supplies as an exclusive distributor with an indefinite contract.[15] This was the simple part. Much more complex was the corporate structure of the new entity. Figure 1 illustrates the intricate way in which this particular takeover was structured. It was only one of many such complex creations by lawyers expert in helping to make disinvestment a less painful and costly affair.

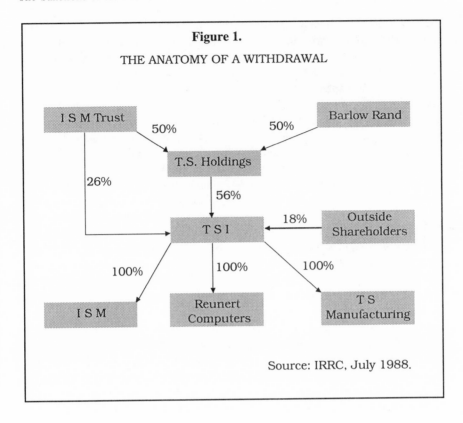

Figure 1.

THE ANATOMY OF A WITHDRAWAL

Source: IRRC, July 1988.

ISM Trust and South Africa's Barlow Rand each ended up owning 50 percent of TS Holdings, which in turn controlled 56 percent of TSI, which owned 100 percent of ISM, Reunert Computers (Barlow subsidiary) and TS Manufacturing. Of the remaining 44 percent of TSI, 18 percent was held by outside shareholders and 26 percent by ISM Trust.[16] This complex corporate checker box was, critics claimed, designed to obfuscate the lurking presence of IBM itself, to make it easy for the American parent to step back into the open as soon as the sanctions pressure abated and the economy improved.

A company that wished to disinvest from South Africa had seven options:

1. Sell its assets to South African companies
2. Sell to local management
3. Close down its South African operations
4. Sell to another multinational company
5. Move its operations to a neighboring country
6. Sell shares to the public
7. Transfer its assets to a trust

No two disinvestment contracts were completely alike. However, in reviewing the basic methods favored most by the 114 US companies that disinvested between 1 January 1986, and 30 April 1988, the Investor Responsibility Research Center (IRRC) found that forty-five sold their operations to South African companies or investors, twenty-seven sold to local management or employees, fifteen closed their operations thirteen sold to foreign multinationals and six to other US companies, one donated its assets to a church, one moved its operations to a neighboring country, one sold shares to the public and seven did not disclose what they have done with their assets.[17] Whatever their reason for departing, the IRRC found that "companies could structure their disinvestments to promote their public image, to maintain their market share in South Africa, to maximize the dollars they receive for their assets, or to retain some measure of control over their former subsidiary." They could chose between a range of disinvestment methods, each with its own drawbacks and advantages—"some of which entailed complex financial maneuvers which the companies had little interest in explaining to the public."[18]

To beat the financial rand, designed by the South African authorities to discourage disinvestment and attract new investment, US firms came up with interesting variations. Instead of selling out at fire-sale prices and then repatriating this capital in financial rand at a substantial loss, some US firms opted for an off-shore trust. By "loaning" money to this trust, the US corporation could "purchase" its own subsidiary, which would then start paying dividends at the commercial rand rate to the trust, which in turn would pass it along as repayment of the "loan."[19] The IRRC found toward the end of the 1980s that while 100 companies had claimed to have disinvested, only thirteen plants were actually closed down.[20]

Although it was one of the fifteen American corporations that claimed to have closed down operations in South Africa altogether, even Kodak discovered that a clean break was difficult to attain. Initially, Kodak's announcement in 1986 that it was not only ending its operations but prohibiting all sales of its products in South Africa drew applause from activists in the United States. But it also earned the ire of 460 workers and praise in US anti-apartheid circles soon turned to scorn when it was discovered that Kodak products were still freely available in South Africa many months after its announced departure.[21] Kodak had trouble maintaining a complete embargo on its product. Early in 1988 news leaked out that its Paris advertising agency chose sunny South Africa as the site for the filming of a commercial to be used on European television during the Olympic Games. Featured were South African children and athletes. Embarrassed by this kind of exposure, Kodak was forced to recall its camera crew and shelve the film footage.

In November 1987 the American authorities, acting on a complaint by Kodak, cautioned Japan to stop Fuji from taking advantage of the "gap" left in the South African market by the departure of the American film maker.

Kodak was not only losing business in South Africa. In 1989 3M, which persisted with its operations in South Africa, was chosen by the city of New York over Kodak as a supplier of microfiche equipment. "David Dinkins, Manhattan borough president and a mayoral candidate, wants New York to stop granting service and purchase contracts to Minnesota Mining & Manufacturing Co. (3M) which has a subsidiary in South Africa," reported the *Wall Street Journal* in 1989. "Easier said than done. The city looked hard and found an alternative microfiche reader-printer from Eastman Kodak Co., but it cost twice as much." The "service 3M supplies on this is phenomenal," a city official was quoted as saying. So despite New York law, Kodak, the "clean" bidder, was passed up in favor of a "contaminated" 3M.[22]

Others, however, found the pressures on the local government level too much to bear. In March 1987 Xerox became the twenty-fourth company to announce its withdrawal from South Africa since the beginning of that year. Xerox Chairman David T. Kearns, an outspoken opponent of disinvestment, admitted that the company had been forced to do so by local governments that boycotted its products and services because of its South African links. Not every US executive displayed the same candor as Kearns, but it was clear that the potential loss of business at home was an important incentive to disinvest.

The Massachusetts state legislature started a trend in 1983 by passing a bill, over the veto of its governor, requiring divestment of all pension fund monies invested in corporations and banks doing business with South Africa. Connecticut soon followed suit by prohibiting state funds from investing in corporations with South African links. So did Michigan. On 26 September 1986, when California's Republican Governor George Deukmejian signed a law requiring the withdrawal of $11.4 billion in public funds from companies operating in South Africa, his became the nineteenth state to apply such sanctions. As a conservative and close associate of Reagan, Deukmejian strongly opposed sanctions in principle, but he had no alternative. It had become politically prudent to support disinvestment. Los Angeles Mayor Tom Bradley, however, was driven by more than political expediency as he steered his city toward sanctions against South Africa. As a prominent Black American with strong anti-apartheid convictions, he had long been in the front of the anti-apartheid struggle.

In November 1989, the giant brokerage firm Merrill Lynch followed others that had succumbed to stringent rules adopted by the city of Los Angeles, when it announced cessation of all trading in South African stock. This decision, prompted by the fear of losing out on billions of dollars in city pension fund business, required Merrill's precious metals division to produce research reports on gold without ever mentioning South Africa—the world's major producer. It was a matter of choosing between handling billions in local pension funds or making a few millions on South African gold and industrial stock trading.

But US firms with operations in South Africa faced not only pressures at home but a worsening economy. "To date, the greatest force for disinvestment appears to be South Africa's three-year-old recession," wrote the *Wall Street Journal* on 30 April 1985. At that time, however, the number of departures was still a mere trickle—with only 16 recorded as having left South Africa between 1983 and 1985. Soon, however, the trickle turned into a flood as the economy continued to worsen and disinvestment pressures intensified. Many US companies simply reached the point where dwindling profits in South Africa no longer justified the hassle at home.

While Crocker and Shultz tried their utmost to prevent Congress from stealing their show in Washington, city and state authorities had a field day in making their own foreign policy decisions by introducing sanctions against South Africa. The State Department showed no hesitation in taking legal action against the state of Maine when it dabbled in foreign policy by boycotting Canadian potatoes in a trade dispute with its northern neighbor. But it preferred not to challenge local governments on the South African sanctions issue. There were, however, some unsuccessful challenges from private quarters. In mid-July 1987 the pro-disinvestment forces won a major battle when Judge Martin Greenfield's Circuit Court ruled that Baltimore was within its rights in adopting an ordinance that required the sale by its pension fund of all South African-related stock. Greenfield rejected claims that it would lead to financial losses and violated federal jurisdiction over foreign policy. Even if there were losses, he argued, they "would be insubstantial when compared to the salutary moral principle which generated the ordinance."

In the ten years since 1976, when Madison, Wisconsin, became the first city to give business preference to firms without South African business links, sixty-five cities and an undertermined number of counties had adopted similar sanctions measures. Under constant pressure from the ACOA, the ICCR, and other anti-apartheid groups, State governments followed suit. In the late 1980s the list of cities and counties applying such sanctions ranged from well-known metropolitan centers such as New York, Los Angeles, Detroit and Houston to obscure places such as Cuyahoga, Sonomy, and Bergen County. States that followed Massachusetts' example and legislated sanctions against South Africa ranged from New York to California, Louisiana to Dakota.

In drafting their sanctions legislation, local authorities had a choice between a number of options. Most of them opted for one or a combination of the following:

1. A total ban on any purchase of South African goods.
2. Discrimination in favor of companies without South African links when buying products or services.

3. Prohibiting official transactions with or investment in banks that extended loans or conducted business with South Africa.
4. Divesting pension fund investments in stock issued by firms with South African links.

New York City demonstrated the difficulties in applying the second option when business considerations forced it to select 3M as a supplier over Kodak despite its continuing South African links. And when faced with demands to apply the fourth option, New York State Comptroller Edward V. Regan disclosed that the state pension fund decided not to sell stocks in US corporations with South African links because the estimated cost in extra fees and commissions would have totaled between $300 million to $600 million. "We're talking hundreds of millions of dollars in cost, to achieve nothing—a press release," Regan told the *Wall Street Journal* on 4 June 1987.[23] Regan's was, however, a rare dissent in the American pension fund landscape with its multibillions in public funds where most took steps to rid themselves of South African tainted stocks, regardless of the cost.

"The campuses are astir again and the issue is South Africa," wrote the *New York Times* on 2 April 1978. "Students and teachers want to attack that nation's racist policies through the power of the American corporations doing business there." In a fashion reminiscent of the Vietnam era, students, often mobilized by outsiders such as the ACOA, forced the selling of university stock in American corporations with South African ties. Tactics ranged from talk-to's to sit-ins, from reasoned debate to rowdy destructiveness. Seven years later apartheid was still a burning issue on campuses. Actions during April 1985 included padlocking and blockading a campus building at New York's Columbia University, a rally by 4,000 students at the Berkeley campus of the University of California, a sit-in at Rutgers University in New Brunswick, New Jersey, and the occupation of the administration building by students at Cornell University in Ithaca, New York. They were all designed to force universities into action on the issue of disinvestment.

Starting with the withdrawal at the beginning of 1977 of a modest $40,000 by Hampshire College from firms with South African connections, the list of divesting universities and colleges rapidly grew to an estimated 100 in 1986. While this small New England college set a trend, the funds involved in this first withdrawal paled in comparison with the hundreds of millions pulled out later by larger academic institutions. Soon corporations with South African links were confronted with threats from tens of colleges and universities, ranging from Ivy League institutions such as Yale and Princeton to lesser knowns with substantial monies at stake. In most cases the demands were quite specific. On 12 February 1985, the trustees of Stanford University at Palo Alto, California, voted to sell stock worth $5 million in Motorola if the company resumed sales of electronic gear to the South African military and police. On 14 February 1985, Harvard University revealed that it had sold its stock in Baker International after the company failed to produce proof that its South African operation followed "reasonably ethical standards."

It took Harvard some time to implement total disinvestment from firms with ties to South Africa. Its first partial divestment, involving some $50 million, came in 1981. This was followed by the action against Baker International in 1985 and another decision in 1986 to withdraw $2.8 million from companies with South African involvement. But this gradual divestment could not prevent the final day of reckoning. It came in June 1987 when Bishop Tutu joined forces with students and other alumni demanding a complete sell-off of "tainted" stock by Harvard, his alma mater. The call for total divestment from companies with interests in South Africa was made during the election of Harvard's new board of overseers and affected some $250 million (500 million rand) of the university's total of $2.5 billion (8 billion rand) in stock.

At the beginning of 1979, when the first calls were made for divestment by Harvard University, President Derek Bok made an impassioned plea for its rejection in an open letter. It was, he felt, his responsibility to manage Harvard's resources to further the normal academic purposes of the university and not to support causes or combat injustices for which it was not directly responsible. "Unless we choose to live like hermits in the desert, we must all be linked in direct and innumerable ways to the wrongs of the world—through the goods we buy, the taxes we pay, the services we use, the investments we make," Bok wrote. In any event, "universities cannot actually exert much direct economic pressure against American corporations by selling their stock, because such action will scarcely depress the value of the shares, let alone force management to change its policies."[24] Bok, as it turned out, was only half right. While the sell-off by universities of "tainted" stock rarely depressed share prices, their disinvestment pressures and all the accompanying unsavory publicity did nudge several corporations toward ending their involvement with South Africa.

At Harvard as at most other campuses, disinvestment piggy-backed on a variety of other "social responsibility" issues, including demands for better funding of Black studies programs, scholarships for minority students, and increased minority teacher recruitment. In view of the continuing US cooperation with South Africa in the nuclear field, an alliance was formed on the Dartmouth campus under the leadership of the ACOA that called for divestment from both nuclear and apartheid-linked stock. While Derek Bok and other administrators were reasoning in the boardrooms and academic journals against such divestment, the anti-apartheid activists blared out their message in stadiums and the streets. At the time when Bok's open letter appeared, the Amandla concert was held at Harvard Stadium. This "Benefit Concert to Celebrate Liberation in Southern Africa" with its all-day performances by Black stars in July 1979 drew a crowd of 18,000. It not only raised money for Black African nationalists, but also the level of awareness for disinvestment.

"The South African issue of apartheid was responsible for rejuvenating student organizations and action on college and university campuses," George Houser, founder of the ACOA, contends.[25] In the end this issue had more staying power than Vietnam. Pressures for disinvestment on American campuses continued unabated for the next ten years. Such was the pressure that even the prestigious apolitical Smithsonian Institute could not escape. On 13 May 1987, it finally announced that it had decided to sell all its holdings, worth $27 million, in US firms with ties in South Africa.

Some corporations fought back. Although its control resided outside the United States, Royal Dutch/Shell was targeted for boycott action in the United States over its involvement in South Africa. However, when its filling stations across America were picketed, the Dutch oil giant showed the same resoluteness that later prompted it to go to court over similar boycotts by local authorities in Holland and Britain. It won in both instances. The Dutch government ruled that the town of Hilversum did not have the authority to discriminate against Shell because of its South African business ties. In Britain the Lewisham borough of London was restrained by court order from boycotting Shell for the same reason.

The American oil giant, Mobil, escaped consumer boycott action at the pump with good deeds in both South Africa and the United States. In 1977 it became one of the original signatories of the Sullivan Principles. In the person of Sal Marzullo, Mobil maintained an able presence in the Sullivan Committee that monitored compliance to these principles by American firms active in South Africa. He was chairman of the Committee's Industry Support Unit for ten years and later its administrator. When the US Corporate Council was formed to give further weight to American business responsibility in South Africa, Mobil chief executive Allan Murray was elected one of its three co-chairmen. In South Africa Mobil made grants to a variety of Black programs and its American beneficiaries included Coretta Scott King, who received $20,000 toward her trip to South Africa in September 1986, to attend the enthronement of Archbishop Tutu.[26] King's last-minute cancellation of a scheduled meeting with President P. W. Botha at the insistence of anti-apartheid activists in South Africa made this donation something of an embarrassment at the time.

Still, Mobil seemed to have developed an impenetrable armor against sanctions pressures. Even the decision by the Rev. Leon Sullivan on 3 June 1986, to abandon his code of conduct and call for a complete corporate pullout from South Africa "within nine months" did not derail Mobil. "We will now have to carry out the Sullivan Principles without Sullivan," Mobil head Allan Murray announced. Said Sal Marzullo about Mobil's future plans: "A circle of hard-core companies will always remain."[27] But even Mobil finally had to pack up and leave in 1989. The straw that broke the camel's back was an obscure tax provision—dubbed "the Rangel Amendment" after its sponsor,

Rep. Charles Rangel (D-New York)—that slipped through as part of the 1988 Deficit Reconciliation Bill.

This Bill, originally introduced at Reagan's request to enact federal tax increases and savings to help reduce the nation's deficit, became the vessel for non-related items. The Rangel Amendment and a number of other measures were attached like barnacles to the main bill to ensure passage through Congress and the White House. It disallowed foreign tax credits on the income earned by American companies in South Africa and made the cost of doing business in South Africa prohibitive by slapping an additional 57 percent to 72 percent in taxes on business operations there. Congressional sources claimed that it would raise the price of operating in South Africa by some $57 million between 1988 and 1990. Although President Reagan personally opposed this new sanctions measure, he had no alternative but to sign it into law together with the main bill, which he originally requested.

On 28 April 1989, Chief Executive Allan Murray was finally forced to announce Mobil's withdrawal from South Africa after having operated there for more than ninety years. The decision was taken on economic grounds, Murray explained, as the Rangel Amendment, which prevented it from taking credit for taxes paid in South Africa, meant that Mobil would be shelling out 72 percent of its profits in taxes. Although he found it difficult "because we continue to believe that our presence and our actions have contributed greatly to economic and social progress" in South Africa, "very foolish laws" made it impossible to remain. "The economics were such," he said, "that it was in our shareholders interest to make the sale."[28]

The anti-apartheid forces were elated to see the largest remaining American corporate presence in South Africa disappear. It was chalked up as a major victory in the sanctions battle. Mobil sold its $400 million in assets (including a refinery and 1,150 gasoline stations) to a South Africa's General Corporation (Gencor) at fire-sale prices. Gencor reportedly paid $155 million, after taxes, plus $10 million of the 1989 earnings. This deal was of such magnitude and impact that it caused the financial rand to drop to its lowest level in more than two years—$0.2372 or 4.2150 rand to the dollar.

In June 1987, however, Mobil and others were still standing firm. Even a call by Leon Sullivan, then a member of the Reagan advisory committee, for everyone to pack up and leave South Africa, could not move it or several other signatories of the Sullivan Principles to fold their tents. Apart from Mobil, giants such as American Cyanamid Corp., Goodyear Tire & Rubber Co., Union Carbide, Minnesota Mining & Manufacturing Co., Johnson & Johnson, Unisys Corp., and RJR Nabisco refused to disinvest. Some spoke about continuing the Sullivan Principles without Sullivan, while Nabisco talked about establishing a new independent review process of its own.[29] Sullivan's decision to call for total withdrawal, however, robbed corporate America and the Reagan administration of one of their most useful defenses against disinvestment—one that helped US corporations to defeat no less than 127 anti-apartheid-inspired shareholder resolutions demanding disinvestment during the first half of 1987. Linked to a fiery activist like Leon Sullivan, the Sullivan Principles, with their call for desegregated workplaces, equal employment practices and pay, training for non-Whites and other Black advancement programs, had validity. Without Sullivan's endorsement they had lost their effectiveness.

Left to its own devices, corporate America tried to come up with alternative strategies to blunt the attacks on its presence in South Africa. Union Carbide announced that profits from its South African operations would go into a fund to aid the Blacks. Coca-Cola offered shares to Black retailers. But for some the writing was on the wall. In June 1987 when Sullivan deserted their ranks, the corporations in Table 2 were listed by the IRRC as the top twenty American employers that still had a presence in South Africa.

Table 2.
Top 20 US Companies in South Africa —May 1987

Company	Employees
Mobil Corp.	3,013
RJR Nabisco Inc.	2,479
Goodyear Tire & Rubber Co.	2,471
USG Corp.(Formerly US Gypsum Co.)	2,239
Caltex Petroleum Corp.	2,140
Johnson & Johnson	1,376
Emhart Corp.	1,159
United Technologies Corp.	1,060
American Brands Inc.	1,044
Joy Mfg. Co.	1,000
Minnesota Mining & Mfg. Co.	878
Xerox Corp.	824
Baker International Corp.	749
Colgate Palmolive Co.	696
H.H. Robertson Co.	694
Crown Cork & Seal Co.	693
Unisys Corp.	693
American Cyanamid Co.	689
PepsiCo Inc.	688
Dresser Industries Inc.	682

Source: Investor Responsibility Research Center, Washington, D.C.,1987.

At that stage Emhart, Xerox and Pepsi had already indicated their intention to withdraw. Eventually Mobil, Nabisco, Unisys, Black & Decker, Foster Wheeler, Sentry, and Union Carbide joined the exodus.

A special UN report released on 28 August 1989, found that more than half of the 277 companies that pulled out of South Africa since 1984 were American firms. Both the International Chamber of Commerce and the Washington-based Investor Responsibility Research Center (IRRC) disputed these figures as too low. The chamber told UN hearings in Geneva during September 1989 that over 550 foreign firms had disinvested from South Africa since 1985, leaving large-scale unemployment and poverty among Blacks. In its report, *International Business in SA 1990*, the IRRC claimed that 393 companies had disinvested since 1984 with US companies leading the way with 209 departures, followed by British companies (84), German (34), and Canadian (16). Disinvestment, according to an estimate by the South African Reserve Bank Governor Gerhard de Kock on 6 February 1989, caused a net capital outflow of 25 billion rand (more than $10 billion) during the previous four years.

Toward the end of 1986, the Comprehensive Anti-Apartheid Act and a spate of other congressional, state, and city sanctions laws forced a growing number of American corporations to curtail their business with South Africa. It was, however, not only these laws themselves, but sagging profits and continuing unrest and violence in South Africa that caused many of them to reduce their exposure or to pull out altogether.

The larger American firms that still remained followed the example of South African business, circumventing the Botha government and trying to cut their own deal with the ANC, which had now begun to look like a government-in-waiting. Despite frantic efforts by the Botha government to regain the confidence of the local and overseas business community, the rift continued to grow. The sanctions of the markets were taking their toll.

NOTES

1. Herman Nickel interview, August 1993.
2. *Sunday Tribune*, 25 November 1979.
3. De Villiers, D. and J., *PW*, pp. 160-161.
4. *The Citizen; The Star*, Johannesburg, 2 February 1981.
5. De Villiers, op. cit. p. 162
6. Ibid., p. 164.
7. *Rand Daily Mail*, 8 October 1983.
8. Pottinger, B., *The Imperial Presidency: PW Botha-The First Ten Years*, p. 121.
9. Leape, J., Baskin, B., and Underhill, S., *Business in the Shadow of Apartheid*, p. 137.

10. *Business Day,* 10 October 1985.

11. *The Airmail Star,* Johannesburg, 17 November 1987.

12. *Wall Street Journal,* 26 October 1986.

13. *Wall Street Journal,* 6 November 1986.

14. *Wall Street Journal,* 24 August 1987.

15. *Computer Mail,* Supplement of *Financial Mail,* Johannesburg, 26 February 1988.

16. Kibbe, J., and Hauck, D., *Leaving South Africa: The Impact of US Corporate Disinvestment,* IRRC, July 1988.

17. Ibid., p. i.

18. Ibid., p. 33.

19. Ibid., p. 4.

20. *New Nation,* Johannesburg, 28 April 1991.

21. *Washington Post,* 19 March 1987.

22. *Wall Street Journal,* 1 September 1989.

23. *Wall Street Journal,* 4 June 1987.

24. Bok, Derek, "Reflections on Divestment of Stock: An Open Letter to the Harvard Community," Supplement to the *Harvard University Gazette,* 6 April 1979, p. 6.

25. George Houser interview, May 1993.

26. Sal Marzullo interview, June 1993.

27. *Wall Street Journal,* 4 June 1987.

28. *Wall Street Journal* and *New York Times,* 29 April 1989.

29. *Wall Street Journal,* 4 June 1987.

SANCTIONS APPLIED AGAINST SOUTH AFRICA
BY ITS MAJOR TRADING PARTNERS
IN 1989

	IMPORT BANS						EXPORT BANS				FINANCIAL			
	Iron & Steel	Coal	Agricultural Products	Parastatal Products	Krugerrands	Uranium	Oil & Petroleum	Computer Equipment	Nuclear Cooperation	Arms	Private Loan	Government Loans	New Investment	Air Links
Australia	●	○	●		●	○	●	●	●	●	○	●	●	●
Austria		○		●				●		●		●		
Belgium	●			●			●		●	●				
Canada	●	●	●		○	●	●	●	●	●	○	●	○	●
Denmark	●	●	●	●	●		●	●	●	●		●	●	●
France	●	●			●				●	●			●	
Germany	●				●					●			●	
Israel	●				●					●		●	●	
Italy	●									●		○		
Japan	●			●				●		●	●	●	●	
Netherlands	●	○			●		●		●	●				
Norway	●	●	●	●	●	●	●	●	●	●	●	●	●	●
Portugal	●			●			●		●			●		
South Korea											●	●	●	
Spain	●			●			●		●	●		○		●
Sweden	●	●	●	●	●	●	●	●	●	●	●	●	●	●
Switzerland									●			●		
Taiwan														
United Kingdom	●			●			●	●	●	●	●	●	○	
United States	●	●	●	●	●	○	●	●	●	●	●	●	○	●

● Mandatory   ○ Voluntary

Illustration by author.

12

Erecting Barriers

> For the past few months Crocker and his team have been absorbed in the dreary business of erecting the new barriers required by the law. For Congress this is an interlude before the imperatives of the 1988 [US] elections produce another round of sanctioneering.
>
> *Simon Barber, Washington, early 1987*[1]

Early in 1987 not only the Americans but also the South African government were busy erecting barriers of their own. While shying away from counter-sanctions out of necessity, the Botha government took every opportunity to express its displeasure with the actions of Congress and its disappointment with the Reagan White House for failing to prevail. Pressures were already building in Washington for additional sanctions.

Instead of resigning, as many had expected after the apparent demise of constructive engagement, Chester Crocker decided to stay on until the end of the Reagan term. Anxious to rescue some kind of victory out of the jaws of a bruising defeat, he decided to take up the Namibian issue, where he left off when the battle with Congress over sanctions interfered. First he had to win back the trust and confidence of Pretoria. It would not be easy. He now found even the formerly friendly Pik Botha most uncooperative. In December 1986, when he offered help in furthering negotiations between South African Whites and Blacks, Crocker was rebuffed by Foreign Minister Pik Botha. "How reliable is it? What would Congress do with any deal I made with your government?" a newspaper reported Botha as saying.[2] On 23 December 1986, Botha, citing congressional sanctions, announced that visas were refused to two groups of twenty US congressmen who asked for permission to visit South Africa on "fact-finding" trips during January 1987.

But not all of Crocker's problems in trying to get the Namibia talks back on track were related to the chill that had descended on Pretoria after the adoption of the CAAA. Some were of the Reagan administration's own making. On 10 February 1987, it was hoisted on its own petard when an advisory committee, appointed in terms of the preemptive presidential executive sanctions order of 1985, brought out its report calling for more sanctions and "a new policy" to replace "constructive engagement." The report recommended stronger ties with South Africa's Black opposition and urged the United States to press its allies into passing sanctions as tough as those contained in the CAAA. It suggested "additional diplomatic and economic steps," including a total trade embargo and a ban on the purchase of South African gold, if other steps failed to bring the Botha government to its senses.

As required by the CAAA, the State Department on 2 April 1987, submitted a report to Congress on the sanctions performance of other nations. It cited violations by several nations of the UN arms embargo against South Africa. It identified Israel, a valued ally of Pretoria, and several European manufacturers as culprits. To the chagrin of the Botha government, the United States not only coerced Israel into ceasing its arms sales to South Africa but also into adopting wide-ranging economic sanctions. Japan was taken to task for having filled the trade gap left by the United States. Anxious not to put its lucrative multibullion dollar favorable trade balance with the United States at risk for a much smaller volume of business with South Africa, Japan readily agreed to adopt more severe sanctions of its own in March 1988.

President Botha started 1987 in a surprisingly conciliatory fashion. His New Year's message on 1 January 1987, was a calm review of the events that led to the adoption of the CAAA. Although he felt it "ironic and disturbing that all this came about while we were in the very process of moving forward with our reform program" Botha now conceded that South Africa could not stand in isolation in the international economic order. Therefore, the normalization of its foreign relations would receive his highest priority "without abandoning the principles which should guide a country like South Africa."

Opening the new session of parliament on Friday, 30 January 1987, the South African leader once again stressed the need not "to become isolated from the international community" despite "the regrettable trend of international interference and regardless of the motives behind it." The previous year, he complained, "South Africa's international position was characterized increasingly by intensified pressures and punitive actions." But this, he pointed out, was not of recent origin. "Today we are witnessing an accumulation of historical forces and events that have been gaining momentum, especially since the end of the Second World War," Botha explained. "This was starkly evident before the National Party came to power. Even the internationally-acclaimed United Party Prime Minister of South Africa, General Jan Smuts, had cause to complain bitterly about the prejudice, abuse and dishonesty South Africa had to endure at the hands of cynical and sanctimonious antagonists abroad. That was in 1946."[3]

Botha had called an election on 6 May 1987—the first in six years—to silence critics who claimed that as a result of large-scale defections to both the left and right, the National Party had lost its mandate to rule. "South Africa must stand united against the unwarranted interference in our domestic affairs," Botha explained.[4] Like his predecessor, John Vorster in 1977, he also chose to play the anti-American theme to win votes. While Vorster attacked the Carter administration for threatening sanctions against South Africa, Botha targeted Congress. Just as Vorster did in 1977, President Botha now relied on the able and enthusiastic assistance of Foreign Minister Botha.

On 3 February 1987, Pik Botha launched a scathing attack on the United States Congress. Speaking at a briefing for foreign correspondents, he charged Congress with shared responsibility for killings in South Africa's Black townships. Referring to the lawmakers in Washington as "hopeless, vengeful and ignorant," he announced that anti-United States rhetoric would be part of the election campaign to help ensure a victory in the May 6 general election. By imposing sanctions on South Africa, Botha claimed, Congress had encouraged Black militants and made it more difficult for moderates who wanted dialogue with the government. The Americans, he said, can send rockets to the planets, but when it comes to judging decisions on earth, they were "hopeless." Citing his recent refusal of visas to group of American congressmen, he said it was time to show the American Congress that it would not determine South Africa's future.[5] An equally combative President Botha told a National Party convention that the outside world should not "underestimate" the Afrikaner: "I'm not a jellyfish, we're not a nation of jellyfish," he said. He threatened punitive economic measures against neighboring states in retaliation for their own calls for sanctions. "South Africa," Botha claimed, "is the scapegoat for America's bad conscience."[6]

South Africa's other nemesis, the ANC, also served as a convenient target during the hard-fought election campaign. By attacking the exiled organization, the Botha government not only tried to keep its own right wing from defecting to Andries Treurnicht's Conservative Party but to discredit the liberal PFP for having talks with "terrorists." The PFP had initiated talks with the ANC on 12 November 1985, when its leader, Frederik van Zyl Slabbert, accompanied by the party's foreign affairs spokesman, Colin Eglin, and law and order expert Peter Gastrow, journeyed to Zambia to meet with ANC Secretary-General Alfred Nzo. In a joint statement at the conclusion of the talks, both sides stressed the need to end apartheid and to establish a "united, non-racial democratic South Africa." They expressed differences, however, over the use of force.

The National Party returned to power after the May 1987 elections with a slight increase in parliamentary seats despite a marked shift in the popular White vote to the political right. Andries Treurnicht's right-wing Conservative Party made a strong showing and won several extra seats to become the country's official opposition. The main loser in the election was the liberal PFP, which lost eight of its previous twenty-seven seats, and its electoral ally, the New Republic Party, which lost four of its five seats.

While the PFP lost in White support for talking to the ANC, the banned organization itself had gained stature abroad, as evidenced by the meeting between US Secretary of State George Shultz and exiled Oliver Tambo in Washington on 28 January 1987. Both sides called the exchange "serious and substantive," and Tambo took the opportunity to urge the United States to encourage other Western nations to follow its example and impose tough sanctions against South Africa.

It was no longer possible to summarily dismiss the ANC as a Communist "terrorist" organization. But the Botha government kept trying. Reacting to a suggestion by US Secretary of State Shultz that South Africa should negotiate with the ANC, Foreign Minister Botha responded sharply. Shultz, he said, should realize that the onslaught against South Africa was aimed in the first place against the United States and that there were many African leaders who were "just as concerned as the South African Government about America's weak and wavering action against Communist intervention in Africa."[7]

Despite their government's disapproval, private South Africans continued contact with the ANC. After a nationwide furor in the press over refusal of passports to eight Stellenbosch university students for a meeting in November 1986 with the ANC, the Botha government grudgingly allowed a large group of academics and politicians to travel to Dakar for discussions with the ANC in July 1987. Van Zyl Slabbert, now president of the newly established Institute for a Democratic Alternative in South Africa (IDASA), led the group. Even President Reagan felt obliged to personally praise Senegalese President Abdou Diouf for acting as host to these talks in the Senegalese capital. "The Dakar meeting constitutes a double victory—a prelude to a kind of legitimization of the liberation movement and an acceptance of the fact that nothing positive can happen inside South Africa without the participation of the ANC," commented *The Citizen* on 20 July 1987.

Despite official disapproval of the Dakar conference and continued attempts to discredit the ANC as a Communist-inspired terrorist organization, the Botha government had already started secret talks of its own. Much of it revolved around meetings with the imprisoned Nelson Mandela. The public got its first glimpse of this behind-the-scenes activity on 16 June 1987, when Deputy Minister of Information Stoffel van der Merwe deemed it necessary to defend in public his willingness to meet with imprisoned Black activists. "I have a job to do, and if it is part of the job to talk to someone in jail or detention, that mere fact will not stand in my way," he said. In September

1987, however, Constitutional Development Minister Chris Heunis officially denied rumors that the South African government had conveyed its desire for discussions with the exiled ANC leadership through intermediaries such as Van Zyl Slabbert's Dakar mission. Later it would be revealed, however, that at about this time an official delegation journeyed with President Botha's approval to Frankfurt in Germany, where members conferred in secret with the exiled ANC leadership. Tambo publicly challenged Pretoria on 25 September 1987, to back up its "approaches" with the necessary steps that could lead to negotiations. At a minimum, he demanded, the government had to lift the state of emergency, legalize the ANC, and free its jailed leaders.

By 1987 it had become clear that something had to be done with the world's most celebrated prisoner—ANC leader Nelson Mandela. When diagnosed in August 1988 as suffering from tuberculosis, Mandela was hastily transferred from Cape Town's Pollsmoor Prison to a state-run hospital for treatment. Afterward he was sent to a private facility for convalescence. On 7 December 1988 he was moved once again to comfortable quarters at a guarded house on the grounds of the well-appointed Victor Verster prison farm at Paarl, thirty miles from Cape Town. Outsiders interpreted these moves as release-in-stages to avoid an outburst of Black revolutionary fervor and to dampen possible right-wing backlash. The South African government, it was believed, not only wished to get Mandela off its hands to avoid anything happening to him in prison, but to stave off further sanctions as the international economic sanctions campaign kept feeding off the ANC leader's imprisonment. Mandela's frequent relocation and the release in November 1987 of another prominent ANC leader, Govan Mbeki, fueled rumors that Mandela's freeing was imminent.

The clamor for additional sanctions was growing stronger. In South Africa the most powerful Black trade union gave its support. At its second national meeting in July 1987 the Black Congress of South African Trade Unions (COSATU) voted unanimously in favor of sanctions and disinvestment and called for the complete withdrawal of all foreign companies. Previous withdrawals of American and other multinationals were dismissed as "nothing more than camouflage." COSATU also called for the banning of emigration by South Africans, overseas travel by South African tourists, business managers and public servants, the recruitment of skilled workers abroad, and landing and air space rights for South African Airways.[8] Reviewing the first year of US sanctions in terms of the CAAA in October 1987, Archbishop Tutu also demanded tougher measures, such as denying South Africa access to international money markets, cutting off landing rights everywhere for South African Airways, and an embargo on telephone and telex links.[9]

In the meantime, President Reagan had the onerous task of reporting to Congress the progress made in South Africa during the first year after the passing of the Comprehensive Anti-Apartheid Act (CAAA) of 1986. This report on 2 October 1987, was required by the CAAA to help Congress determine whether further sanctions were necessary. His ambassador to South Africa, Edward Perkins, had already expressed his own viewpoint in a speech in Johannesburg on 19 August 1987. While conceding that it was hard to assess its effect "in practical terms," the Black envoy described sanctions as "a great success" insofar as it expressed "the anguish of the American people about the plight of Black South Africa."[10] In his October review President Reagan regretted being "unable to report significant progress leading to the end of apartheid and the establishment of nonracial democracy in South Africa in the 12-month period since the enactment of the act." But he implored Congress, instead of passing new sanctions that would have a "negative rather than positive" effect, to allow a "period of active and creative diplomacy" to help to bring Black and White together at the negotiating table.[11]

Responding to a leaked copy of the report, a bipartisan group of thirty-three members of the House of Representatives sent a letter to the White House on 1 October 1987, demanding further measures against South Africa in view of the "abominable and deteriorating situation." After the official release of the report on 2 October, the chairman of the House Subcommittee on African Affairs, Rep. Howard Wolpe (D-Michigan), accused Reagan of being "an apologist for the regime in South Africa." At a press conference the next day, Wolpe and his colleagues in the Congressional foreign policy committees urged Reagan to "apply the law" and introduce new sanctions. Shortly afterward the House began hearings to consider proposals for new sanctions and the Senate followed suit on 22 October 1987. Senator Edward Kennedy (D-Massachusetts) released a report by the General Accounting Office (GAO) accusing the Reagan Administration of having failed to carry out some provisions of the CAAA and ignoring other measures of the sanctions Act.[12]

Suddenly Pretoria was on the move again, trying to strengthen Reagan's hand in the new sanctions battle. In a speech on 23 November 1987, before the prestigious Bavarian Hans-Seidel Foundation in Munich, Foreign Minister Botha made promises of further reforms. "We accept that White supremacy must end and that the division of power is the only way to govern South Africa justly," he said. He gave no specifics. Earlier that same month President P. W. Botha shared a platform with Chief Mangosuthu Buthelezi for the first time in two years. The occasion was the launch of a government-inspired Joint Executive Council (JEC) in Natal. The Zulu, by far the majority in this province, were allocated five seats as opposed to two for Whites, two for Asians and one for Coloreds. But the JEC had no real legislative or fiscal authority beyond making recommendations on matters such as health services, roads and conservation affecting the province. Buthelezi, a pragmatic politician, nonetheless accepted the new authority as a first step toward merging Natal and KwaZulu into one multiracial government. A detailed plan for such a merger had already been stitched together at the so-called Natal *Indaba* or constitutional conference in 1986. It was rejected by the Botha government because it did not provide guarantees for the White minority.

Instead, the government pushed its own concept of power-sharing on a nationwide basis. It envisaged a National Statutory Council consisting of a thirty-six member Black advisory body representing a mix of homeland leaders, representatives of Black urban communities, and other racial groups— presided over by President Botha. The idea had little chance of acceptance among Blacks. Still, Botha, with the help of his billowing bureaucratic machinery, kept tinkering and tuning, trying to find the right formula to get something suitable for Blacks on the road of reform without endangering the White minority. In a speech before parliament in April 1988, Botha rolled out the latest version of the National Council plan. The final plan proposed nine regional elected bodies for Blacks living in a "common South Africa." They would function on an equal footing with the provincial councils and the non-independent homelands. Drawn from this layer of bodies would be another layer of "multi-racial policy makers." Ultimately a few Blacks could be appointed to the cabinet. The bottom line was preservation of White dominance.

With this as his best offer, it was obviously not within Botha's power to satisfy overseas demands or the expectations of either the radical Black opposition in South Africa or its more moderate opponents such as Buthelezi. "How can I as a Black leader believe that the State President is serious about his commitment to reform?" asked Buthelezi during an address before a White audience in Pretoria early in 1988, "What does he mean by reform? I just do not know."[13] Shortly afterwards, in a major policy statement before the KwaZulu Legislative Assembly in Ulundi, Buthelezi administered final rites to the Botha efforts of reform. "Botha's lack of courage compounds the tragedy of him as an Afrikaner on the crossroads of history," Buthelezi said. "He is a political Midas gone wrong. He touches gold and it turns to ashes."[14]

Buthelezi's view was shared by a growing number of Whites—frustrated liberals and White business managers who were now feeling the pinch of sanctions and a worsening economy. But from the right, President Botha was assailed with the same vigor for giving in to demands and endangering White privilege and power. Faced by the gaping abyss between his concept of partial power-sharing and real majority rule as demanded by the world, Botha elected not to jump but to turn around and try to regain the support of the right. On 24 February 1988, he clamped down, banning seventeen leading Black opposition groups, including COSATU, and prohibiting them from engaging in any political action to prevent "a revolutionary climate." This action sent shock waves through South Africa and around the world.

Coming shortly before two important parliamentary by-elections in the Transvaal, this drastic action did not, as apparently intended, prevent the Conservative Party from winning decisive victories with increased majorities in Standerton and Schweizer-Reneke on 3 March 1988. Instead, this clampdown early in 1988 provided Nobel Laureate Tutu with a golden opportunity to place the issue of sanctions back on the front-burner. "The government's idea of reform is to smash all possible political opposition in the country, no matter how peaceful and lawful, and to rule with the jackboot," he complained. Fellow UDF patron, the Rev. Allan Boesak, echoed the sentiments. "Every single peaceful action we can take has now been criminalized," he said.[15] In Washington, State Department spokesman Charles Redman announced that the United States was "appalled" at what it considered "a giant step backward." In protest, the Reagan administration instructed its diplomats to boycott South Africa's Republic Day functions, he said.

Not satisfied with mere words of condemnation and symbolic gestures, the House of Representatives sprang into action. Its Foreign Affairs Committee approved legislation barring all investment in South Africa and imposing a near-total embargo on trade. The legislation, sponsored by African Affairs Subcommittee Chairman Howard Wolpe was passed along to the floor of the House by a vote of twenty-seven against fourteen. The Wolpe proposal prompted a spate of other new sanctions bills over the next few months. The most comprehensive was one introduced on 22 March 1988, by Rep. Ron Dellums (D-California) and co-sponsored by ninety-five other members. It proposed a ban on all US investment in and loans to South Africa and prohibited all imports from South Africa except strategic minerals. It also proposed to preclude US subsidiaries of foreign companies with South African investments or links from obtaining US coal, gas or petroleum leases—a measure that was aimed at foreign multinationals such as Royal Dutch/Shell, British Petroleum, and Total Petroleum. Dellums also joined Senators Alan Cranston (D-California), Edward Kennedy (D-Massachusetts) and Carl Levin (D-Michigan) in pushing for a ban on the importation of strategic minerals from South Africa—unless the president could certify that supplies were not available elsewhere. There was no mention in their proposal of any ban on purchases from the Soviet Union.

The Reagan administration lobbied hard to defeat the Dellums Bill, arguing that it would end virtually all American exports to South Africa, costing America more than a billion dollars in earnings, and force US companies to get rid of their total assets worth almost $1 billion at "fire sale prices." In response to White House claims that the Dellums Bill would result in the loss of jobs for Black South Africans, its supporters in Congress countered that only 46,000 jobs were at stake—and that the short-term suffering would be well worth the long-term gain of eliminating apartheid. Republicans complained that the sanctions bill was rammed through by the Democratic leadership hoping that any opposition to it could be portrayed as pro-apartheid in the upcoming US elections. Voting on the Dellums Bill, the Republicans contended, was conveniently timed to take place on the eve of the Republican National Convention.

At their convention in Atlanta the Democrats had made "comprehensive sanctions," as proposed by the Dellums Bill, part of their platform at the insistence of presidential aspirant the Rev. Jesse Jackson and Rep. Dellums himself. "The Democrats had to choose between helping the Blacks of South Africa or helping their own political interests," wrote Max Singer. "It was no contest." Singer charged them with hurting the Blacks under the pretense of helping. This was done according to "prescriptions insisted on by TransAfrica, the Congressional Black Caucus and Jesse Jackson."[16]

In his quest for the presidency, Jackson kept the South African issue alive in all his debates with the other Democratic primary contenders. The importance of this issue as a vote-getter was not lost on the other Democratic presidential hopefuls. During a primary debate in Miami in October 1987, Congressman Richard Gephardt from Missouri promised that as president he would be willing to arm the ANC to fight the South African government.[17] In many constituencies with substantial Black votes, a candidate's stand on apartheid and sanctions had become a litmus test for fitness to serve in Congress.

On 11 August 1988, the House of Representatives passed the Dellums Bill with its sweeping new set of sanctions by 244 votes against 132. The prospects of the measure passing into law, however, seemed unlikely in view of significant resistance in the Senate. But to make certain that the White House try its best to defeat this new sanctions legislation, President Botha warned on 12 August 1988, that if the Dellums Bill became law, it might "obstruct or make impossible" the tentative peace process underway in Angola and Namibia.

At this stage Chester Crocker was on the verge of an important breakthrough in Namibia. After allowing for the immediate anger in Pretoria in the wake of the CAAA to subside, Chester Crocker had brought all the interested parties together and brokered a deal whereby both Cuban and South African troops would withdraw and Namibia gain its independence under UN supervision. The first day of November 1988 was set as the target date for the implementation of UN Resolution 435, which called for South Africa's withdrawal from Namibia and independence. UN-supervised elections was scheduled for July 1989. It was at this critical stage that President Botha threatened to scrap the tentative agreement on Namibia unless the Dellums Bill was defeated. So the Reagan administration doubled its efforts to ensure a vote against it in the Republican-controlled Senate. The Dellums Bill was rejected and the Namibian initiative saved.

In an apparent attempt to demonstrate to the world that South Africa still had friends and allies on the continent and even enjoyed the respect of a Communist neighbor, President Botha embarked on a whirlwind tour of four African countries during September and October 1988. First stop was Mozambique where he joined Marxist head of state Joachim Chissano on an inspection tour of Cabora Bassa Dam—damaged by the Renamo rebels who

once drew their support from the SADF. Botha promised assistance with re-
pairs before setting off to Malawi for a visit with South Africa's longtime
friend and ally, President Hastings Banda. Next he called on Zaire's poten-
tate, Mobutu Sese Seko, who had received millions in aid from South Africa
over the years and apparently expected more. Finally, he met with President
Felix Houphet-Boigny of the Ivory Coast, whose friendship with South Africa
dated back to the days when Mulder's Information Department first be-
friended him. Although critics noted that these visits, aside from the meeting
with Chissano, hardly broke new ground, P. W. Botha and his traveling companion, Foreign Minister Pik Botha, were elated. "Africa is talking to South
Africa," President Botha told reporters on his flight home on 2 October 1988.
"We are going to other African countries as well where we will be busy this
year and next."[18]

On 6 October 1988, the Bothas journeyed again—this time to Germany,
where they attended the funeral of Premier Franz Josef Strauss, a longtime
friend of South Africa. They spent the following ten days in meetings with
bankers, business leaders, and politicians in West Germany and Switzerland.
In a speech before a group of bankers in Zurich, President Botha accused
those who insisted on sanctions of furthering the objectives of forces hostile
to democracy and free enterprise: "Our case is that sanctions are aimed at
the destruction of the free enterprise system which, in turn, would lead to increased unemployment, lower standards of living, poverty and hunger." Those
who clamored for more sanctions "misjudge the people of South Africa if
they believe that pressure will influence them to deviate from their course,"
he said.[19]

The punitive measures under the CAAA together with European and
Japanese sanctions were evidently taking their toll in jobs and causing a certain degree of suffering. No one, however, seemed able to determine exactly
how much and where it hurt most. If the South African authorities knew, they
were not saying. So observers were left to their own devices to gauge the
damage, often weighing conflicting bits and pieces of information against
each other. In the United States, Congress relied on its General Accounting
Office (GAO) to assess the damage. After the first year it reported to the
Senate Foreign Relations Committee that sanctions imposed by the CAAA
had cut South Africa's exports to the United States by $417 million. South
Africa's total international trade loss as a result of sanctions was $624 mil-
lion, Congress was told. The US Department of Commerce revealed, however, that in 1988 South African imports from the US hit their highest level in
four years. Figures showed an increase of 37 percent to $1.24 billion between
January-September 1988, compared with the same period in 1987.

In December 1988, after the CAAA had been in place for more than two
years, South Africa reported exports worth 4.5 billion rand—the second highest monthly figure ever recorded. It represented an increase of 1.1 billion rand
or 32 percent over the figure for December 1987. At the same time, imports

dropped to 3.25 billion rand, the lowest since special surcharges were introduced in May 1988 to discourage "rampant imports as a result of boom
growth in certain sectors." Even after taking into account the almost 20 percent drop in the value of the rand against major currencies from December
1987 these December 1988 figures were described by analysts as remarkable.
At the same time, South Africa's important coal mining industry reported a
drop in exports during 1987 of between 5 million and 7.5 million tons.

According to a study by the Johannesburg brokerage firm of David Borkum
Hare, Americans in 1988 still held the largest chunk of South Africa's mining
stocks under foreign ownership—despite severe sanctions and disinvestment
pressures. Although US shareholding had dropped slightly from 11.5 percent
to 10.4 percent in 1988, it still exceeded British ownership, which dipped
from 7.7 percent to 7 percent, and European holdings, which increased
slightly from 2 percent to 2.2 percent. Even more astounding was the
performance of the Johannesburg Stock Exchange. In the first quarter of 1989,
according to the London *Financial Times,* the JSE outperformed virtually all
other exchanges around the world. The newspaper's index showed the JSE
exceeding the world average by 17 percent in dollar terms. Ascribing the
soaring price of South African industrials in part to a "hothouse" economy
despite efforts by the government to cool it, the *Times* found the performance
of precious metals shares scarcely logical in view of the low gold price, high
interest rates, and double-digit inflation.

Early in 1987 the first cases of sanctions-busting surfaced. In February 1987
American officials accused South African exporters of transferring cargoes
between ships in foreign ports to disguise their origin and re-registering South
African ships under other flags. One contravention under investigation was
the alleged entry of millions of dollars of South African lobster tails into
Massachusetts from Uruguay. In March 1987 the US authorities filed the first
criminal case under the CAAA against two Californians, George Pose and
Edward Bush. They were charged with attempting to smuggle sensitive military manuals to the South African military attaché in Washington. In
November 1989 a grand jury in Washington indicted two Americans and
three South Africans on charges of trying illegally to export thirty-eight
military gyroscopes to Armscor, the South African state-owned arms
manufacturer.

These and other instances were suspected to be only the surface ruptures of
a substantial underground flow of contraband materials between the United
States and South Africa. The South African government itself had set up a
committee to find ways to circumvent trade and financial strictures under the
leadership of an experienced expatriate Rhodesian. They were helped, in part
at least, by bureaucratic bungling in the United States. On 19 August 1989,
the General Accounting Office (GAO) complained to Congress that sanctions
against Pretoria had been hurt because the State Department failed to give

US Customs Service a specific list of South African goods barred from entering the country.

One of the first pieces of legislation to be introduced after the newly elected 101st US Congress was sworn in early in 1989 was yet another Dellums Bill—a harsher version of the one defeated by the Senate the previous year. In South Africa, however, this development almost went unnoticed as high political drama unfolded, starting on 18 January 1989, when President P. W. Botha was rushed from Westbrooke, his official residence in Cape Town, to nearby Constantiaberg clinic, after suffering a stroke. While convalescing in the same clinic where Nelson Mandela was treated for tuberculosis only a few months earlier, the South African leader's silence gave rise to speculation over his possible retirement. Constitutional Minister Chris Heunis was appointed acting president but Botha, back at Westbrooke in a matter of weeks, was reported to be working from a desk in his bedroom.

On 2 February 1989, Botha sent a surprise note to the National Party caucus meeting, announcing that he intended to separate the functions of state president and leader of the National Party. It was his wish that a new party leader be elected. After several votes, starting with four candidates—Constitutional Minister Heunis, Education Minister and Transvaal leader F. W. de Klerk, Finance Minister Barend du Plessis, and Foreign Minister Botha—de Klerk emerged the victor. On 2 March, Botha resumed his role as state president, putting an end to rumors that he would be relinquishing the presidency to de Klerk as well. In the power struggle that ensued, the National Party parliamentary caucus lined up almost unanimously behind de Klerk. After several weeks of in-fighting, the South African Broadcasting Corporation reported on 23 March 1989, that a tentative agreement had been reached at a cabinet meeting the day before. The deal was confirmed on 6 April, when Botha announced to parliament that he would resign as president after a general election on 6 September 1989, on the completion of his five-year term, instead of staying on until March 1990, as he originally intended.

Accompanied by his erstwhile opponent, Pik Botha, now a constant public companion, de Klerk's education in foreign affairs started with a trip to Western Europe during June 1989. The former education minister, however, needed little tutoring. His smooth and easy manner—in contrast to the more rigid and domineering style of his predecessor—solicited a good response in meetings with West German Chancellor Helmut Kohl, British Prime Minister Margaret Thatcher, and the leaders of Italy and Portugal. President-in-waiting de Klerk also stopped in at the Vatican before returning to South Africa on 27 June 1989. At an airport press conference in Johannesburg, de Klerk described his reception abroad as "polite" and "warm" and noted with satisfaction that no one had "expressed unrealistic expectations." His confidence under the bright lights and the smiling Pik Botha at his side reminded some onlookers of other times, when the now lonely and deserted P. W. Botha also returned from triumphant tours abroad with the same foreign minister.

Lonely P. W. Botha may have been, but not without the power of the highest office still at his command. Midway through his press conference de Klerk was signaled by telephone to cut his airport press conference short and return to Pretoria for a meeting with the president. This peremptory summons was seen by outsiders as another in a series of thinly veiled insults aimed at de Klerk as Botha reluctantly relinquished his post.[20] The final confrontation came on 11 August 1989, barely three weeks before the general election. At the center of the storm stood President Kenneth Kaunda of Zambia, who had told the press that he was receiving de Klerk on 28 August for discussions in Lusaka. President Botha responded by issuing a terse statement saying that his permission for such a visit had not been sought—as it should have been in terms of the constitution.

Foreign Minister Botha insisted that he had indeed consulted the state president before setting up this meeting. A public debate ensued. On 14 August 1989, President Botha summoned the cabinet to Tuynhuys in Cape Town. As he took his seat at the top of the horseshoe-shaped table of the cabinet room, Botha found himself faced with a choice between impeachment or resignation. In their riveting account of this final round, Alf Ries and Eben Dommisse described the atmosphere as quite tense and Botha as testy. At one stage when reference was made to his physical condition, President Botha reportedly snapped: "How many of you are sitting here with pills in your pockets?"[21]

In a nationwide telecast that same evening he informed the country of his decision to resign. During his announcement P. W. Botha repeated his version of the Kaunda controversy. He also revealed that if he were approached beforehand, he would have vetoed de Klerk's intended trip to Lusaka. As Kaunda aided and abetted the ANC which threatened to disrupt the upcoming election, the outgoing President Botha felt that it was unwise to have meetings with the Zambian leader at this time. There was no reason to believe that P. W. Botha felt any personal animosity toward Kaunda, with whom he also had meetings as early as April 1982. When news about Botha's illness was released, the Zambian president was one of the first heads of state to wish him a speedy recovery, "as Southern Africa needed his presence."[22] Now, despite Botha's protestations, de Klerk kept his appointment with Kaunda in Lusaka, arriving not as president-in-waiting but as acting president—a post in which he would be confirmed by the new parliament shortly after the general election of 6 September 1989.

On 6 September 1989, the National Party suffered its biggest electoral setback since assuming power in 1948. For the first time in twenty-eight years it failed to win at least half the support of the White electorate. The Conservative Party increased its seats from twenty-two to thirty-nine and the liberal Democratic Party grew from twenty-one to thirty-three seats. This left de Klerk's Nationalists with only ninety-three of the 123 seats it held before the election. An accomplished politician, de Klerk set out rationalizing near defeat into a resounding victory. By adding the votes in favor of the liberal Democratic Party to that of the National Party, he argued that "seventy percent of the whites voted for parties favoring renewal and reform" and "granting political rights" to Blacks. He called it a "clear mandate" for reform. But he hastened to deny that he had any plans to follow the "fatally flawed" agenda of the DP. Instead he espoused the merits of the "five year action plan" adopted by the National Party's Federal Congress in Pretoria on 29 June 1989. This vaguely worded program for the future promised South Africa's 23 million Blacks "democratic participation" in a new national government, but ruled out universal voting rights that would allow them to "dominate" the White minority.

De Klerk received what was described as "a routine" message of congratulations from President George Bush on 7 September 1989. It was left to a State Department spokeswoman, Margaret Tutwiler, to be more specific. Noting that de Klerk had received a "mandate for real change in South Africa" she announced that the Bush administration now expected him to take "concrete, specific action," including the release of Nelson Mandela and Walter Sisulu, the lifting of the state of emergency, the unbanning of the ANC and "all other anti-apartheid groups," and an end to violence from all sources. From the Capitol came a warning by Congressman Howard Wolpe (D-Michigan), chairman of the House Foreign Affairs Subcommittee on Africa, that the new South African state president should move quickly if he wished to keep the US Congress from passing further economic sanctions against South Africa.

George Walker Bush had been sworn in as America's new president on 20 January 1989. While no one expected him to stand as firm on South Africa as his conservative predecessor, his eagerness to promote harmony with Congress on this issue caught Pretoria by surprise. During a South African policy review in May 1989, the Bush staff made it clear they wanted to avoid the mistakes of President Ronald Reagan, whose "constructive engagement" had led him on a collision course with South African and American Black leaders as well as Congress. While Bush as vice president under Reagan had opposed the CAAA in 1986, his officials now publicly conceded that sanctions may have forced the White government to think more seriously about reforms. At the same time, new Secretary of State James Baker asked Congress to hold off on additional sanctions legislation to give the Bush administration time to implement its own, more dynamic South African policy.

As part of the new approach, Bush invited three prominent South African activists to the White House. Bishop Tutu and the Rev. Boesak were accompanied by the veteran White Afrikaner anti-apartheid cleric Beyers Naude on their mission to Washington to hear President Bush promise to use "pressure" and "leverage" to "influence Pretoria." Although Bush did not mention new sanctions, Tutu, who had accused Reagan of being "a racist pure and simple," found the new man in the White House to be a "catalyst for change" and "a positive influence." Also invited for tea and talks in the Oval Office was Albertina Sisulu, co-president of the UDF and wife of Walter Sisulu, an ANC leader who had been imprisoned together with Mandela for a quarter of a century. Pretoria lifted a travel restriction on Mrs. Sisulu to enable her to lead this delegation to the White House on 30 June 1989.

In an interview on a *Worldnet* program produced by the official US Information Agency, an Atlanta mayor and former UN Ambassador during the Carter presidency, Andrew Young, confidently predicted that President George Bush would be more supportive of economic sanctions against South Africa than his predecessor. This prediction turned out to be accurate. In its first report to Congress in terms of the CAAA, the Bush administration warned that while it welcomed "new thinking" on the part of de Klerk, it fully intended to introduce new sanctions of its own unless legislative steps were taken to end apartheid before June 1990. But de Klerk's "new thinking" at this stage was limited to vague generalities. While conceding on 12 May 1989, during his first major policy speech in the House of Assembly as National Party leader that "the present system cannot last indefinitely," he gave no specifics. In an interview with the *Washington Post* on 24 November 1989, de Klerk ruled out the idea of an interim multiracial government while the nation's Blacks and Whites negotiated a new constitutional order. The expectations of some in the United States that South Africa could overhaul its political system in six to nine months were unrealistic, he contended.

Nevertheless, speculation persisted that de Klerk was about to announce far-reaching reforms at the opening of parliament early in 1990. The dreaded word "Rubicon" cropped up again, bringing up unpleasant memories of an opportunity lost in August 1985 when President P. W. Botha spoke in Durban.

NOTES

1. Barber, Simon, Washington correspondent of *Business Day,* in *Optima*, Vol. 35, No 2 (1987).

2. *Wall Street Journal,* 10 December 1986.

3. *Debates of the House of Assembly, Fourth Session, Eighth Parliament,* 30 January to 6 February 1987, col. 10.

4. *Debates of the House of Assembly*, op. cit., col. 20.

5. *Business Day, Beeld,* and *The Citizen,* Johannesburg, 4 February 1987.

6. P.W. Botha speech at National Party gathering, Lichtenburg, 25 March 1987.

7. *Beeld* and *The Citizen,* 13 January 1987.

8. *Africa Research Bulletin,* Economic Series, 1987/8, p.778.

9. *New York Times*, 11 October 1987.

10. *Facts-on-File—Weekly World News Digest,* 1987, p. 836.

11. Ronald Reagan report to Congress in terms of CAAA, State Department, 2 October 1987.

12. *Facts-on-File—Weekly World News Digest,* 1987, p. 836.

13. Mangosuthu Buthelezi speech before the Student Representative Council of Pretoria University, 22 February 1988.

14. Mangosuthu Buthelezi policy speech, Debates in the KwaZulu Legislative Assembly, March 1988.

15. *Facts-on-File—Weekly World News Digest,* 1987, p. 113.

16. Singer, Max, "Reconstituting ANC Is Too Good an Idea for US," Op Ed article, *Wall Street Journal,* 4 August 1988.

17. *Business Day,* 7 October 1987.

18. *Facts-on-File—Weekly World News Digest,* 1988, p. 765

19. *Business Update,* New Canaan, Connecticut, Vol. 2, No. 11, November 1988.

20. *Financial Times,* London, 28 June 1989.

21. Ries, Alf, Dommisse, Eben, *Leierstryd,* p. 243.

22. Ibid., p. 83.

13

Rubicon Revisited

> All and sundry had cautioned against a second "Rubicon," [but]
> now, in the run-up to the 1990 opening address, the Rubicon
> specter was abroad with a vengeance.
>
> *Willem de Klerk*[1]

F. W. de Klerk's older brother, Willem, was among those who expressed concern over the Rubicon expectations created around the new president's first parliamentary opening address on 2 February 1990. President de Klerk, in contrast to his liberal brother, was an unlikely candidate for drastic reform. He was not only deeply rooted in the conservative wing of the National Party but rumored to have been among those who held predecessor P. W. Botha back on the banks of the Rubicon in 1985.

During the months leading up to the opening of parliament in February 1990, the newly elected state president found himself under the same pressure as P. W. Botha in August 1985.

Once again the world expected to see apartheid slain and buried in one single speech. Many wondered in the weeks and months of speculation preceding the speech whether de Klerk too would earn a political obituary instead of acclaim, as did his predecessor. Would he also, in the words of *The Star*, "stumble on the banks of the Rubicon," turn around "rush back to the laager?"[2]

As in the case of Botha in the days leading up to this crucial date with destiny early in February 1990, de Klerk was heavily burdened by demands at home and from abroad. Everywhere President de Klerk turned, reported Roger Thurow of the *Wall Street Journal,* he heard "the same mantra of demands—release, lift bans, dismantle, negotiate—be it from local anti-apartheid activists or from foreign governments."[3] Inevitably the subject of sanctions reared its head. In the United States, Congress warned about additional and tougher sanctions. The Bush administration threatened similar action unless de Klerk finally stepped across the Rubicon into a new land without apartheid.

As early as October 1989, shortly after he was sworn in as president, de Klerk had been cautioned by American Assistant Secretary for African Affairs Herman J. Cohen that the Bush administration would consider punitive measures of its own unless South Africa took legislative action before June 1990 to abolish apartheid. During his appearance before the Senate Foreign Relations Committee, Cohen became the first State Department official to set a specific deadline for change in South Africa. Laws such as the Group Areas Act, he said, would have to go during the next parliamentary session. If at the end of June 1990 "there is little to show for it," Cohen told the senators, the administration would consult with Congress, Europe, and Japan on imposing further "appropriate" punitive measures.[4]

Even shorter deadlines were issued by members of Congress, some of whom gave the new South African leader only until the beginning of 1990 to get his house in order before another round of stricter sanctions would start. Sen. Edward Kennedy did not want to wait. He had already proceeded with another more comprehensive sanctions bill. A "grace period," he argued, was inadvisable when there was "no question" that trade and financial sanctions passed by Congress in 1986 had worked and that more were in order.[5]

Under mounting pressure from anti-apartheid activists not to reschedule the $8 billion in South African debt due for repayment in mid-1990, international bankers were also waiting anxiously for de Klerk to cross the Rubicon into "the new South Africa." On 1 June 1989, four prominent South African anti-apartheid church leaders, under the leadership of Anglican Archbishop Desmond Tutu, had sent a letter to American bankers urging them not to reschedule South Africa's debt repayments until the government granted political power to the Black majority.[6] This action touched a raw nerve, following closely on an admission by the governor of South Africa's Reserve Bank, Gerhard de Kock, that a further drain in foreign reserves and economic stagnation could be expected unless adequate progress was made with political and constitutional reform.

In the second week of October 1989, South African Finance Minister Barend du Plessis returned from a visit to the United States and Europe angered by overseas bankers and government officials who were being "misled" by anti-apartheid activists. The "wrong perception" is being spread, he complained, that the government, having received a mandate, is not going to do anything.[7] "What the government does understand is pressure," retorted Terry Crawford-Browne, a former South African banker advising church leaders on sanctions strategy. "It is a fallacy that Pretoria reacts badly to pressure. In fact, it's the only thing that works."[8]

In September 1989 de Klerk inherited from his predecessor an ailing economy. The South African rand had fallen to 36 US cents, compared with $1.40 a decade ago. Prices in the stores were soaring at an inflation rate of 16 percent. Unemployment lines were growing by the day. Although a variety of other factors, such as severe drought, a drop in the price of gold, labor unrest, and a global recession, contributed to this dismal state of the South African economy, nobody could deny any longer that sanctions and disinvestment were hurting. At the center of the problem was South Africa's $20.5 billion foreign debt, of which $8.5 billion was frozen in 1985 when international banks demanded repayment of short-term loans. This made South Africa a capital exporter despite its weak rand. An increasing number of foreign corporations, mostly American, departed as the violence and labor unrest continued, profits plunged, and sanctions pressures mounted.

Some 200 of the estimated 350 American firms with operations in South Africa had withdrawn by the end of 1989.[9] To illustrate South Africa's ability to withstand sanctions, its officialdom liked to parade strategic import replacement undertakings such as Armscor (armaments), Soekor (oil exploration), Sasol (oil from coal), the Atlantis diesel engine plant, and Valindaba (enriched uranium production). Yet the billions spent on these projects served to further drain capital needed for social programs that may have helped prevent unrest and violence resulting in part from Black poverty and joblessness.

To those who were looking for signs of willingness by the new South African leader to take that final irreversible step across the divide on 2 February 1990, de Klerk's initial actions were encouraging. In September 1989 he won praise for allowing the "Big March" on parliament to proceed despite the state of emergency. Organized by the Mass Democratic Movement (MDM), this protest against the exclusion of Blacks from the elections drew 35,000. On 15 October 1989, Walter Sisulu and seven other political prisoners were released. With de Klerk's permission, they were welcomed back to Soweto township at a huge ANC rally—the first in South Africa in twenty-five years. On 16 November 1989, de Klerk declared all South Africa's beaches open and scrapped the Separate Amenities Act, which segregated public facilities. On 24 November 1989, he announced that the Group Areas Act, one of the cornerstones of apartheid, would no longer apply in four "free settlement areas" to be established. Members of all racial groups would be allowed to live side-by-side in these integrated areas. On 13 December 1989, de Klerk received jailed ANC leader Nelson Mandela at his official residence in Cape Town. In contrast to the ANC leader's reportedly cordial but unproductive visit with P. W. Botha a few months earlier, the meeting with de Klerk was said to have been an in-depth discussion about power-sharing in South Africa—and Mandela's release.

Although these actions drew some applause and raised hopes, critics were wondering whether de Klerk, like his predecessor, was merely trying to put a kinder and gentler face on apartheid. Would he also, like P. W. Botha, turn around and seek solace in the "laager" when the going gets tough? De Klerk's gesture in allowing mass protest in the streets turned sour. Accolades soon made way for acrimony and accusations as violence spread and the police were obliged to resort to tougher action. "The sun was just beginning to rise on F. W. de Klerk's 'new South Africa' when the casualty figures from fresh police clashes with anti-apartheid protesters started escalating," reported Roger Thurow of the *Wall Street Journal* early in September 1989. "Eleven dead in Mitchell's Plain, four dead in Lavender Hill, two dead in Khayelitsha. In all, church groups said 25 people died (police confirmed 12 deaths) and more than 100 were injured in the black townships around Cape Town." De Klerk's president's seat "sits now in a pool of blood," the Rev. Allan Boesak charged. "If he doesn't move quickly, nothing that he says, politically or otherwise, will have any meaning whatsoever."[10]

During January 1990, as the opening of parliament drew closer and Foreign Minister Botha implored the United States to hold back on further sanctions until de Klerk had spoken, visions of another doomed Rubicon recurred. It was Botha as foreign minister, it was recalled, who helped to foster great expectations abroad before President P. W. Botha delivered his disappointing Rubicon speech in August 1985.

The 500 foreign media personnel, including all the major American television networks, did not, however, assemble in Cape Town toward the end of January 1990 simply to cover de Klerk's speech. They were there to witness the freeing of world's most celebrated political prisoner. Any doubts about Mandela's release were finally dispelled by the publication on 25 January 1990, of a 5,000-word memorandum in *South,* a left-wing Cape Town weekly newspaper. In his first detailed political statement to be published in South Africa in twenty-six years, Mandela outlined a strategy for talks between the ANC and the South African government. His appeal for negotiations to save the country "'from civil strife and ruin" was seen as the signal of "willingness" to be released. But Mandela's tone was not altogether conciliatory. He refused to renounce the armed struggle before negotiations began, or to break the ANC's alliance with the South African Communist Party. As it was this same refusal to denounce violence that thwarted his release by P.W. Botha in the past, some observers wondered how de Klerk would respond.

As President Frederik Willem de Klerk mounted the rostrum in parliament on the morning of Friday, 2 February 1990, to deliver his opening speech, only he and his cabinet had an inkling of what was to follow. It soon became apparent that this, the forty-first annual opening of a parliamentary session under National Party rule, was to make every other one pale in comparison. De Klerk stunned the world and shocked many of his own supporters. In a sensational address he signaled a future hitherto unthinkable. He unbanned several "terrorist" organizations, announced the release from jail of ANC leader Nelson Mandela, and expressed a desire to renegotiate the future of the country with all concerned. In short, he announced the end of the existing order, including the very parliament he was addressing. He promised a new South Africa under Black majority rule. He finally crossed the Rubicon. "Incredible," Bishop Tutu gasped. "It took my breath away. Give him credit, man. I do." The Rev. Allan Boesak exclaimed euphorically: "If he had given us more we would not have known what to do with it." In Johannesburg young black men and women were dancing in the street, punching the air and shouting "Viva Comrade Nelson Mandela!" interspersed with an equally enthusiastic "Viva Comrade F. W. de Klerk."[11]

What really caused de Klerk's conversion on the road to Cape Town? Apparently anticipating some backlash within his own ranks and severe attacks from the right-wing Conservative Party, State President de Klerk took time trying to explain this about-face during his parliamentary address on 2 February 1990. He mentioned growing violence, tension, and conflict as reasons for his decision to negotiate a new South Africa where Whites would no longer be in complete control. He also cited the demise of "Stalinist Communism" in the Soviet Union and Eastern Europe as "an historical opportunity" to set aside "conflicts and ideological differences" and to reach a "negotiated understanding among the representative leaders of the entire population." Without further Communist support from Europe, the banned liberation movements posed less of a threat, he felt.

Speaking at a foreign correspondents' dinner in Cape Town a few weeks before this dramatic announcement in parliament, de Klerk had linked a promise to remove "class, race and other barriers" in South Africa with similar trends in post-Communist Europe.[12] In a flurry of public appearances following his parliamentary speech of February 1990, de Klerk would often revisit this theme. He believed that the political and economic upheaval in Eastern Europe and the Soviet Union had "developed into an unstoppable tide."[13] It opened "a door which did not exist before" in what seemed to be "a blank concrete wall" and offered South Africa "a marvelous opportunity."[14] According to de Klerk, the collapse of Communism served as a warning to those "who insist on persisting with it in Africa." Those who sought to force "this failure of a system on South Africa," he believed, were bound to engage in "a total revision of their point of view."[15]

A year later, in his second parliamentary opening speech on 1 February 1991, de Klerk raised the topic once again. "The exploitation of regional conflict in our part of the world to further ideology and power has come to an end," he noted. No longer could "the two major powers" be played off against each other "for the achievement of questionable political objectives" and revolution was no longer "a marketable product," de Klerk said. What remained unsaid by him was that the crumbling of Communism and the end of the Cold War cut both ways. It also meant that his government had finally lost one of its most important bargaining chips. The perception of a White-ruled pro-Western South Africa as a vital bulwark against Communism in Africa that had been such an important US policy consideration for more than forty years had lost validity. No longer would the Bush administration be able, as its predecessors had done since 1946, to argue against sanctions and other punitive measures on the grounds that it would weaken a valuable ally against Communism.

"The season of violence is over," de Klerk announced during his famous Cape Town speech on 2 February 1990. "The time for reconstruction and reconciliation has arrived." Hundreds of congratulatory telegrams, telephone calls, and letters from foreign governments included messages from UN Secretary-General Perez de Quellar, French President François Mitterrand, British Prime Minister Margaret Thatcher, and American President George Bush. "Rubicon Crossed," proclaimed the *Natal Mercury* on 3 February. "F.W. has saved South Africa, says Business Leaders," wrote *Beeld.* "Bush Wants to Review Sanctions," reported *The Star.*

Oddly, sanctions were not at all mentioned in de Klerk's historic speech and afterward he went to great lengths to deny that it had anything to do with the far-reaching reforms. Yet the dramatic steps announced on 2 February 1990, showed a close resemblance to the actual conditions set by the US Congress for the lifting of sanctions under the Comprehensive Anti-Apartheid Act (CAAA) of October 1986. Was that purely coincidence?

For several months State President de Klerk continued to deny that his actions were dictated or influenced in any way by sanctions. Why? In answer to a question during his appearance before the National Press Club in Washington in September 1990, he finally let the cat out of the bag. "We don't like, as a country, to be prescribed to by other countries," de Klerk explained, "and there is emotional reaction which is brought about by that." De Klerk like his predecessors, could not afford to concede that the dictates came from abroad. In Afrikaner politics this was tantamount to committing the ultimate sin—something akin to treason.

On Sunday, 11 February 1990, the focus shifted away from de Klerk as Nelson Rolihlahla Mandela stepped out of the gates at Victor Verster Prison near Cape Town after an incarceration of more than a quarter-century. Holding hands with his wife Winnie and flashing a Black power salute, the world's most celebrated prisoner stepped onto television screens into a multitude of living rooms in America and around the world. His first public announcement from the balcony of Cape Town's city hall sounded more militant than de Klerk may have anticipated. "We call on the international community to continue to isolate the apartheid regime," Mandela said. "To lift sanctions now would be to run the risk of aborting the process toward the complete eradication of apartheid. Our march to freedom is irreversible."

He spent his first night of freedom in the home of Archbishop Desmond Tutu, where he gave a press conference the following morning. While he went to great lengths to reassure Whites that the ANC regarded them as "fellow South Africans and want them to feel safe," he ruled out an end to sanctions before majority rule was in place. "You must remember that the demand in this country is for a non-racial society," he told the press. "We are very far from that and it is too early for anybody to expect us to call for the lifting of sanctions." In interviews with several American and other overseas television networks, the ANC leader repeated this need for continued sanctions. His calm and dignified demeanor added power to the message. The feedback from Washington was reassuring. George Bush, while praising de Klerk as a man "who is making dramatic changes," told a press conference on 12 February 1990, that he would not ask Congress to lift sanctions until South Africa had met certain conditions.

The White House extended invitations to both de Klerk and Mandela to visit Washington—separately. But first Nelson Mandela had another mission to fulfill in Africa. On 27 February 1990, he arrived in Zambia for an emotional reunion with ANC comrades. Among them stood PLO leader Yasir Arafat, who "repeatedly hugged and kissed" Mandela, "then stepped back to smile at him and kissed him some more." In his airport speech, Mandela, "trim and upright and in a dark blue suit," praised the international community for supporting the ANC's cause "through sanctions and other forms of pressure."[16] The next day, after a meeting with the leaders of the six Frontline states, Mandela issued a call to the United States and other members of the international community to keep sanctions in place until the United Nations had decided that they could be lifted.

On 1 March 1990, a delegation of seven Democratic and two Republican congressmen under leadership of Congressman William Gray 3rd (D-Pennsylvania), House Majority Whip and long-time sanctions supporter, arrived in Lusaka to pay respects to Mandela. He in turn thanked the US Congress for its "priceless gift" by supporting the anti-apartheid struggle over the years. The legislators were urged to stand firm on sanctions and oppose a rumored trip by Vice President Dan Quayle to South Africa—as well as the proposed one by de Klerk to Washington. On 28 February 1990, Chief Mangosuthu Buthelezi had, however, already visited the White House to urge the lifting of sanctions. He emerged from the meeting telling reporters that he had asked President Bush to do so as soon as possible. "The vast majority of black South Africas," Buthelezi said, "reject sanctions and the isolation of South Africa which minimizes economic growth and maximizes black misery."

Despite the demise of constructive engagement, Reagan's Assistant Secretary of African Affairs, Chester Crocker, did manage to accomplish the seemingly impossible—independence for Namibia. Brokering an agreement between widely disparate parties, ranging from Castro's Cuba to P. W. Botha's South Africa, Crocker had left office with a diplomatic coup that made up in part for his resounding rebuke by Congress on the question of sanctions. There were, however, those who contended that South Africa would never have given up Namibia if it were not for the very sanctions opposed by Crocker. Pretoria, they insisted, was forced to seek relief from further and tougher punitive measures by making concessions on this front.

Attending Namibia's independence celebrations on 21 March 1990, were the new Secretary James Baker and his African assistant, Herman Cohen. There to hand over the keys, instead of P. W. Botha was newly elected President F. W. de Klerk. The only remaining link with the past was Pik Botha, who accompanied de Klerk to Windhoek. As South Africa's foreign minister, he had been involved in deliberations over Namibia for fourteen years with four different US administrations. Even though Botha had openly sided with Sam Nujoma's opponents during the elections in the belief that the Democratic Turnhalle Alliance and other minor groupings could win the election against SWAPO, it did not seem to hamper the cordiality on stage. Ultimately, the smooth transition in Windhoek would serve to hasten developments in South Africa as it made arguments against the "dangers" of Black majority rule seem unfounded.

Attending the celebrations and attracting as much attention among the visiting dignitaries as de Klerk, was Nelson Mandela. De Klerk "appeared solemn" in contrast to the "broadly smiling" newly elected President Sam Nujoma as the South African flag was lowered and the new Namibian flag raised. Namibian Home Affairs Minister Hifikepunye Pohamba told reporters that 21 March 1990 was picked as independence day to express solidarity with "South Africa's black majority in its struggle against apartheid." It happened to be the thirtieth anniversary of the Sharpeville shootings.[17] In handing over the reins in Namibia to Nujoma and SWAPO, de Klerk declared himself "an advocate of peace" and pronounced the "season of violence" over for Namibia and the whole of Southern Africa. Echoing this last phrase first used in his historic address in South Africa's parliament on 2 February 1990, proved to be a trifle too optimistic—at least for South Africa.

South Africa had enjoyed only a brief peaceful respite in February 1990. After a two-week interlude following the release of Mandela, violence once again erupted in Black townships across the country. Alarmed officials described this new wave of unrest and killing as the worst violence since the mid-1980s. It was felt in some circles that much of this violence was the work of Black radicals intent on wrecking the upcoming talks between de Klerk and Mandela, scheduled to begin on 11 April 1990. On 26 March police opened fire on a crowd of tens of thousands of Black protesters at Sebokeng, a township near Vereeniging, in de Klerk's former constituency. Initially eight were reported dead, then eleven. Hundreds were wounded. The ANC called off the talks.

On 5 April 1990, de Klerk invited Mandela to Tuynhuys in Cape Town. After a three-hour meeting, the two leaders emerged to announce a rescheduling of the talks. Delegations from the ANC and de Klerk's Nationalist government finally met in Cape Town on 5 May. At the conclusion of a three-day conference the so-called Groote Schuur Minute was issued—a joint communiqué that set guidelines for ongoing negotiations between working groups on both sides. In Natal, in the meantime, open war between cadres of Buthelezi's Inkatha Freedom Party and "comrades" of the pro-ANC United Democratic Front (UDF) continued to take a heavy toll. Over a three-year period, the death toll amounted to more than 3,000—including women and children. On 7 June 1990, de Klerk decided to lift the four-year old nationwide state of emergency in three of South Africa's four provinces—excluding Natal. The partial lifting was welcomed by the White House in Washington as "another significant step toward creating a climate conducive to negotiations." The next step required for lifting of sanctions, the State Department pointed out, would be the freeing of political prisoners.

In May 1990 the battle over sanctions had shifted overseas, where de Klerk and Mandela dogged each other's footsteps across Europe, meeting with heads of state to press their opposite views on sanctions. During his visit with President François Mitterrand on 7 June 1990, Mandela insisted that sanctions should remain. A month earlier, on 10 May, de Klerk in his meeting with the French leader had requested that sanctions be lifted.[18] De Klerk exploited his new-found acceptance abroad by staging a nine-nation tour of Europe between 8 and 25 May. Apart from his meeting with Mitterrand in France, he managed to see heads of state in Greece, Portugal, Italy, Belgium, Britain, Germany, Switzerland, and Spain. "Sanctions are crumbling," he announced at an airport press conference in Johannesburg on his return on 26 May 1990.

Mandela undertook a six-nation trip in Africa from 9 to 22 May 1990, and briefly returned to Johannesburg for a bladder cyst operation before embarking on another grueling tour. The highlight was to be the United States, where he intended to keep sanctions in place.

NOTES

1. De Klerk, Willem, *F. W. de Klerk: The Man in His Time*, p. 17.

2. *The Star,* Johannesburg, 3 January 1987.

3. Thurow, Roger, "Clock is Ticking Loudly for South Africa," *Wall Street Journal,* 8 September 1989.

4. *Washington Post,* 4 October 1989.

5. Ibid.

6. *Washington Post,* 2 June 1989.

7. *Wall Street Journal*, 12 October 1989.

8. Ibid.

9. Cooper, A., *US Business in South Africa,* Investor Responsibility Research Center, 1990, p. 11.

10. *Wall Street Journal,* 8 September 1989, p. 8.

11. *Cape Times,* Cape Town, and *The Citizen,* Johannesburg, 3-4 February 1990.

12. F. W. de Klerk speech at Foreign Correspondents Dinner, Cape Town, 13 November 1989.

13 F. W. de Klerk remarks about German reunification, German Embassy, Pretoria, 3 October 1990.

14. F. W. de Klerk speech before the Harvard Business School Club of South Africa, Johannesburg, 12 June 1990.

15. *Debates of Parliament, Second Session - Ninth Parliament,* 2 to 9 February 1990, cols. 14-17.

16. *New York Times,* 28 February 1990.

17. *New York Times,* 21 March 1990.

18. *The Citizen,* 8 June 1990.

14

Irreversible Change

"During the past two years we've seen a profound transformation in the situation in South Africa—I really firmly believe that this progress is irreversible."

President George Bush[1]

With this announcement on 10 July 1991, President Bush lifted the sanctions imposed on South Africa under the Comprehensive Anti-Apartheid Act (CAAA) of 1986.

Even though South African President F. W. de Klerk had met all five conditions laid down by the CAAA for its lifting, Bush still felt it necessary to stress that he had taken this step because he regarded the changes as "irreversible."

The Democratic leadership in Congress had sided with Nelson Mandela in opposing the scrapping of the CAAA before there was sufficient proof of "irreversible" change in South Africa.

As early as September 1990, nine months before the CAAA was lifted, the word "irreversible" had become a crucial element of the ongoing debate between de Klerk and Mandela over sanctions. Addressing the Washington National Press Club on 24 September 1990, de Klerk expressed his satisfaction over President Bush's acceptance of the "irreversibility" of change in South Africa during a ceremony in the Rose Garden that same morning. He used the word "irreversible" no less than five times: "My Government's commitment to remove the last pillars of apartheid is final and *irreversible*...the *irreversibility* of my Government's commitment to the removal of racial discrimination...we provide also final and *irreversible* proof that we mean what we say...The process of creating this new and just South

Africa is *irreversible,* and I thank your President for yesterday publicly and privately accepting this *irreversibility."*

While uninformed outsiders may have been tempted to ascribe this repetitious use of the word to sloppy speech-writing, insiders recognized its significance. No one quite knows exactly where the word "irreversible" first entered the sanctions debate, but Mandela had not been slow in repeating this condition for the lifting of sanctions at every opportunity. The ANC leader kept insisting that he first wanted to see a Black transitional government in place before he would accept the process as "irreversible." At the same time de Klerk needed some reward for his drastic steps to contain defections to the White right. So he set out for Washington in September 1990 determined to convince both the Congress and the White House that the reform process in South Africa was indeed "irreversible." It was not an easy task, following, as he did, Mandela's triumphant tour of Washington and seven other American cities during the last ten days of June 1990.

On 20 June 1990, Nelson Mandela arrived to a hero's welcome in New York. Traveling as a private citizen, Mandela was accorded honors last extended to the Pope. He was a guest at Mayor David Dinkins' official Gracie Mansion residence, received a ticker-tape parade down New York's Broadway, and made a stadium appearance replete with rock music and memorabilia vendors. Wherever he went, an entourage of local politicians and public figures crowded around him, trying to apportion some of this saturation publicity on the electronic and in the print media for themselves. On 22 June 1990, Mandela met at breakfast with 150 American corporate executives at the World Trade Center, assuring them that there would be room for a mixed economy in post-apartheid South Africa. Afterward he proceeded to the United Nations, where he told the Special Committee Against Apartheid to remain vigilant and keep sanctions going.

Next Mandela and his entourage traveled to Boston as a tribute to Sen. Edward Kennedy (D-Massachusetts) in recognition of his leading role in pushing for sanctions against South Africa. On the evening of 24 June 1990, Mandela arrived in Washington with a large following of news people, admirers, and supporters. The next day the ANC leader proceeded to the White House for a meeting with President Bush. Afterward at a Rose Garden appearance, Bush described his guest as "a man who embodies the hopes of millions." But the American president's call on "all parties to renounce the armed struggle" struck a discordant note with Mandela. The ANC leader testily dismissed it as a sign that Bush "has not as yet got a proper briefing from us."[2]

Mandela was reserving that briefing for a much larger occasion—his anxiously awaited address before a joint session of Congress. After a breakfast meeting with the Black Caucus on 26 June 1990, Mandela was escorted onto the podium under thundering applause from a packed Congress. His 35-minute speech was interrupted nineteen times by applause—three times by prolonged standing ovations. It contained an impassioned appeal to Congress to keep sanctions in place until "irreversible reforms" were made. Among the legislators attending were Congressmen Ron Dellums, William Gray, Stephen Solarz, Howard Wolpe, and Senators Richard Lugar, Edward Kennedy, Nancy Kassebaum, Alan Cranston and Paul Simon—all key figures in the bipartisan push for sanctions against South Africa. In the gallery sat the debonair Randall Robinson of TransAfrica, prime sanctions lobbyist and strategist. "We still have a struggle on our hands," Mandela insisted. "Our common and noble efforts to abolish the system of white minority domination must continue. We are encouraged and strengthened by the fact of the agreement between ourselves [and] this Congress, as well as President Bush and his administration, that sanctions should remain in place." Thanking Congress for its adoption of "the historic" Comprehensive Anti-Apartheid Act, "which made such a decisive contribution to the process of moving our country forward towards negotiations," Mandela insisted that "sanctions should remain in place because the purpose for which they were imposed has not yet been achieved."[3]

Assessing the results of the Mandela visit on 1 July 1990, the *Washington Post* noted that apart from winning public adulation and accomplishing superstar status in the American media, Nelson Mandela had achieved his major goal. He ensured, said the *Post*, that United States would keep sanctions "against South Africa's minority White regime" in place for the time being.

This was the formidable challenge that faced President F. W. de Klerk when he landed on board a South African Airways jumbo jet at Andrews Air Force Base in Virginia on 23 September 1990, to begin a much shorter and more modest visit. As the aircraft taxied toward the gate, where a small welcoming party of medium-level American officials led by Assistant Secretary of State for African Affairs Herman Cohen waited, members of de Klerk's entourage luxuriated over the significance of being passengers on the first SAA flight to be allowed to land in the United States since the ban imposed by the CAAA. Stepping behind the microphones on the tarmac, de Klerk remarked upon the "historical significance of his visit." He recalled the "words and deeds" of Presidents Washington and Lincoln and Martin Luther King Jr. as emblematic of his own struggle to achieve equality in South Africa. Change in his country, he told the larger American television audience, was "irreversible." The word "irreversible" rolled easily from de Klerk's lips. It had become part of almost every speech and pronouncement since his sensational parliamentary speech of 2 February 1990, and had assumed even greater importance after Mandela's visit to the United States.

"By now there should not be any doubt either about the process being irreversible," he had told the Cape Town Press Club on 30 March 1990. On 17 April 1990, he reminded parliament that "an irreversible process has been initiated." In Zurich on 23 May 1990, he assured the Swiss South Africa

Association that "the process is irreversible, and the time has come for Europe, for the total international community, to accept that." Even at a Sport Merits Award ceremony at Tuynhuys in Cape Town on 3 May 1990, he did not pass up on the opportunity. "Those in sport who are concerned about reforms in other areas," de Klerk said, "should realize that an irreversible process regarding constitutional negotiation and the elimination of discrimination has started."

On the morning of 24 September 1990, President de Klerk stepped out in the Rose Garden to exchange public pleasantries with President Bush after a meeting in the Oval Office. "We believe the process of change in South Africa is irreversible," de Klerk said. He made no reference to sanctions and South African officials insisted afterward that he did not push for its lifting during the meeting with Bush. The process of change in South Africa was indeed "irreversible," Bush acknowledged in his reply, and this was "a fact" that would be borne "squarely in mind" as the administration consider specific issues in the future. The most important issue Bush was referring to happened to be sanctions.

"Our goal," the US president added, "must be to support the process of change. And of course, I will consult fully with the Congress on these issues and, as you know, all the conditions set in our legislation have not yet been made, in spite of the dramatic progress that we salute here today. But let me emphasize that these conditions are clear-cut, and are not open to reinterpretation, and I do not believe in moving the goal posts." To those familiar with the issues on hand and capable of sorting through the syntactic shortcomings of a president never known for eloquent off-the-cuff speaking, it translated as follows: South Africa has gone a long way toward making the changes required by the CAAA for the repeal of US sanctions but it still had some way to go. We are convinced that this process is irreversible and will approach Congress to rescind sanctions as soon as all our conditions are met. We will stick to the original conditions and will not change the rules.

During de Klerk's appearance at the National Press Club, the next day the word "irreversible" danced off his lips five times—and was repeated a few more times in the question-an-answer session that followed. The South African president declared his visit to Washington a resounding success because "your president yesterday publicly and privately" accepted the "irreversibility" of the changes introduced in South Africa. This, he said, would serve as encouragement to proceed along the road which that he had taken. "We intend, because we believe it must be done, to do all the things to which the CAAA legislation refers," de Klerk said in answer to a question and then hastily added: "Whether the legislation was instituted or not, we would have done it according to the policies which we have accepted." He was still trying to deny the influence of sanctions on his actions.

De Klerk departed from Washington apparently satisfied that his main mission was accomplished. While he could not claim heavy inroads into

Congress, he succeeded at least in having the American president acknowledge publicly that change in South Africa was "irreversible." Shortly after
his return to South Africa de Klerk told the Natal Chamber of Industries that
"it is important to know that this irreversibility has been accepted by many
key countries and also during my recent visit, by the United States Government." As a result, he promised, South Africa could now look "forward to the
lifting of sanctions and the restoration of our relationships with international
financial markets."[4] But the acceptance of the "irreversibility" of change was
not only an important step toward having existing US sanctions lifted; it was
also crucial to help stave off further sanctions. In October 1990 the American
president was required by the CAAA to report to Congress on the progress
made in South Africa.

Barely days after de Klerk left Washington, President Bush submitted his
findings to Congress. "Progress in South Africa toward negotiations and the
establishment of a nonracial and democratic society has been dramatic and
irreversible," Bush reported. Further sanctions were therefore "not appropriate
at this time and would be counter-productive in view of the positive steps
being taken within South Africa to bring about change through peaceful
means," he concluded. Congress concurred and South Africa's leadership
welcomed the development as a victory.

With new sanctions averted, the de Klerk government could now go about
in earnest to eliminate the remaining stumbling blocks that still prevented
the lifting of US sanctions under the CAAA. Toward the end of 1990,
Foreign Minister Botha informed the president of the UN General Assembly
that more "than 100 discriminatory laws and regulations have been repealed." The State of Emergency had been lifted totally in October 1990 and
"only three apartheid laws" still remained. Two of these, the Group Areas
Act and the Land Acts, Botha promised, would be repealed when parliament
resumed early in 1991. The third, the Population Registration Act, would,
however, only fall away when a new constitution was adopted."[5] The
Population Registration Act was a cornerstone not only of apartheid but of
the existing constitution and removing it would in effect bring down not only
apartheid but the whole government, leaving a void. This Act therefore
appeared to be the one item in the American CAAA checklist that remained
an immovable obstacle.

Opening parliament on 1 February 1991, de Klerk announced, as everyone
anticipated, the imminent repeal of the Group Areas Act. Once again, however, he sprung a surprise by indicating that the Population Registration Act
would also be scrapped, despite earlier indications that such a step would be
constitutionally impossible. "On the part of the Government," he explained,
"the view was held that the Population Registration Act would have to be repealed eventually, but that this could not be done immediately because the
Act was technically necessary for the maintenance of the present constitutional dispensation. Therefore it would be possible to repeal the Act only

once a new constitution had been implemented." Further investigation, he announced, showed that it was, in fact, possible to repeal this Act, provided that it was accompanied by the adoption of temporary transitional measures toward the acceptance of a new constitution.

The US State Department responded positively on the same day. "We welcome President de Klerk's historic announcement that his government will introduce legislation to repeal the Group Areas Act, the Land Acts, and the Population Registration Act," it said. "Once enacted, these dramatic and far-reaching measures will abolish the remaining legislative pillars of apartheid. They are the latest evidence that an irreversible process of change is under way, and that substantial progress continues to be made toward dismantling the system of apartheid and establishing a non-racial democracy in South Africa."

Repealing apartheid laws proved, however, to be easier than coping with the chaos and violence that threatened to engulf South Africa as the government loosened its grip. Figures released by Law and Order Minister Adriaan Vlok early in 1991 showed that instead of abating, as de Klerk had hoped after his speech of 2 February 1990, the season of violence continued with a vengeance. A total of 17,088 incidents of unrest in 1990 set a new record.[6] The war between the Inkatha Freedom Party (IFP) and the ANC had spread from Natal to the townships around Johannesburg. There were claims of police complicity by the ANC and counterclaims by the IFP. Despite a peace agreement between ANC Deputy President Nelson Mandela and IFP leader Mangosuthu Buthelezi on 29 January 1991, and another joint statement on 30 March 1991, the violence that had claimed more than 5,000 lives in five years continued. De Klerk found himself in the middle, accused by the White opposition Conservative Party for being naive in thinking that he could abandon apartheid, ignore tribal and national aspirations, and expect an end to the season of violence.

Even more disheartening was the effect that this violence had on Washington. On Sunday, 24 March 1991, twelve members of the ANC were killed and one policeman was hacked to death during a clash in Daveyton. The next morning at a State Department news briefing in Washington, spokeswoman Margaret Tutwiler deplored the "police killings." In security quarters there were charges that the state of emergency was lifted prematurely under sanctions pressures from abroad. Some of his advisers wanted de Klerk to reimpose emergency measures to enable the police to cope with the worsening situation. But de Klerk realized that this would halt the progress toward fulfilling the conditions for lifting the CAAA sanctions. So he pressed on. In the second week of February 1991, he signed his own peace accord with Mandela, only to be rebuffed a month later when the ANC leader threatened to suspend further peace talks with the government unless Defense Minister Magnus Malan and Law and Order Minister Adriaan Vlok were removed from office.

It was in this troubled atmosphere that President de Klerk had to try fulfilling the last and most difficult requirement of the CAAA—the release of all political prisoners. Addressing a seminar on sanctions in Johannesburg on 13 February 1991, American Ambassador William Swing noted that there had been much speculation regarding the lifting of international sanctions against South Africa. "There is, I believe, widespread recognition that South Africa's move away from apartheid to a new political reality is, as President Bush has stated, irreversible," but sanctions, Swing noted, would only go after the release of political prisoners.

But a row over what constitutes a political prisoner in South Africa and how many there were had erupted between the government and the African National Congress. It threatened to delay not only de Klerk's moves toward fulfilling all the requirements of the CAAA, but his constitutional talks with the ANC. A broad spectrum of prisoners, including many whose crimes were considered to be not even remotely political, was released by de Klerk. This concession still failed to satisfy ANC demands. In the end the Bush administration decided to use its own narrower definition of a "political prisoner" instead of the much wider one preferred by the ANC. "The American definition of a political prisoner is a person who is imprisoned for his political beliefs or legitimate political actions," reported *The Star* on 23 June 1991. "It does not include people who rape for liberation or murder for freedom." The ANC definition, the Johannesburg newspaper argued, reflected that organization's "totalitarian ideological bias," which "does not flinch at atrocity" and classified as political prisoners people who have committed "the most dreadful acts of violence, claiming to do so for the noblest motives." The South African government, according to the newspaper, took "an intermediate position, freeing prisoners from both left and right who have resorted to depraved methods in pursuit of political ends." The questions of "how much depravity, and what outrageous deeds, may be condoned by political intentions" were "neither simple nor amenable to facile answers."[7] The American Embassy in Pretoria was assigned the onerous task of monitoring the release of prisoners. Its reports back to Washington led the State Department to conclude in July 1991 that the South African government no longer held "prisoners or detainees" in terms of the CAAA.

In late April 1991, in the midst of all the turmoil at home, the sanctions battle between de Klerk and Mandela had shifted overseas once again. Before their departure both men made separate but equal appearances at a closed-door conference in Cape Town arranged by the American Aspen Institute under the direction of former Senator Clark—the author of the Clark Amendment. Inkatha leader Mangosuthu Buthelezi was also invited to speak. Attended by Assistant Secretary of State for Africa Herman Cohen and some seventeen US congressmen, the four-day conference had assumed special significance as the US president was preparing to consult with Congress over the lifting of the CAAA. Among the legislators in attendance were the new chairman of the African Affairs Subcommittee in the House, Rep. Mervyn Dymally, his predecessor Howard Wolpe, and his fellow Black Caucus member Donald Payne. Representing the Senate were Democrats Charles Robb, Paul Sarbanes, and Howard Metzenbaum and Republican Alan Simpson.

The South African president headed for Europe once more to try to convince foreign leaders to lift sanctions, while Mandela journeyed to Japan to insist on the opposite. Sanctions, Mandela urged, should remain in place until reform was truly "irreversible." Both men ended up in London, only days apart, to visit with newly elected British Prime Minister John Major and Labor opposition leader Neil Kinnock. Predictably, de Klerk got a better response from Major, while Kinnock sided with Mandela. Buthelezi also went overseas. On 20 June 1991 the IFP leader turned up at the White House, urging President Bush to lift economic sanctions "because my people are suffering." The American president assured him that he intended to do so as soon as possible.

Six days later, at a special ceremony in his office at the Union Buildings in Pretoria on 27 June 1991, President de Klerk signed off on the last three remaining apartheid laws in full view of the world press and television cameras—"ahead of the deadline promised to the international community." The scrapping of the Population Registration Act, the Group Areas Act, and the Land Act meant, according to de Klerk, that the book on apartheid was closed.

All this had been accomplished at a political price. In May 1991, the Conservative Party (CP) scored a massive victory in the Ladybrand by-election, defeating the National Party (NP) by increasing its majority from a mere seventy in the 1989 election to 1,258 votes. A swing toward the right in by-elections in Maitland, Randburg, and Umlazi was seen as "disturbing—one that the government dare not ignore."[8] But President de Klerk had moved beyond the narrower confines of the past into what he believed would be a new South Africa devoid of discrimination. A survey by the Human Sciences Research Council now showed him slightly ahead of ANC leader Nelson Mandela in overall popularity in a non-racial South Africa. The findings gave Mandela the support of 44 percent of Blacks, 1 percent of Coloreds and 5 percent of Indians, but no White support. De Klerk polled 25 percent support among Blacks, 51 percent among Whites, 66 percent among Coloreds, and 48 percent among Indians.[9]

On 10 July 1991, President George Bush repealed the CAAA, ending the US federal trade embargo against South Africa. This was justified, Bush explained during a press conference, not only because President de Klerk had met all five conditions of the law, but because the progress was "irreversible." Nelson Mandela, whom Bush called before he signed the executive order lifting the sanctions, expressed disappointment—insisting that he should have waited for more progress. The same view was echoed with "passion" and "anger" by leading Democrats in Congress, the Congressional

Black Caucus and the National Association for the Advancement of Colored People (NAACP). But in the absence of a two-thirds majority these critics in Congress were unable to override the president's decision.

The White House staff had a seven-page fact sheet ready to explain in full the reasons for this step. South Africa, Bush felt, had met the following five conditions listed under Section 311 of the CAAA for the lifting of sanctions:

1. "Release all persons persecuted for their political beliefs or detained unduly without trial, and Nelson Mandela, from prison;
2. repeal the state of emergency in effect on the date of enactment of this Act and release all detainees held under such state of emergency;
3. unban democratic political parties and permit the free exercise by South Africans of all races of the right to form political parties, express political opinions, and otherwise participate in the political process;
4. repeal the Group Areas Act and the Population Registration Act and institutes no other measures with the same purpose;
5. agree to enter into good faith negotiations with truly representative members of the black majority without preconditions."[10]

Section 311 entitled the American president to remove with the stroke of a pen trade bans on textiles, steel, iron, agricultural products, and computers. It also made it legal once again for banks to extend loans to the South African government and for Americans to invest in that country. It gave the president the power to return landing rights to South African Airways. Although not specifically mentioned by President Bush, the Rangel Amendment was considered invalidated as it was closely tied, by intent at least, to the CAAA. On 24 July 1991, Senator William Roth (R-Delaware) declared invalid this amendment, which disallowed tax credits for US companies doing business in South Africa. The Rangel Amendment, he contended, was "vitiated" when Bush certified that the South African government had met the various conditions laid down by the CAAA.[11]

President F. W. de Klerk had accomplished what he set out to do, starting in February 1990. He had convinced the United States and the world that change in South Africa was "irreversible." He fulfilled the conditions of the CAAA at breakneck speed. In less than eighteen months he demolished the bastion of apartheid that took his predecessors more than forty years to build. Welcoming the lifting of the CAAA, he thanked the American president for his positive action, "especially in the face of pressure to shift the goal posts." South Africa, de Klerk said, was now looking forward to a "new era of cooperation with the United States." Noting that certain measures restricting investment and trade still remained at federal, state, county and city level in the United States, de Klerk expressed the belief that the termination of the dreaded CAAA would soon lead to their removal as well.

At his press conference in Pretoria, Foreign Minister Pik Botha showed less restraint. "This is a great day for us," he announced. "We can now look forward to South Africa achieving greater economic growth." He expressed confidence that "this momentous decision will lead all over the world to the termination of sanctions, particularly by those governments who indicated that they are waiting for the lead of the United States."[12]

This important victory gave President de Klerk something meaningful to purvey at the opening of parliament on Friday, 24 January 1992, where results were very much in demand to help stave off further defections to the right. The prosperity and progress to which everyone was aspiring were inextricably linked to South Africa's "return to the world arena," de Klerk insisted. Looking back over the past two years, he felt that South Africa was indeed well on its way to achieving this aim because sanctions were crumbling. New opportunities on a global basis were offered by the lifting of sanctions and the "ending of our isolation has also become irreversible."

Speaking during the debate that followed de Klerk's speech, Foreign Minister Botha felt at liberty for the first time to admit openly that the trip to Washington—and the drastic reforms that preceded it—were primarily aimed at having sanctions lifted. "I had the privilege of standing next to the state president on the lawns of the White House during his historic visit to the USA in September 1990," Botha recalled. "While we stood there, the state president took the historic initial steps which led to the lifting of sanctions against this country by President Bush."[13]

In response to jeers from the Conservative opposition benches, Botha accused his erstwhile compatriots of having cheered on Prime Minister John Vorster when he made a "rousing" speech against sport integration. In a matter of one heated debate it had become evident just how large a political price had to be paid to accomplish the partial lifting of the US sanctions. Not only did Pik Botha repudiate Vorster—his former leader and mentor. He now declared himself enthusiastically in favor of full power-sharing, a concept totally rejected by both Vorster and P. W. Botha, whom he as foreign minister once enthusiastically supported. "The ANC tried to take over this country by means of violence," Botha contended. They tried to do it "by means of foreign pressure, economic embargoes and sports boycotts, and what is the position today? We are sitting around a table where we have to negotiate on how we are going to share power in this country."

H. D. K. van der Merwe of the Conservative Party shouted: "Surrender!"

Pik Botha replied: "We are going to share it—not surrender! Let the ANC also take note of this. We are not handing over the country. We are in the process of negotiation on how to share power in this country."[14]

With a chameleon-like ability reminiscent of Kissinger in the 1960s, Botha had changed colors to blend in with the new landscape and adopted alien policies as if they were his very own creation. But revelations about his role in the secret funding of the Inkatha Freedom Party proved to be a trifle more trying than this encounter in parliament.

After revelations about secret payments to the IFP, published in the *Weekly Mail* on Friday, 19 July 1991, Botha acknowledged responsibility in an interview with the Johannesburg *Sunday Times* over the weekend. He admitted authorizing payments of nearly $100,000 to "subsidize" two IFP rallies in 1989 and 1990—"strictly within the mandate to combat sanctions against South Africa."[15] After further revelations Botha on 25 July 1991, held a press conference to explain further contributions totaling more than $35 million to seven political parties that opposed SWAPO in the November 1989 elections. "We were at war with SWAPO," Botha argued, denying at the same time that South Africa tried to subvert the independence of Namibia. At this "tempestuous" press conference, Botha once again defended the secret payments to the IFP as part of a "broader campaign against international sanctions" totaling $28 million over five years. In response to a journalist who referred to these covert operations as "dirty tricks," Botha retorted: "I do not consider it a dirty trick to try to keep the economy of the country strong."[16] From Kingston, Jamaica, where he stopped over before proceeding to Cuba for a hero's welcome by arch-Marxist Fidel Castro, Nelson Mandela demanded a complete accounting for the past five years—and a replacement of the de Klerk regime by an "interim government of national unity."[17] In contrast to the late 1970s when the so-called Information Scandal or Muldergate led to large-scale investigations and resignations, however, Inkathagate was weathered without much political damage. Botha and de Klerk remained in their posts while Law and Order Minister Vlok and Defense Minister Magnus Malan, whose departments allegedly handled the payments, were shunted to minor posts.

While these embarrassing revelations, shortly after the lifting of sanctions under the CAAA by American President Bush, put a damper on the celebrations, it was only a temporary setback. Reporting the lifting of federal sanctions under the CAAA on 11 July 1991, the *New York Times* proclaimed: "De Klerk's Victory—Without Resolving the Issue of Power Pretoria Regains World Acceptance." Randall Robinson, executive director of TransAfrica, concurred. "We lost—de Klerk Won," he complained in a guest editorial in *Newsweek* on 29 July 1990. "After 25 years of victories culminating in the Anti-Apartheid Act of 1986, the anti-apartheid community has lost a round," Robinson complained. De Klerk, according to Robinson, "parlayed the release of a single person, Nelson Mandela, and the repeal of a handful of apartheid laws into an apparently credible picture of sweeping reforms." The South African president understood that "in America, image is more important than substance."

Those familiar with the sanctions scene in America dismissed Robinson's response as overreaction—a wake-up call to prevent his team from going to sleep. TransAfrica and its allies lost this round, but they were still ahead in the sanctions fight. While Japan and other European nations followed the American example and lifted sanctions, there remained in place in the United States widespread and damaging city and state sanctions against South Africa. It soon became clear that those would only be removed once Nelson Mandela himself gave the word.

NOTES

1. *New York Times,* 11 July 1991.

2. *New York Times* and *Washington Post,* 26 June 1990.

3. *New York Times* and *Washington Post,* 26 June 1990.

4. F. W. de Klerk text of speech before the Natal Chamber of Industries, 4 October 1990.

5. R.F. Botha letter to the president of the General Assembly, UN Document A45/828, 5 December 1990.

6. It exceeded 1985 by twelve incidents (*Business Day,* Johannesburg, 7 February 1991).

7. *The Star,* Johannesburg, 23 June 1991.

8. *The Citizen,* 24 May 1991.

9. *Information Update,* Human Sciences Research Council, Pretoria, 1990.

10. White House Fact Sheet, "Justification for Conclusion that the South African Government has met the Conditions for Sanctions Lifting," Washington, DC, Wednesday, 10 July 1991, US Department of State files.

11. *Congressional Record, Proceedings and Debates of the 102nd Congress, First Session,* Wednesday, 24 July 1991, Congressional Record 137, S10715-03.

12. *The Citizen,* 11 July 1991.

13. Ibid., col. 267.

14. *Debates of Parliament, Fourth Session, Ninth Parliament,* 22 to 31 January 1992, cols. 283-285.

15. *Weekly Mail,* 19 July 1991; Sunday Times, 22 July 1991.

16. *New York Times,* 26 July 1991.

17. *New York Times,* 30 July 1991.

15

The Time Has Come

> To strengthen the forces of democratic change, and to help create
> the necessary conditions for stability and social progress, we be-
> lieve that the time has come when the international community
> should lift all economic sanctions against South Africa.
>
> *Nelson Mandela, 24 September 1993*[1]

Although ANC leader Nelson Mandela lost a round against President F. W.
de Klerk when President George Bush lifted the CAAA in July 1991, he remained firmly in control as far as remaining US federal and local sanctions
and UN embargoes were concerned.

For more than two years Mandela steadfastly refused to release this hold,
insisting that he required further proof of the irreversibility of change in South
Africa.

In the beginning of July 1991, the ANC held its first national convention in
South Africa in thirty years. Two thousand delegates attended. The site was
the same resort city of Durban where former President Botha only six years
before disappointed the world with his defiant Rubicon speech. This time the
main attraction was Nelson Mandela. There was intense speculation over
whether he would finally call for the lifting of all sanctions. Instead,
Mandela invited American and other diplomats to his beach-front hotel for
private talks the evening before his speech. He expressed concern over
President Bush's imminent lifting of the sanctions imposed by Congress
under the CAAA and urged these diplomats to have their governments stand
firm. He was against a relaxation of these measures, he told them, because
there were still lingering doubts in the minds of many of his supporters, who
feared that the whole process might just be "a gigantic trick on the part of

de Klerk."[2] The next evening Nelson Mandela publicly expressed opposition to the lifting of sanctions. "We want to continue to hold the line on sanctions," the ANC leader told his audience on 7 July 1991. The ANC should seek ways to stop the "erosion of sanctions" as a weapon; otherwise it would be left "holding a shell and nothing else."[3]

Mandela, commented *Business Week* on 22 July 1991, may have been unduly despondent. Under the headline "How Mandela Can Still Lean on the Sanctions Lever," the magazine wrote: "That shell may prove more durable than Mandela is letting on." State and local sanctions laws against South Africa were "likely to become a new lever in Mandela's drive to negotiate a transfer of political power to South Africa's black majority."

Even though President Bush lifted federal sanctions in terms of the CAAA, all city and state sanctions remained firmly in place, awaiting ANC clearance. Mayor David Dinkins of New York spoke for most local governments by vowing not to let up on sanctions until Nelson Mandela gave the signal. Still applying sanctions were thirty states, and more than 100 cities and counties.[4] Some 100 universities were still withholding investments from American corporations with South African ties. More than 160 pension funds, representing hundreds of billions in investment dollars, were scrupulously maintaining their ban on any involvement with South Africa—either directly or indirectly.

Instead of taking steps to re-establish links after the federal sanctions in terms of the CAAA were lifted by Bush, companies such as Xerox and Motorola were putting even greater distance between themselves and South Africa. Fearful of losing big city contracts, they continued erasing any semblance of contact with South Africa. These local laws even forced Dell Computer to sever its distribution agreement with a Black-owned South African company, Incorporated Data Systems. "The prohibitions enacted in several cities and states against US firms doing business with South African companies leave us no choice," Dell explained.[5]

Still remaining in force after the lifting of the CAAA were punitive federal measures such as the Gramm Amendment and Export-Import Bank ban, both of which could only be scrapped by majority vote in Congress. The Gramm Amendment to the Bretton Woods Agreement Act required the White House to seek congressional approval before it supported any South African request for credit from the International Monetary Fund (IMF). In reality, this meant a ban on such loans. In terms of congressional legislation passed in the late 1970s during the Carter era, American exporters to South Africa were still precluded from receiving trade credit assistance from the US Export-Import Bank. Also left intact was US adherence to the UN Security Council's mandatory arms embargo of 4 November 1977, and the subsequent voluntary UN ban on the importation of arms from South Africa in terms of Security Council Resolution 558 of 13 December 1984. US intelligence cooperation with South Africa was still banned under Section 107 of the 1987 Intelligence Authorization Act.

In the months leading up to the lifting by President Bush of sanctions under the CAAA, there was much speculation in South Africa about the future, and in some quarters at least, an attempt to look back at the dismal past. The South African Foreign Trade Organization (SAFTO) estimated the cost of market closures, rerouting export shipments on detours, back-handers to middlemen and special price cuts as sweeteners to overseas buyers—so-called "sanctions premiums"—at no less than 3 billion rand a year.[6] South African exports to the United States slumped by almost 1.9 billion rand during the sanctions years, SAFTO found.[7]

"Opportunistic middlemen" would be the losers as their "premiums" and "vast profits" fall "victim to freer trade" after the lifting of CAAA, wrote the *Financial Mail* on 22 March 1991. Steel, textile and sugar producers that have been "outrightly prejudiced" were bound to benefit greatly. But with the lifting of the CAAA, President Bush not only removed the US federal ban on imports of iron and steel, sugar, textiles and agricultural products. He also once again allowed new US investment and loans by American banks to the South African government. It was the lack of foreign capital, most experts agreed, that caused the greatest damage to the South African economy during the sanctions years. Starting in 1984 with the outbreak of violence in South Africa, continued US capital flight had a debilitating effect. "We handled trade sanctions well, so their removal won't make much difference," contended business commentator Ronnie Bethlehem. "Financial sanctions are what matter."[8]

In Cape Town during May 1991, Finance Minister Barend du Plessis informed the annual conference of the National Association of Home Builders that these international financial constraints had cost South Africa 1 percent in gross domestic product (GDP) growth every year since 1985. If it weren't for these capital constraints, he added, the GDP would have totalled an additional 18 billion rand in 1991, giving the government an extra 5 billion rand to spend.[9] From the Investor Responsibility Research Center (IRRC) in Washington came estimates that South Africa—in fear of shortages as a result of sanctions—spent in two decades until 1991 the equivalent $27 billion on import substitution. This represented a loss of 1.5 percent in real income growth a year.[10] Between 1985 and 1988, Reserve Bank Governor Gerhard de Kock estimated, the capital outflow was $11 billion—or 4 percent of the GDP in 1988.[11] "In the early sixties, South Africa had all the opportunity to grow like one of the Asian tigers," observed Colorado University economist Charles Becker in 1991. "Instead, it restructured its economy to look like a sick Latin American country."[12]

Early in May 1991 there was an air of new optimism in private South African financial and government circles as the lifting of US sanctions under the CAAA seemed imminent. The *Sunday Times,* under the heading "Dollars to Roll as SA Rejoins World," reported on 5 May 1991, that numerous "high-powered delegations" visited South Africa in the previous two months in anticipation of the lifting of US and other bans on business and investment. The newspaper quoted President de Klerk as saying that 1 billion rand in foreign capital flowed into South Africa in a single week and another 2 billion rand were anticipated from the United States.[13]

The American Chamber of Commerce in Johannesburg also felt that economic growth would follow shortly after the repeal of the CAAA. "A surge of investment in South Africa by US companies" was bound to result, the chamber said.[14] But the new governor of the Reserve Bank, Chris Stals, remained skeptical. "Large sums of money" will not be pouring into South Africa, he contended, in part because loans from the International Monetary Fund (IMF) and certain investment and trade would still be hampered by US legislation unrelated to the CAAA.[15] Chester Crocker, Reagan's former assistant secretary for African Affairs and now a consultant in Washington, confirmed that he had been approached by some US companies for advice, but, he added, it was "absurd to think there's a queue of Americans salivating to return."[16] Former US ambassador to the United Nations under Carter, Donald McHenry, believed that most corporations would play "wait and see." None, he said, are "chomping at the bit to get back in."[17]

Nelson Mandela still held tight on the remaining sanctions early in July 1993 when both he and F. W. de Klerk arrived separately in the United States to jointly receive the Liberty Award in Philadelphia from newly elected President Bill Clinton for their respective roles in creating a new South Africa. In the preceding days they had gone their own separate ways—de Klerk trying to convince Americans that the time had come to lift the remaining sanctions in cities, states, and on federal level, and Mandela asking the opposite. Back in South Africa the Nationalist government hastily worked toward the adoption, over objections by Chief Buthelezi's IFP and several other Black and White conservative groupings, of 27 April 1994, as the date for "free elections." Although Mandela conceded that the election date introduced "an element of irreversibility," he was still not ready to give the signal. When de Klerk once again raised the question of sanctions during their joint press conference in Philadelphia, Mandela dismissed him as "irrelevant" to the lifting of sanctions. "Nothing and nobody is irrelevant when it comes to the issue of sanctions," protested de Klerk. But it had now become clear that although de Klerk had won the first round, Mandela was in full control of this final round.

In the months leading up to the annual meeting of the IMF in Washington in September 1993, the de Klerk government worked feverishly toward the establishment of a multiracial Transitional Executive Council (TEC). Formal acceptance of such an interim government, de Klerk believed, would finally enable Mandela to pull the lever and lift all the remaining sanctions, allowing once again a free flow of trade and investment between the United States and South Africa. Reversing his original strong opposition to any form of transitional or interim government, de Klerk instructed his chief negotiator Roelf Meyer to speedily take the TEC proposal to the White parliament in Cape Town. De Klerk monitored the parliamentary proceedings from the United States, where he was scheduled to visit the UN and the IMF, and speak at economic seminars—all arranged on the premise that sanctions would be lifted. By being in New York, de Klerk saved himself the public embarrassment of being branded a "despicable traitor" by the Conservative Party opposition as Meyer was when he asked parliament to approve the TEC Bill. On 23 September 1993, the TEC and majority rule finally became law. South Africa's White parliament had in effect voted itself out of existence, and all that remained to be done was to confirm an interim constitution in November.

The next day President de Klerk emerged from a "constructive and friendly" meeting with Secretary-General Boutros-Boutros Ghali, expressing confidence that the latest development in South Africa would result in a call by Mandela for the lifting of all sanctions. During his visit to the United Nations—the first for a White South African leader since Smuts' unhappy experience in 1946—de Klerk finally admitted publicly that international pressures had played a part in bringing about change in South Africa. Sanctions, he said, had "a marked effect on the internal debate."[18]

This time Nelson Mandela, already in New York in anticipation of these developments, felt that the Rubicon had finally been crossed and that change was indeed irreversible. On 24 September 1993, not long after de Klerk had left the UN building, he turned up in the company of New York Mayor David Dinkins and Black activists Jesse Jackson and Al Sharpton, ready to pull the lever on sanctions. Proclaiming that "the countdown to democracy in South Africa had begun," he called for the lifting of all remaining economic sanctions against his country, leaving only the arms embargo in place.[19]

He made this call for the lifting of all sanctions (except the arms embargo) in the UN Special Committee Against Apartheid, which like the White South African parliament was about to lose its reason for existence.[20] Still, Mandela's announcement was welcomed by this committee with warm applause—in contrast to the tepid reaction from erstwhile supporters in and outside Congress in Washington. The Congressional Black Caucus reacted to Nelson Mandela's call for the lifting of sanctions with "extremely bad grace," reported Simon Barber from the American capital. He quoted Black Congressman Donald Payne (D-New Jersey) as saying that the Mandela announcement was made "under enormous pressure" to which the ANC leader had evidently felt obliged to cave in. This was, Payne said, "unfortunate for Blacks in South Africa" because "the time when one person, one vote will really be counted will be 1999."[21]

Anti-apartheid groups such as TransAfrica, the ACOA, ICCR, and the NAACP in a sense became rebels without a cause. With Mandela now directing himself toward the business community to help reconstruct the new

South Africa, these groups, with their expertise at erecting barriers and imposing sanctions, were in danger of becoming irrelevant. Needed now were capital, technology, and trade to revitalize post-apartheid South Africa. This could only be provided by corporate boards, investors, fund managers and other business executives—Mandela and the ANC's "new friends."[22]

Immediately after Mandela's announcement in the UN, President Bill Clinton called on American states, counties and cities to move quickly to lift their sanctions. The Namibian experience has shown, however, that the removal of local sanctions can be a time-consuming affair. More than three years after this territory became independent from South Africa and all US sanctions against it were officially called off, Namibia was still trying to have some cities and states repeal their sanctions laws and ordinances. Namibia, reported The Argus on 26 September 1993, should be "a cautionary lesson for South Africa." The US ambassador in Windhoek was even obliged to start a letter-writing campaign to assist in the dismantling of redundant sanctions legislation still in effect against this country.

When in September 1993, Mandela finally called for the lifting of all sanctions against South Africa, the IRRC reported that 179 local entities—thirty states, 109 cities, thirty-nine counties and regional authorities, and the Virgin Islands—were still applying punitive measures against companies doing business in South Africa. It contended that these sanctions measures below federal level would take time to fall away and that in the meantime US companies would continue to respect them.

After his UN appearance Mandela flew to Washington, where he joined some sixty South African officials and business executives in an appeal to American and world business executives to invest in South Africa. "We appeal to you who are important players in the world economy to seize this historic moment of the lifting of the economic sanctions on South Africa, to look afresh at our country in terms of investment, trade and other economic opportunities," he said. The ANC leader's first reward came in the form of a pledge of $850 million (2.6 billion rand) in economic aid to South Africa from IMF chief Michel Camdessus on Saturday, 25 September 1993. Camdessus chose to announce the IMF's first multilateral assistance to South Africa since sanctions were first introduced in the early 1980s after a breakfast meeting with Mandela.[23] In the meantime President de Klerk utilized a news conference at the World Economic Development Congress in Washington to challenge the contention that sanctions were lifted in response to Mandela's call at the UN. "The world reacted before Mr. Mandela made his speech," de Klerk claimed. He also criticized the ANC leader's appeal to the international community to recognize the TEC rather than the Pretoria government.[24] In the American capital at this time such squabbles seemed irrelevant—even petty—while ANC specialists, Nationalists, and DP-minded financiers and officials took limousines together from one meeting to another, attending seminars and receptions, soliciting trade and investment.

On 8 October 1993, the UN General Assembly adopted a resolution sponsored by Nigeria that ended most economic sanctions against South Africa and allowed for the removal of the oil embargo once the TEC became operational. On the same day, South Africa's Foreign Affairs Department announced that India would be sending a high-powered delegation to South Africa "to talk trade."[25] So ended the sanctions saga at the UN that started when India became the first nation to apply a trade embargo against South Africa in 1946 and, spurred on by its failure, took the campaign first to the world organization and ultimately the United States.

On 24 September 1993, American President Clinton called for an end to all remaining sanctions. Within hours the Senate adopted by voice vote Bill 1493, sponsored by Senators Nancy Kassebaum (R-Kansas) and Paul Simon (D-Illinois). It proposed an end to US restrictions on loans to South Africa by the IMF and urged local and state governments to remove their sanctions as well. This initial step by the Senate enabled the International Monetary Fund to extend credit to South Africa while Mandela and de Klerk were still in Washington seeking its financial assistance. The ultimate signing off on sanctions by Congress took much longer.

Only on 19 November 1993, the House of Representatives responded by adopting Bill HR 3225 and passing it along to the Senate for endorsement. Speaking in the Senate the next day, shortly after it ratified the House bill, Republican Senator Nancy Kassebaum, who played such a key role in the passing of the CAAA in 1986 over her own president's objections, now welcomed South Africa back into the international community. "The days of isolation and sanctions are over," she announced. The United States stood ready "as partners" to support South Africa's efforts to create "a new, democratic and non-racial nation."[26]

The bill repealed all the remaining bans on the importation of products from South Africa and elevated it to most-favored-nation trade status. It made clear, however, that the United States would still abide by UN Security Council resolutions imposing bans against South Africa on arms sales and purchases and the transfer of nuclear technology. At the same time, 179 state and local legislatures were urged to remove trade and investment barriers against South Africa before October 1995. Those who failed to do so would risk forfeiting valuable federal transportation subsidies.

Finally Congress had signed off on one of the most debilitating pieces of American sanctions legislation, which required US representatives at the IMF and World Bank to vote against any form of financial aid to South Africa. It also urged the Overseas Private Investment Corporation (OPIC) and the Export-Import Bank to assist Black-owned companies in South Africa and authorized the American president to grant foreign aid through the Development Fund for Africa.[27]

At a ceremony on the South Lawn of the White House on Tuesday, 23 November 1993, President Bill Clinton signed into law HR 3225—the South

African Democratic Transition Support Act. It was attended by civil rights leaders and congressmen who played a key role in the US sanctions campaign. Citing "Nkosi Sikelel' i-Afrika" (God bless Africa)—the first line of the song favored by many to be the anthem of the new South Africa—Clinton brought with a stroke of his pen an end to all remaining federal sanctions.

On 10 December 1993, de Klerk and Mandela shared the stage at Oslo's city hall as joint recipients of the Nobel Peace Prize. They were not the first South Africans to become Nobel laureates. First in 1960, Chief Albert Luthuli, a prominent Zulu and former president of the ANC, and then in 1984, Anglican Archbishop Desmond Tutu were honored in this fashion—both men for their stand against apartheid. De Klerk, about to be eclipsed by his former prisoner as he received his just reward for negotiating himself out of power, and Mandela, the Black freedom fighter, ready to step into the highest office in a land where he spent most of his adult life in jail, presented vastly different views on why and how White minority rule and apartheid were dismantled.

Nelson Mandela, citing American civil rights leader Martin Luther King as an inspiration, credited millions of his own people who "dared to rise up" and the "millions of people across the globe, the anti-apartheid movement [and] the governments and organizations" who helped to ostracize and isolate South Africa. De Klerk in turn, denied that either international sanctions or the armed struggle brought about the downfall of apartheid. Fundamental reforms, he argued, came not because of "external pressure" but as a result of "social changes which economic growth generated," especially the movement of millions of people into the cities, and "the exposure to realities" brought by television and radio. The single most important factor, he concluded, was "a fundamental change of heart" that had "occurred on both sides."

Whether it was the heart or the stomach that spoke the loudest will be debated for many years to come as historians, economists, and political scientists revisit the South African sanctions saga. There is, however, little doubt that sanctions, while not the only factor, was a major force for political change in South Africa. US sanctions, in particular, served not only to sever South Africa from the world's leading and largest trade and capital market, but from other important business partners as they also shut their doors on business under apartheid in fear of retribution from Washington.

NOTES

1. *New York Times*, 24 September 1993.
2. *The Sowetan,* Johannesburg, 3 July 1991.

3. *Business Week*, "How Mandela Can Still Lean on The Sanctions Lever," 22 July 1991.

4. These figures vary according to source. Even the New York Times in two reports during he same week cited conflicting statistics. On 1 July 1993, it stated: "Although the Bush Administration ended comprehensive Federal sanctions, at least 28 states, 24 counties and 92 cities, including New York, also passed laws against doing business with South Africa." On 3 July 1993, the same newspaper wrote that "some 29 states and more than 100 cities, including New York, maintain [sanctions]" (*New York Times*, 1 and 3 July 1993).

5. *US Business in South Africa 1991*, IRRC report, 1991.

6. *The Star*, Johannesburg, 11 February 1991.

7. *SAFTO Exporter*, April/May 1991.

8. *Financial Mail*, 19 April 1991.

9. *The Star*, Johannesburg,17 May 1991.

10. *Business Day*, Johannesburg, 2 May 1991.

11. Ibid.

12. Ibid.

13. *The Star*, Johannesburg, 3 May 1991.

14. *Business Day*, Johannesburg, 26 June 1991.

15. *The Citizen*, Johannesburg, 11 July 1991.

16. *The Citizen*, 13 February 1991.

17. Holmes, Paul M., "Reinvestment in a Post-Apartheid South Africa?" *AQ, The Aspen Institute Quarterly*, Spring 1991, Vol. 3, No. 2, p. 122.

18. *The Argus*, Johannesburg, 24 September 1993.

19. Ibid.

20. It was requested that the arms embargo stay in place until after the elections, when a Black majority government was in place.

21. *Business Day*, 12 October 1993.

22. Ibid.

23. *Sunday Star*, Johannesburg, 26 September 1993.

24. *The Argus*, 27 September 1993.

25. Ibid.

26. *Congressional Quarterly, Weekly Report*, Vol. 51, No. 38, 25 September 1993, p. 2574.

27. Aid was, however, specifically excluded from going to the government of South Africa or any group supported by it until after multiracial elections took place. Also excluded were groups that have not renounced violence as a tactic to gain power.

16

Conclusion

Question: "So did sanctions work?"
Answer: "Oh, there is no doubt."

Nelson Mandela
Time, 14 June 1993

In sharp contrast to this unequivocal affirmation by Nelson Mandela stand numerous denials by President F. W. de Klerk that sanctions played any role in his decision to end apartheid and accept Black majority rule.

When de Klerk set this process in motion with his now famous February 1990 parliamentary opening speech in Cape Town, he mentioned violence, tension, and conflict in South Africa as considerations. He saw the demise of Communism in Europe as a window of opportunity for unbanning and allowing the ANC and others to freely participate in the South African political process. Without Communist support, de Klerk reasoned, these organizations posed much less of a threat. Not once did he mention sanctions.

Almost four years later, during his acceptance speech at the Nobel Peace Prize ceremony in Oslo, after all significant sanctions had been lifted, de Klerk still denied that external pressures played a role in the dramatic dismantling of apartheid. Speaking on the same occasion, however, fellow laureate Nelson Mandela went out of his way to thank all those who had helped the cause by ostracizing and isolating South Africa.

Disagreement over the relative importance of sanctions in bringing about the final capitulation of White rule in South Africa is, of course, not confined to these two prominent personalities. It exists on many other levels in government, business, church, and academic circles in South Africa and abroad.

The purpose of this study was to determine the role, if any, that sanctions played in moving South Africa's White leadership from totally rejecting any form of power sharing to embracing majority rule in a unified country. What effect did sanctions, and more specifically US sanctions, have on the decision-making process in South Africa? The spotlight is on the United States as the one country that held the key to the ultimate success of sanctions against South Africa. Not only was it one of South Africa's foremost business partners; it alone had the superpower ability to coerce others into following its example.

There is hardly any debate over the goal of the sanctions campaign against South Africa. India, the first nation to apply a trade embargo against Pretoria in the 1940s, had hoped that its action would result in better treatment for expatriate Indians living in South Africa. When this effort failed, India proceeded to the United Nations, where it tried to muster world support for such punitive action.

Initially, UN sanctions were sought simply as a remedy for the "injustices" under apartheid or a means to coerce South Africa into adopting more humane policies towards its non-White citizenry. However, with the growing influence and numerical strength of newly independent Black African nations in the General Assembly, the goal posts shifted. Imbued with a strong sense of anti-colonialism and resentment toward White rule, Black Africa insisted that the continent would be free only when the last vestiges of White rule were removed and replaced by Black "majority" rule.

Sanctions were seen as the only means to accomplish this goal in South Africa—short of outright warfare. Pretoria presented such a formidable challenge on the military front that the direct involvement of one or more of the major powers would have been required to forcibly remove its White rulers from power. The unlikelihood of the Soviet Union, let alone any of the major Western powers, involving itself in such a confrontation made sanctions the only viable alternative.

But while the Soviet Union and its satellites, as well as the Scandinavian countries, readily supported numerous UN General Assembly sanctions resolutions, the rest of the West demurred. And without support from South Africa's major Western trading partners, these resolutions amounted to little more than posturing. Needed to enforce sanctions was a decision by the UN Security Council, where the United States, Britain, and France continued to hedge.

In the early 1950s ANC President Albert Luthuli echoed the call for sanctions even though, he conceded, it might cause suffering to Blacks. He and other prominent Black South African leaders provided grist for the mill at several newly established anti-apartheid organizations (AAOs) in major cities abroad. From New York the American Committee on Africa (ACOA) spearheaded the anti-apartheid drive and became the first non-governmental organization (NGO) to press for sanctions in the United States.

These AAOs, however, needed something more dramatic than appeals from South Africa to kindle interest and rally support for the cause. It happened in 1952, when the so-called Defiance Campaign started as a local boycott action, spread, and turned violent. The world took notice. In the United States the ACOA exploited this newfound interest to its fullest, steadily gaining support for its sanctions calls among churches, universities, and civil rights organizations.

In March 1960 Sharpeville shook the world. This tragic event finally made apartheid a matter of global concern. It provided the AAOs with new means to promote their cause. In the United States Sharpeville added a new sense urgency to ACOA calls for action against apartheid as it pressured private corporations and Washington officialdom into severing their business ties with South Africa.

It was largely in response to pressures from organizations such as the ACOA and allied civil rights groups, as well as pleas from Black African rulers, that President John Kennedy first took official action on the sanctions front. He saw US support for a UN Security Council arms embargo against South Africa as the least disruptive step against a valuable anti-Communist ally in Africa—but sufficient, he hoped, to appease the anti-apartheid forces for the time being. Kennedy and his advisers were under no illusion. They knew that further and greater demands would follow. And so they did.

In subsequent years, other American presidents found themselves under similar pressures and also tried to get by with sanctions in small doses on a piecemeal basis. All of them from Truman to Reagan—with the possible exception of President Carter—considered White-ruled South Africa a staunch and vital ally against Communism at the tip of Africa. In the mid-1980s when President Ronald Reagan found himself locked in a final and fierce battle with Congress over sanctions, the specter of Communism was once again raised—to no avail.

Sharpeville did more than push South Africa and apartheid to the fore at world forums. It caused a flight of foreign capital and placed heavy strains on an economy hitherto seemingly invincible. This chip in South Africa's armor encouraged the sanctions supporters to double their efforts. So convinced was the Kennedy administration of the inevitable fall of White rule in the wake of Sharpeville that it instructed its new envoy to Pretoria to prepare dealing with a Black government within eighteen months. But these projections did not take into account the economic and political resilience of South Africa in the 1960s. Barely two years after Sharpeville, South African Finance Minister Eben Dönges could marvel at his country's strong economy, which stood like a bulwark against foreign sanctions pressures.

In the next twenty years the proponents of sanctions invariably found themselves up against this seemingly impenetrable economic bulwark as they tried to cripple the country with sanctions. US corporations resisted disinvestment pressures for the sake of outstanding profits in South Africa.

Successive US administrations went out of their way to find excuses for continued trade with and investment in South Africa. Picking up on the so-called Polaroid experiment, the Nixon and Ford administrations emphasized the role that business could play by undermining apartheid through economic integration. President Carter, and Reagan after him, used the Sullivan Code to justify a continued US business presence in South Africa.

This all changed in the 1980s. While some observers saw the Soweto riots of 1976 as the watershed event that marked the beginning of the end for Pretoria's white rulers, a prominent American policymaker in the Carter administration, Richard Moose, in 1980 painted a South Africa impervious to outside pressures. The economy, he noted, was booming as gold reached an all-time peak, and the Botha government was in total control.

In 1984, however, violence erupted once again. Despite repeated efforts by the authorities to clamp down, a multitude of protest movements under the UDF umbrella managed to grab overseas newspaper headlines and TV prime time with continued acts of violence. Instead of creating understanding and sympathy for the security forces in their efforts to quell the violence, as the Botha government had hoped, the horrid scenes on American TV screens did the opposite. US Congress found itself under increasing pressure "to do something" to stop the "brutal repression" by the South African "regime." At the same time, many American businesses left in panic.

A debilitating debt crisis resulted as American and other overseas banks refused to roll over loans to South Africa in August 1985, after Botha's disappointing Rubicon speech had left them without hope for the country's political and economic recovery. Leading South African and foreign economists saw these unofficial "financial sanctions" or "sanctions of the markets" as more devastating than any official measures passed before or since.

Loss of business confidence in South Africa was of course not limited to Americans and other foreigners. In September 1985, a group of South African business leaders risked Botha's opprobrium by journeying to Lusaka in a desperate attempt to seek an independent settlement with the exiled leadership of the ANC. The friendly partnership formed between President Botha and the moguls of South Africa when he assumed power in 1978 unraveled as it became evident that he had no remedy for the growing pressures from abroad.

American and other foreign corporations that once pledged to stay in South Africa regardless of disinvestment pressures—ostensibly for the welfare of its Black population—now found it necessary to fold their tents and leave. The "hassle factor" at home had begun to outweigh dwindling profits in South Africa with its rapidly worsening economy—the result of a world economic recession coupled with a devastating drought, persistent violence, disturbances at the work place, and sanctions.

It was at this stage that Congress finally stepped in to take charge of US policy toward South Africa. In 1985 President Reagan could still manage to stall Congress with a sanctions decree of his own. This was much to his own distaste, as he remained throughout his tenure totally opposed to sanctions against South Africa, which he considered to be a staunch friend and ally against Communism. In 1986 he risked a sure and crushing defeat by vetoing the Comprehensive Anti-Apartheid Act (CAAA) despite overwhelming bipartisan congressional support for this sanctions legislation.

When Congress took matters in its own hands with the passing in 1986, over Reagan's veto, of tough sanctions under the CAAA, it finally put an end to the quiet diplomacy as practised by the State Department. Under successive American presidents with widely differing political philosophies, the professionals at State had somehow managed to stick steadfastly to the *status quo* in dealing with South Africa. Even during the Carter presidency, with its penchant for promoting human rights around the world by punitive measures if necessary, little happened. While many thought South Africa would be targeted for sanctions, the Carter administration merely toughened the UN arms embargo originally passed in the Kennedy era, and reluctantly accepted credit restrictions passed by Congress. At the same time, it discouraged and blocked more than twenty sanctions bills.

Why did it take Congress so long to wrest control over South African policy away from the State Department? First, South Africa was never perceived to be an issue of war and peace that required US intervention. Second, there were no special treaties at stake that necessitated congressional endorsement. Third, South Africa remained a low priority issue for many years. Even the Sharpeville shootings and Soweto uprising were occasions not for serious congressional policy review, but for public posturing on the floors of the Senate and House of Representatives.

In 1985 all this had changed. Violence in the Black townships and a constant vigil outside the South African Embassy in Washington brought the "crisis" right to the doorstep of Congress. The issue was no longer merely South Africa or apartheid. The Black American voter had become a bargaining chip as legislators were cautioned that their vote on sanctions would be used as a litmus test for their stand on racism at home. In their own self-interest even conservative Republicans could no longer resist joining liberal Democrats in their call for sanctions—over the objections of their own president.

During the heated Senate debate that preceded the adoption of the CAAA, one of the few conservative Republicans who stuck with the Reagan position, Senator Malcolm Wallop of Wyoming, pictured his peers as middle-class, comfortable Whites playing up to the Black and liberal population of America. Senator Edward Kennedy, who fought long and hard for sanctions proclaimed South Africa "the new civil rights issue" of America.

Despite de Klerk's denials, it is evident that much of what happened in South Africa since February 1990 was driven by an urgent desire to have sanctions lifted, especially US sanctions. To ascribe, however, every drastic change to sanctions alone would not only be too simplistic but inaccurate. It was a combination of international and domestic economic and political factors that prompted this decision.

An insider privately likened de Klerk's dilemma when he assumed the presidency in September 1989 to that of a new chief executive taking charge of a company on the brink of bankruptcy. He had to weigh the debit side against the credit column in making tough decisions to ensure survival.

On the credit or plus side de Klerk found comfort in the demise of Communism. It had practically disappeared from the face of Europe and the Black liberation movements could therefore no longer rely on assistance from these quarters. Therefore it seemed safe to unban organizations such as the ANC, PAC, and SACP.

But the collapse of Communism had, of course, a negative flip-side that de Klerk, publicly chose to ignore, but privately must have considered. The end of the Cold War meant that South Africa could no longer exploit its role as an anti-Communist stronghold in Africa to curry favor with the United States and other Western nations.

Also on the credit side was Namibia's independence which brought an expensive and unpopular war to a close. The territory's smooth transition to majority rule could help to dampen White fears of a similar direction in South Africa.

The debit side showed an economy in shambles. This was in part the result of a long drought, some mismanagement, and a global recession that affected not only the price of gold and the sales of strategic minerals but every other facet of the South African economy. While trade sanctions could be circumvented through middlemen, the premiums required to do so made exports less lucrative and imports more costly.

The country was committed to a tough repayment schedule in terms of a debt standstill arrangement with American and other major overseas banks. Very little capital was flowing in as business confidence reached an all-time low. South Africa, which always relied heavily on foreign financial sources for much of its development financing, had in effect become a capital exporter.

Large expenditures on strategic import replacement industries, or "inward industrialization" such as Valindaba, Sasol, Mossgas, and Armscor, had drained away funds needed for social services. Black unemployment was exceeding 40 percent.

Even though de Klerk's militaristic predecessor's security apparatus seemed to have stymied the armed struggle waged by the ANC from bases in neighboring states, Black internal revolt appeared beyond control. Despite the state of emergency the widespread violence and political uncertainty that prompted large-scale capital flight in the mid-1980s, continued unabated.

More than making up for the ANC's apparent rebuff on the battlefield were the inroads that the exiled organization made in Western diplomatic circles abroad. After a meeting between Reagan's secretary of state, George Shultz, and exiled ANC leader Oliver Tambo, came urgent appeals from Washington for Pretoria to initiate talks as well.

No longer was it possible to convince the Americans that the ANC amounted to nothing more than a Communist-inspired terrorist organization. The ANC, in fact, was increasingly beginning to look like a government-in-exile. Unbanning it and allowing it to compete openly with other political parties in South Africa could be one way of stripping it of its mystique.

The September 1989 White election had shown that by trying to steer a middle road between liberal reform and the traditional hard-line policies, the National Party was losing support on both sides. Adding the votes in favor of the liberal Democratic Party to those who remained loyal to the National Party, de Klerk now perceived a potential new constituency composed of 70 percent of the Whites who voted for reform and endorsed granting political rights to Blacks.

This would more than compensate for the inevitable loss to the right-wing Conservative Party if radical reforms were introduced. De Klerk was subsequently proven correct in this assumption as he won almost 70 percent of the total votes in a referendum on reform.

Finally, and of major importance, were several new bills before the US Congress aimed at adding further sanctions to the already tough measures contained in the CAAA. Even President George Bush, who as Reagan's deputy strongly opposed sanctions, was now threatening to take punitive action unless Pretoria started complying with the CAAA's conditions before the end of June 1990.

In short, de Klerk had inherited from President P. W. Botha a nation under siege, a country beleaguered. It was evident that only drastic change could help it to break out of the walls surrounding it. How drastic?

The CAAA clearly spelled out the conditions for the lifting of sanctions. There were five steps to be taken, ranging from the release of Mandela to the unbanning of all political organizations, the lifting of the state of emergency, the repeal of the Group Areas Act and the Population Registration Act, and good-faith negotiations with the Black majority. De Klerk went to work trying to fulfill all these requirements. He did so with an alacrity that surprised both friend and foe.

He was, incidentally, not the first or only South African leader to respond to sanctions—or the threat of sanctions. In the early 1960s Verwoerd saw the need to introduce modest changes and to take extra precautions to prevent a recurrence of Sharpeville in fear that it would invite punitive action from abroad. In the 1970s Vorster turned the screws on Rhodesia to avert possible US support for UN sanctions against South Africa. In the mid-1980s P. W. Botha, to the disenchantment of his own securocrats, prematurely lifted the state of emergency in an attempt to stave off sanctions.

President de Klerk was not the first either to recognize the need to negotiate with the ANC or to free Mandela. When he took office several prominent
jailed ANC leaders had already been released, and his predecessor, President
P. W. Botha, had discussions with Nelson Mandela over his own imminent
release. Top-level official contact, although secretive, had been initiated
with the exiled ANC leadership abroad in Botha's time. But whereas
President Botha resisted Black majority rule at all costs, even at the risk of
additional and total US sanctions, de Klerk chose to meet this demand.

During the February 1992 no-confidence debate in the South African parliament, Foreign Minister Pik Botha recalled how President F. W. de Klerk
took the necessary steps that led to the lifting of sanctions by American
President Bush. All of South Africa, he contended, was pleased to be back
in the international arena. Instead of being the target of sanctions and
boycotts, he noted, the government was now "sitting around a table"
negotiating with the ANC on how "to share power in this country."

Pik Botha finally confirmed what observers had suspected all along but
few in government wished to admit: American sanctions played a key role in
the drastic changes announced by President de Klerk in the same parliament
two years earlier.

He also illustrated the extent to which US sanctions helped force a political transformation in the upper ranks of the governing National Party. During
most of his career Foreign Minister Botha stood solidly with both Vorster and
his successor, President P. W. Botha, in their defiance of the outside world—
inviting sanctions rather than adopting majority rule. Now he was distancing
himself from his former political mentors and colleagues in the conservative
opposition, who saw majority rule in exchange for the lifting of sanctions as
surrender.

Was it a matter of reform in exchange for the lifting sanctions? The response most frequently heard from de Klerk and his top advisers is that other
important domestic imperatives, not sanctions, dictated change. The lifting of
sanctions happened to be merely a welcome bonus, an encouragement, they
claim, but hardly the prime reason for reform.

Witness, for example, the triumphant trip to Washington about which
Foreign Minister Botha spoke in parliament in February 1992. During his call
on President Bush at the White House and in a subsequent appearance at
the National Press Club, de Klerk went to great lengths to deny that he was
making any effort to conform to the conditions set out for the lifting of
sanctions the CAAA. South Africa, he claimed, would have scrapped
apartheid and adopted majority rule regardless of whether the CAAA existed.

Yet, in the months following his Washington visit, de Klerk left no stone
unturned to work speedily toward the fulfillment of every one of the five conditions set by the CAAA. Even the repeal of the Population Registration Act,
which was initially deemed impossible under the existing South African
Constitution, was almost miraculously accomplished overnight. Seemingly

insurmountable squabbles with the ANC over the freeing of political prisoners were settled in such expedient fashion by de Klerk that even the liberal South African media complained about the indiscriminate release of hardened criminals.

Why then this persistent denial by President de Klerk that sanctions had any influence on his actions? Under questioning after his speech at the Washington National Press Club in September 1990, he provided some insight. South Africa did not like to be prescribed to by other countries, he explained. As an astute politician, de Klerk was evidently not willing to admit to the ultimate sin in White, and especially Afrikaner, South African politics: listening to and acting according to dictates from abroad or caving in to foreign pressure.

In 1992, when Foreign Minister Botha credited President de Klerk with breaking South Africa out of its isolation, most, but not all US sanctions against South Africa had been lifted. While de Klerk succeeded in having the CAAA repealed, ANC leader Nelson Mandela still held the key to the removal of the remaining federal, state, and city sanctions in America. These, it was made clear, would not be lifted until the ANC leader gave the word.

Contrary to de Klerk, Nelson Mandela made no secret of his belief in the value of sanctions as a tool to coerce South Africa's White rulers into accepting majority rule. He refused to let go of it until he was totally convinced that change was indeed irreversible. Not even acceptance of an election date shortly before he and de Klerk arrived separately in Philadelphia in the United States in July 1993 to jointly receive the Liberty Award could move the ANC leader to call off the remaining US and UN sanctions.

Only after the Transitional Executive Council (TEC) was endorsed by parliament did Mandela finally accept the irreversibility of change. Informed of this development in New York only hours before he was due to address the UN Special Committee Against Apartheid on 24 September 1993, Mandela finally agreed to call for the lifting of all remaining economic sanctions. This prompted both the United Nations and the United States to act.

De Klerk, who was also in the United States at the time for his own series of meetings, insisted during a press conference that the sanctions were lifted not as a result of Mandela's call, but because of the establishment of the TEC. US President Clinton, Congress, and several American mayors and governors, however, left no doubt that the scrapping of the remaining sanctions were in specific response to Mandela's speech.

As a politician, de Klerk was evidently electioneering for a position of power against the man that he saw as his main rival in the new South Africa that he heralded in February 1990. There was much to be lost and very little, if anything, to be gained by giving Mandela or sanctions any credit.

Apart from the obvious need to deny the influence of sanctions and other external pressures in a country where Whites expect their leaders to defy the outside world, support could be also be gained by such denials in Black, Colored, and Indian communities. It allowed de Klerk and his colleagues to claim that they acted out of the goodness of their hearts in scrapping the "failed" and "cruel" policies of the past and opting for a new "democratic" and "just" multiracial South Africa.

In Oslo during the Nobel Peace Prize ceremony, President de Klerk once again dismissed the role of external pressures in his decision to turn his back on apartheid. It was de Klerk, the competent campaigner, apparently speaking with his mind focused on the upcoming April 1994 elections. Nelson Mandela, speaking on the same occasion, followed his own political agenda when he not only thanked those who helped to force the de Klerk government to the negotiating table by ostracizing and isolating South Africa but praised the "armed struggle"—even though the latter seemed to have had little impact.

What the world witnessed in Oslo were not merely two remarkable men who reshaped South Africa in four short years, but experienced politicians ready to do battle in that country's first free elections. They both had potential constituents at home to impress.

On the surface, the US sanctions drama seemed to have played itself out in a matter of eight years, from 1985 until 1993. It was in 1985 that American banks led a run on South Africa and the exodus of US corporations first reached alarming proportions. That same year President Reagan was forced to impose sanctions by executive order as the only means to preempt stronger measures by Congress. The Comprehensive Anti-Apartheid Act of 1986 with its far-reaching sanctions, was adopted by Congress over Reagan's veto. In his historic February 1990 speech President de Klerk set in motion a process that would result in the final elimination of US sanctions with the signing of the South African Democratic Transition Support Act in November 1993.

But these happenings were only the dramatic conclusion of a saga that started rather innocuously in 1946, when India first introduced sanctions as a means to change South Africa's racial policies and then took its case to the UNited Nations. From the very beginning it was clear that any UN sanctions resolution without the support of the United States had little real impact. The United States was not only one of South Africa's major business partners, but it also had the ability to bring other important industrial nations into the sanctions fold.

Ultimately, this US-South African episode met all the requirements for successful sanctions. The United States, the "sender" country, was not only much larger than South Africa, the "target" country, but strong enough to force other nations to comply with its own sanctions. US trade with and investment in South Africa, while constituting a major portion of the smaller target country's foreign business activity, were of minor importance to itself. Unrest, violence, and a sagging economy made South Africa relatively unattractive to US corporations that might otherwise have fought harder to retain business links and prevent official sanctions. The goal enunciated in the CAAA was clear-cut and straightforward. It was eventually attained in full when President de Klerk complied and enabled President Bush to repeal sanctions.

Sanctions against South Africa did not pitch good against evil in a battle between two clearly defined forces. It was rather a series of shifting strategies and alliances. Sanctions were chosen by those opposed to the White South African government as the best method, short of outright war, to end apartheid and introduce Black majority rule. Right until and beyond the adoption of the CAAA in 1986, the debate over the morality of sanctions continued. At times it pitched staunch opponents of apartheid against each other. On one occasion, liberal author Alan Paton, who politically supported the ANC from the very outset at his own peril, accused Bishop Desmond Tutu in an open letter of acting immorally by supporting sanctions.

Sanctions against South Africa was sheer power politics. It was in a sense a war that left many victims jobless and an economy more tattered than it may have been otherwise. Just how severe the devastation was and how many were left destitute as a result of sanctions will no doubt be the topic of future studies.

This historical review does not reveal in exact measure the role sanctions played in the rapid transformation of the South African political scene in the 1990s. This would be an impossible task. But it does prove beyond doubt that US and other punitive measures significantly dictated the form, substance, timing, and pace of these reforms. In this sense—notwithstanding strenuous arguments to the contrary for apparent political reasons—sanctions did work.

Selected Bibliography

Acheson, Dean. *Present at the Creation.* W. W. Norton, New York, 1969.

Ball, G. *The Discipline of Power.* Little, Brown, Boston, 1968.

Bethlehem, Ronald W. *Economics in a Revolutionary Society: Sanctions and the Transformation of South Africa.* A. Donker, Craighall, 1988.

Biermann, H. H. H., ed. *The Case for South Africa: As Put Forth in the Statements of Eric H Louw.* McFadden Books, New York, 1963.

Bissell, R. *South Africa and the United States: The Erosion of an Influence Relationship.* Praeger, New York, 1982.

Blake, Robert. *A History of Rhodesia.* Alfred A. Knopf, New York, 1978.

Brzezinski, Zbigniew. *Power and Principle.* Weidenfeld and Nicholson, London, 1983.

Burgess, J. and Rogers, B., eds. *The Great White Hoax: South Africa's International Propaganda Machine.* Africa Bureau, London, 1977.

Calpin, G. *Indians in South Africa.* Shuter & Shooter, Pietermaritzburg, 1949.

Coker, Christopher. *The United States and South Africa 1968-1985: Constructive Engagement and Its Critics.* Duke University Press, Durham, N.C., 1986.

Crocker, Chester. *High Noon in Southern Africa: Making Peace in a Rough Neighborhood.* W. W. Norton, New York, 1992.

D'Amato, James V. *Constructive Engagement: The Rise and Fall of an American Foreign Policy.* Ph. D. dissertation, University of South Carolina, 1988.

Daoudi, M. and Dajani, M. *Economic Sanctions: Ideals and Experience.* Routledge and Kegan Paul, London, 1983.

De Klerk, Willem. *F. W. de Klerk: The Man in His Time.* Jonathan Ball Publishers, Johannesburg, 1991.

De Villiers, D., and de Villiers, Johanna. *P. W.* Tafelberg, Cape Town, 1984.

De Villiers, Les. *Secret Information.* Tafelberg, Cape Town, 1980.

———. *South Africa: A Skunk Among Nations.* International Books, London, 1975.

———. *South Africa Drawn in Colour: The Smuts Years 1945-1946.* Gordon Publishing, Johannesburg, 1979.

Dexter, Byron. *The Years of Opportunity: The League of Nations 1920-1926.* Viking Press, New York, 1967.

Doxey, M. *Economic Sanctions and International Enforcement.* Oxford University Press, London, 1971.

Du Boulay, Shirley. *Tutu: Voice of the Voiceless.* William B. Erdmans Publishing Co., Grand Rapids, Mich., 1988.

El-Khawas, Mohammed, and Cohen, Barry, eds. *The Kissinger Study of Southern Africa: National Security Study Memorandum 39.* Laurence Hill, New York, 1976.

Esterhuyse, W., and Nel, P., eds. *The ANC and its Leaders.* Tafelberg, Cape Town, 1990.

Fornara, Charles. *Plutarch and the Meganan Decree.* 24 Yale Classical Studies, 1975.

Fourie, Brand. *Brandpunte: Agter die Skerms met Suid-Afrika se Bekendste Diplomaat.* Tafelberg, Cape Town, 1991.

Franck, Thomas M., and Weisband, Edward. *Foreign Policy by Congress.* Oxford University Press, New York, 1979.

Friedman, B. *Smuts: A Reappraisal.* Basil Keartland Press, Johannesburg, 1976.

Geldenhuys, Deon. *The Diplomacy of Isolation: South African Foreign Policy Making.* Macmillan, Johannesburg, 1984.

Hance, W., Kuper, L., McKay, V., and Munger, E. S. *Southern Africa and the United States.* Columbia University Press, New York, 1968.

Hancock, W. K. *The Field of Force 1919-1950.* Cambridge University Press, London, 1968.

Hanlon, J., and Omond, R. *The Sanctions Handbook.* Penguin Books, London, 1987.

Hero, Alfred, and Barratt, John, eds. *The American People and South Africa.* Lexington Books, Lexington, Mass., 1981.

Hill, Adelaide, and Kilson, Martin, eds. *Apropos of Africa.* Frank Cass & Co., London, 1969.

Hoffmann, Stanley. *Primacy or World Order.* McGraw-Hill, New York, 1978.

Houser, George M. *No One Can Stop The Rain: Glimpses of Africa's Liberation Struggle.* The Pilgrim Press, New York, 1989.

Hufbauer, G. C., and Schott, J. J. *Economic Sanctions in Support of Foreign Policy Goals.* Analysis in International Economics No. 6, Institute for International Economics, Washington, D. C., 1983.

Hull, Richard W. *American Enterprise in South Africa: Historical Dimensions of Engagement and Disengagement.* New York University Press, New York, 1990.

Isaacson, Walter. *Kissinger: A Biography.* Simon & Schuster, New York, 1992.

Jackson, Henry F. *From the Congo to Soweto: US Foreign Policy Toward Africa Since 1960.* William Morrow & Co., New York, 1982.

Kissinger, Henry. *White House Years.* Little Brown & Company, Boston, 1979.

Koenderman, Tony, *Sanctions: The Threat to South Africa,* Jonathan Ball, Johannesburg, 1982.

Lake, A. *Caution and Concern: The Making of American Policy toward South Africa 1946-71,* Unpublished Ph. D. dissertation, Princeton University, 1974.

————. *The Tar Baby Option: American Policy toward Southern Africa.* Columbia University Press, New York, 1976.

Lapping, Brian. *Apartheid: A History.* George Braziller, New York, 1986.

Leape, J. Baskin B. and Underhill, S. *Business in the Shadow of Apartheid: US Firms in South Africa.* Lexington Books, Lexington, Mass., 1985.

Leiss, Amelia C., ed. *Apartheid and United Nations: Collective Measures, An Analysis.* Carnegie Endowment for International Peace, New York, 1965.

Lemarchand, Rene, ed.. *American Policy in Southern Africa.* University Press of America, Washington, D.C., 1981.

Lipton, Merle. *The Challenge of Sanctions.* Discussion Paper No. 1, Center for the Study of the South African Economy and International Finance, London School of Economics, September 1990.

Luthuli, A. *Let My People Go.* McGraw Hill Co., New York, 1962.

Martin, Patrick H. *American Views on South Africa, 1948-1972.* Unpublished Ph.D. dissertation, Louisiana State University and Agricultural Mechanical College, Baton Rouge, 1974.

McKeever, Porter. *Adlai Stevenson: His Life and Legacy.* William Morrow & Company, New York, 1989.

McLellan, David, and Acheson, David. *Among Friends: Personal Letters of Dean Acheson.* Dodd, Mead & Co, New York, 1980.

Morris, R. *Uncertain Greatness: Henry Kissinger and American Foreign Policy.* Quartet Books, New York, 1977.

Myers, Desaix. *US Business in South Africa,* Indiana University Press, Bloomington, Ind., 1980.

Orkin, Mark, ed. *Sanctions Against Apartheid.* David Philip, Johannesburg, 1989.

————. *The Struggle and the Future: What Black South Africans Really Think.* Ravan Press, Johannesburg, 1986.

Pachai, B. *The South African Indian Question 1860-1971.* C. Struik, Cape Town, 1971.

Padover, S. K. ed., *Wilson's Ideals.* American Council on Public Affairs, Washington, D.C., 1942.

Paton, Alan. *Hofmeyr.* Oxford University Press, Cape Town, 1964.

Pottinger, Brian. *The Imperial Presidency: P. W. Botha—The First 10 Years.* Southern Book Publishers, Johannesburg, 1988.

Price, Morris. *The Nixon Years (1969-1974): Duplicity in United States Policies Toward Southern Africa.* Unpublished Ph. D. dissertation, St. John's University, New York, 1977.

Prinsloo, Daan. *United States Foreign Policy and the Republic of South Africa.* Foreign Affairs Association, Pretoria, 1978.

Reed, Douglas. *The Battle for Rhodesia.* Devin-Adair, New York, 1967.

Ries, A. and Dommisse, E. *Leierstryd.* Tafelberg, Cape Town, 1990.

Salinger, Pierre. *America Held Hostage: The Secret Negotiations.* Doubleday & Co., New York, 1981.

Schlesinger, Arthur M. Jr. *A Thousand Days: John F Kennedy in the White House.* Houghton Mifflin Co., Boston, 1965.

————. *Robert Kennedy and His Times.* Houghton Mifflin Co, Boston, 1978.

Schoeman, E. ed. *South African Sanctions Directory 1946-88.* South African Institute of International Affairs, Johannesburg, 1988.

Scott, George. *The Rise and Fall of the League of Nations.* Macmillan Publishing Co., New York, 1973.

Segal, Ronald, ed. *Sanctions Against South Africa.* Penguin Books Ltd., Harmondsworth, England, 1964.

Shepherd, George W. *The United States and Non-Aligned Africa.* Optional Paper No. 1, University of Denver, Colorado, 1970.

Shultz, George P. *Turmoil and Triumph: My Years as Secretary of State.* Charles Scribner's Sons, New York, 1993.

Smuts, J. C. *Jan Christiaan Smuts.* Cassel & Company, Cape Town, 1952.

Spence, J. E. *Republic Under Pressure: A Study of South African Foreign Policy.* Oxford University Press, London, 1965.

Spring, Martin C. *Confrontation: The Approaching Crisis Between the United States and South Africa.* Valiant Publishers, Sandton, 1977.

Thomas, Franklin, ed. *South Africa: Time Running Out.* Foreign Policy Study Foundation, University of California Press, 1981.

Vance, Cyrus. *Hard Choices: Critical Years in America's Foreign Policy.* Simon & Schuster, New York, 1983.

Van der Poel, J. *Selections from the Smuts Papers. Vol. VII, August 1945 - October 1950.* Cambridge University Press, London, 1973.

Walshe, P. *Church Versus State in South Africa.* C. Hurst & Co, London, 1983.

Index

About the Author

LES de VILLIERS spent ten years in the United States and Canada as a senior South Africa diplomat before becoming Senior Deputy Secretary of Information in Pretoria. Today, as a consultant in the U.S., his writings on business and international relations appear in newspapers and business and academic periodicals. He is a featured speaker and participant in radio and TV discussions.

ISBN 0-275-94982-6

90000>

EAN

9 780275 949822

HARDCOVER BAR CODE